# Contemporary Issues in Criminal Justice Management

*First Edition*

By Don Lacher
*Union Institute & University*

Bassim Hamadeh, CEO and Publisher
Michael Simpson, Vice President of Acquisitions
Jamie Giganti, Managing Editor
Jess Busch, Graphic Design Supervisor
Mieka Portier, Acquisitions Editor
Jessica Knott, Project Editor
Luiz Ferreira, Licensing Associate

Cover credits: Modern day gladiators, Copyright © 2012 by Depositphotos/Alancrosthwaite; Lance Cpl. Nicholas, Source: http://commons.wikimedia.org/wiki/File:USMC-120604-M-VP013-005.jpg. Copyright in the Public Domain.; Helmet on a police officer, Copyright © 2013 by Depositphotos/Iurii Konoval.; K-9 Unit, Copyright © 2012 by Depositphotos/Mark Hayes.; Police Officers Using Two-Way Radio, Copyright © 2013 by Depositphotos/Craig Robinson.

First published in the United States of America in 2014 by Cognella, Inc.

Trademark Notice: Product or corporate names may be trademarks or registered trademarks, and are used only for identification and explanation without intent to infringe.


Printed in the United States of America

ISBN: 978-1-62661-746-9 (pbk)/ 978-1-62661-747-6 (br)

www.cognella.com          800-200-3908

## Dedication

This body of work is dedicated to my family; my Platoon marching beside me on the path of life; My Village; all my love and admiration;

My loving wife Joan; my Rock

My son Glenn and his wife Brialynn; my heroes;

My parents Wallace and Janet; thanks for your love and encouragement;

My brother Chris his wife Susan my niece Sarah and nephew William;

My step daughters & their spouses; Angela & Bryan; Michelle & Jason; & Elizabeth;

Our grand kids in order of appearance; Bradley; Auburn; Colin, Austin, Tyler; Mackenzie, Madison, & Olivia;

My in-laws; Ida Dale; matriarch & southern belle; her husband Dean; Janet & Bob; Judy & Steve; and Driff;

A prayer for our loved ones who have passed on; Wallace; Janet & Dean; rest in eternal peace until we meet again;

AND; our family of warriors serving the nation in combat and peace; Wallace; US Army AC & Air Force; Dean; US Army AC & Air Force; Jason; US Marine Corps; Glenn; US Army Airborne; Brialynn; US Army Airborne & Scott; US Army Ranger

# Contents

Acknowledgements                                                          vii
    Don Lacher

Foreword                                                                    ix
    Dr. Andrew Harvey

Introduction                                                                 1
    Donald C. Lacher


UNIT 1: INTERNAL IMPACTS

Chapter 1: Organizational Change and the Criminal Justice Manager            7

Future Issues in Criminal Justice Management
    Richard Kania

Chapter 2: Contemporary Trends and Impacts in Police Administration          21

Contemporary Issues in Police Administration
    Gary Cordner

Chapter 3: Doing More with Less: Economic Impacts on American Policing        47

The Impact of the Economic Down Turn on American Police Agencies
    U.S. Department of Justice-COPS

Chapter 4: Breaking the Silence on Law Enforcement Suicide                    85
    Donald C. Lacher, MS, Captain-Retired

Chapter 5: Issues in Community Supervision—Who is Watching Them?        95

Issues in Community Supervision
> Lawrence Travis


Unit 2: External Impacts

Chapter 6: Modern Slavers: The Evil of Human Bondage        127

Trafficking and Human Dignity
> Mark Lagon

Chapter 7: Boot Prints in the Sand: The Global War on Afghan Heroin        139

Gaming the System: How Afghan Opium Underpins Local Power
> Justin Mankin

Chapter 8: Attacks on American Kids: School Threats and the Active Shooter        167

School Security Best Practices
> Kent C. Jurney and Steve Cader

Chapter 9: The Impact of Cannabis Legalization on Human Resource Management        175
> Donald C. Lacher, MS, Captain-Retired

Chapter 10: Looking Toward the Future        191

Looking Toward the Future: Criminal Justice in the 21st Century
> Joycelyn Pollock

Credits        213

# Acknowledgements

By Don Lacher

Editing this book and writing two of the chapters reinforced the importance of the concept of team work. I have wanted to write or edit a textbook for many years. I can finally check this work off my personal bucket list. With that being said, I would like to take a moment of the reader's time to acknowledge the following persons:

First to my team at Cognella Inc. and University Readers; Jessica Knott, Senior Project Editor, Mieka Porter, Acquisitions Editor, Jess Busch, Graphic Design Supervisor, Jamie Giganti, Managing Editor, Sean Adams and Mandy Licata, Associate Editors, Luiz Ferreira, Senior Licensing Specialist, and Chelsey Rogers, Marketing Program Manager;

Secondly, to my Union Institute and University family; thanks to Dr. Roger Sublett, President for your leadership and for all your support; Dr. Soto Nelson, Provost; I appreciate all your efforts helping to move CJM forward; Dr. Elizabeth Pruden; thanks for your mentorship in academic assessment; the Deans who have been so supportive; Dr. Beryl Watnick, Dr. Carolyn Turner, and a special thanks to Dr. Elizabeth Pastores-Pallfy; for your outstanding leadership of the Los Angeles Center and your friendship; to Dr. James Rocheleau thanks for all your encouragement; and a special note of appreciation to Dr. Rich Hanson, Provost-retired; you taught me so much about academic administration.

To my Criminal Justice Management faculty for all your support with special mention to my Curriculum Committee, Andrew Harvey, Jim Babcock, Lawrence Hibbert, and Brian Dragoo; AND; Larry Chavez, Roland Pandolfi, Lee Spector, Andre Risse, Bill Smyser, and Corina Smith; you have all contributed to my success at the University and special thanks for those professors who have helped develop on-line courses for the CJM program; John Andrews, Al Cobos, Jeff Rose, Don Crist, Corina Smith, Greg Frum, Mike Sullivan, Mike Wells, Dr. Rob Kirkland, and Sheila Ingram.

A special note of appreciation to my colleague, Dr. Andrew Harvey, Captain-retired for writing the Foreward to this book; thanks for 30 years of friendship.

A special recognition for my experts; I could not have completed this work without your immeasurable expertise; James Emett, Ron Clark, William Griffin, Corina Smith, Steven Lankford, Sarah Creighton, James Hunt, Glenn Lacher, Jason Lilley, William Couch, and Danielle Tellez;

To the men and women of the Monrovia Police Department; thanks for sharing a wonderful career with me. A special thanks to those officers who shared my youth putting bad guys behind bars; Roger, Doc, Rick , Steve "Scoo", Rich "Smitty", Jim, Alan, Dottie, Don N, Glen C, Steve G, Alex, Tom W, Tom L, Rich D, Jamie A, and Bill. AND Lori L, for all your support and guidance.

AND Teresa St. Peter, retired City of Monrovia Director of HR and Scott Ochoa, former Monrovia City Manager and current Glendale City Manager; I have always appreciated your combined wisdom, support, and friendship.

# Foreword

Dr. Andrew J. Harvey, Retired Police Captain

After having spent the last 35 years involved in the field of law enforcement, first as a police officer, and now as a university criminal justice professor, I've seen the vast changes and challenges that have occurred in, and impacted on this profession. Some of those changes have been for the better, and some, well, maybe not so much. Regardless, our current working law enforcement officers are dealing with those changes and challenges in their typical professional and humble way. Although I didn't write this book, I am of the firm belief it was designed and written to help our brave police professionals better cope with the emerging issues they are facing, both now, and in the future.

As an author myself, and as someone who continually examines and evaluates criminal justice texts, I feel this is a book that is very much needed. Covering current issues such as the impacts of reduction in funding, community supervision, human trafficking, school shootings, and the heart-breaking problem of police suicide, this book provides much needed perspective on key issues. Even better, the book looks toward the horizon, and stimulates officers to examine the issues they will be facing in the future, so they are better prepared to handle these challenges as they arise.

Lastly, this book is constructed and edited by Professor Donald C. Lacher, one of the finest law enforcement professionals I have ever known. Criminal justice professionals who read this book will be in good hands, as Professor Lacher guides them to success both now and in the future. I believe this text will serve as the benchmark in the field for many years to come.

# Introduction

By Donald C. Lacher

## Introduction

This book examines key contemporary issues in the field of criminal justice management. Divided into two units, the book explores relevant and future issues in policing and corrections. The internal impact section centers on contemporary issues for the criminal justice manager, future considerations, and organizational change. The unit on external impacts focuses on issues impacting criminal justice organizations. Peppered throughout the book, topics the reader will become acquainted with on the impact of globalization of crime and the impacts of global issues on the criminal justice system as a whole. Allocation of resources and budget management are the two most critical components of the book. The abundance of resources or lack thereof is the central themes for criminal justice organizational responses to reducing crime and delivery of services to the public.

## Who Should Read This Book?

I selected the readings for this book to stimulate discussion among students, law enforcement, and correctional personnel, professors, and other stakeholders, who wish to improve their knowledge of contemporary issues in criminal justice. This textbook was written for a course entitled "Contemporary Issues in Criminal Justice Management." I designed this required course for the Union Institute and University as part of the Bachelors of Science program in Criminal Justice Management. The course was developed as an upper-level class. This book examines the contemporary and future issues that will impact managers in the criminal justice field. So, from a management perspective, this book explores strategies to impact current and future issues facing the criminal justice system.

## What Will You Find Inside This Textbook?

Much of the book revolves around futurist thinking and managing change. The section on the effects of the economic down turn in policing analyzes best practices for law enforcement agencies forced to do more work with fewer resources.

Breaking the silence on police suicide examines an issue that frankly has been ignored at least on the large scale by American policing and corrections. Why this situation existed for so long is a mystery. Statistics reveal that while suicide by American law enforcement officers is small compared to the total police population, the numbers themselves do not discount its importance as a significant impact. The good news is that chiefs of police on a national level have vowed to work together to develop best practices for preventing suicides by their employees. If this book helps in that mission, it will have been worth my efforts writing the chapter.

"Attacks on American Kids: School Threats and the Active Shooter" explored the phenomenon of violence toward children at our schools. It seems that several times a year some maniac walks into a school in this country and shoots kids and staff. The causal effects in this issue are very controversial and complex. The issues that are raised include gun control, mental health issues, and the lack of adequate numbers of treatment programs, campus security, and violent video games. These issues have created a climate of fear and also have political ramifications. Unfortunately, politicians talk big and make promises to end the violence but never take any appreciable action.

"Issues in Community Supervision: Who is Watching Them?" examines the concept of community corrections. Court decisions in California and perhaps other states have released felons from state prisons into our already overcrowded county jails. Law enforcement and correctional organizations, during a downturn in the economy, have been forced to deal with the impact of hundreds of career criminals "hitting" the streets and neighborhoods. Unfortunately, many communities are dealing with increases in crime and deficiencies in the allocation of personnel to monitor this criminal element.

I stumbled across the human resource implications of the legalization of marijuana quite by accident. I was researching the impact of high THC levels in cannabis-impaired drivers for a lecture in my Drugs in Society course. In our library, I found articles questioning Colorado's recent legalization of marijuana. The voters' decision provoked such controversy that I decided to write a chapter on HR implications on the legalization of marijuana. Today and in the foreseeable future the private, public, and non-profit sectors will be plunged into this controversial topic. I forecast that as new workplace legislation is decided in the courtroom, workplace managers will be forced to reform and modify "drug-free work zones" for the next several decades. I shudder to think what impact marijuana legalization will have on our youth who are the workers of the future.

Globalization of crime figures prominently in this work. The United Nations Office on Drug Policy released a 2010 report listing the top global crime issues facing the world. (See Figure 1.1). I had room to only write about three of the issues including trafficking in persons, smuggling migrants, and heroin.

The chapter on human smuggling acquaints the reader with the sinister topic of modern slavers. Trafficking in persons is divided into two broad areas. Migrant smuggling can be a voluntary activity where desperate unskilled workers enter this country with the dream of making a decent living. On the other side of the equation, men, women, and children are trafficked against their will for the purposes of sexual exploitation. Child pornography is a subset of the human trafficking issue.

In the chapter "Boot Prints in the Sand—The Global War on Afghan Heroin", I had the opportunity to interview my son and son-in-law. They became my story tellers, informing the reader about Afghan culture and custom. These participants and thousands like them left their boot prints in the sand.

America will be woven into the fabric of Afghanistan for many years to come, just like Vietnam; our troops went to fight for the freedom of others.

The fall of the Soviet Union and China opening its borders has fueled the Afghan opium, heroin, and hashish markets. Illegal drugs flourish where licit goods trade. Does anyone doubt that cocaine, heroin, and cannabis cross from Mexico to the United States in NAFTA-licensed trucks? Afghan heroin has made its way into the United States. It is cheaper and more potent than heroin from Mexico. Afghan warlords and at least one extremist group are manufacturing heroin and distributing the drug on a global scale.

These smugglers have decades of experience in warfare and will become more powerful as coalition forces leave Afghanistan in 2014. Assisted by government corruption and little hope for the tribal population of Afghanistan, poppy cultivation has significantly increased over the last few years. Once sold, profits from the heroin trade buy weapons and ammunition for enemy fighters bent on killing American and coalition forces. These are the same folks America, China, and India supported in their war against the Soviet Union. In conclusion, I hope you the student learn some best practices that will help you in your present and future careers.

**Figure 1.1**: United Nations List of Contemporary Global Crime Impacts

**Trafficking in Persons**
**Smuggling Migrants**
**Cocaine**
**Heroin**
**Firearms**
**Environmental Resources**
**Counterfeit Products**
**Maritime Piracy**
**Cybercrime**

# Unit 1

# Internal Impacts

Unit 1 explores selected issues impacting criminal justice organizations today. The methodology for selection of the issues was a simple poll of college professors who teach courses in contemporary issues in criminal justice management. The majority of the topics examined in this book were issues taught by the editor in his courses too. All of these college professors are retired law enforcement and corrections managers with decades of experience in the field.

While not an exhaustive list of trends it is a start for our study. All the topics have shaped or will shape contemporary and future organizational policy responses in the allocation of resources, compensation, training, morale, productivity, liability and discipline. It is my objective that the study of these internal issues will help the student appreciate the vital roles played by line personnel, supervisors, managers, and department heads working in criminal justice organizations today.

## Objectives:

- Summarize and interpret how current issues in the field of criminal justice management impact organizations, personnel and other stakeholders
- Analyze and critique criminal justice policy and service delivery issues in criminal justice

# Chapter 1: Organizational Change and the Criminal Justice Manager

*Ask not what your country can do for you, ask what you can do for your country*
John F. Kennedy

## Student Objectives

1. Examine the three patterns of change
2. Explore future issues in criminal justice management
3. Analyze technology trends
4. Compare and contrast the importance of the media in the field

The article for this chapter, *Future Issues in Criminal Justice Management* was written in 2008. Much of the information is still relevant today for criminal justice managers. The topic of futuristic studies is important to both the student and practitioner alike. To be successful in criminal justice today and in the future we must embrace change management. Failure to change with the times will result in poor service delivery to the public and will likely widen the public's distrust in the system.

The challenge I see is how "do we as a criminal justice industry put theory into practice?" I am issuing a personal challenge to students reading this article. How can you as an individual embrace innovation and change and model behaviors that prepare you for your role in the criminal justice system? So, as you read the article, make a list of items combining theory and practice and place those in your personal toolbox. You might have an answer on your next entry-level or promotional interview when asked; "what changes would you suggest for … ?"

# Future Issues in Criminal Justice Management

## By Richard Kania

What does the future hold for tomorrow's criminal justice managers? While we cannot be certain, forecasts can prepare us for what we may experience in years to come. Forecasting is one of the planning tools mentioned in Chapter 6. Forecasts typically look to the past and consider contemporary developments to predict the future. A criminal justice manager in the twenty-first century can expect to face many of the same issues that challenged managers in the past.

An entire new discipline appeared in the 1960s called **futuristics**, the prediction of the future based on the scholarly study of existing conditions. **Futurologists** (also called **futurists**) in criminal justice have offered numerous insights into what may be in store for your career as a criminal justice manager some decades ahead.

Two organizations have been leaders in the study of the future: the World Futures Studies Federation (WFSF), founded in 1967 in Oslo, Norway, and the World Future Society (WFS), founded in the United States in 1966. The WFS publishes two journals, *Futures Research Quarterly* and *The Futurist*. The *Journal of Futures Studies*, published by the Graduate Institute of Futures Studies of Tamkang University in Taipei, Taiwan, is another scholarly outlet for such studies. Many futurists have looked ahead to the risks that we face from crime and terror. None, though, is more distinguished than Wendell Bell (2000), one of the founders of futurology, and the author of one of its major works, *Foundations of Futures Studies* (1996; 1997).

The Society of Police Futurists International is a nongovernmental organization dedicated to applying futuristics to policing. In 1991, William Tafoya, then with the FBI, cofounded the Society of Police Futurists International. He has lectured and consulted on various futuristic threats, including cybercrime in its infancy. Another leading futurist in criminal justice, studying for more than a quarter century, is Gene Stephens. In a recent report (2005), he summarized some of the predictions that he and others see ahead for American law enforcement, including such things as the expanded use of nonlethal force, customization of police and criminal justice services to meet specific public needs, greater demands on first responders, cybercrime, and terrorist incidents including the threat of bioterrorism.

One of the leading futurists looking at the court system is Sohail Inayatullah (1990; 1992). Having worked on a judiciary improvement project with the Hawaiian courts, Inayatullah writes of futures for judicial bureaucracies (Inayatullah and Monma, 1989). The project initiated a problem-oriented planning process, and considered options for the future, including some low-probability issues such as the rights of robots, sentencing offenders using natural brain drugs, and even the secession of Hawaii from the United States.

Many others also are looking ahead. Georgette Bennett sought to predict future crime trends in her 1987 book, *Crimewarps* (revised in 1989). Her predictions relied heavily on demographic trends and foresaw the problems of cybercrime. Another future-looking expert on demographic trends and crime is Alfred Blumstein whose work (1995; Blumstein and Rosenfeld, 1998; Blumstein and Wallman, 2000; 2006) was recognized with the 2007 Stockholm Prize in Criminology for his predictive work on human rights, age-based crime trends, and studies of incarceration rates in American correctional institutions among other subjects. His advanced statistical analyses have produced complex predictions on the productivity of deterrence, the growth of prison populations, and the problems and future of drug-enforcement policies. He developed the statistical concept of "lambda" as a reliable predictive measurement of an individual's offending frequency within a possible life-long criminal career. Roslyn

Muraskin and Albert Roberts have compiled a collection of essays, *Visions for Change* (2009), that addresses future issues for the twenty-first century. The authors look at recent developments and future directions in technological applications, forensic sciences, globalization, victimology, drug policy, cybercrimes, juvenile justice issues, media matters, gender issues, and all of the components of the justice system.

These leading futurists and others have looked ahead to the future of criminal justice. Others have undertaken efforts to direct that change into improved futures. These kinds of managers are change agents in the pattern of such great criminal justice reformers of the past as Cesare Beccaria, Jeremy Bentham, Zebulon Brockway, Dorothea Dix, August Vollmer, Orlando W. Wilson, Bruce Smith, Arthur Vanderbilt, Katharine Bement Davis, Mary Belle Harris, and George Beto. Future criminal justice managers need to recognize three distinctive patterns of change: (1) straight-line change, (2) rise-plateau-crash change, and (3) cyclic change.

## Natural Patterns in Change

**Straight-Line Change:** Change often will follow a trend in a consistent fashion, either steady-state, rising, or falling. In criminal justice, **straight-line change** patterns have existed involving: training requirements, entry educational requirements, and in-service educational achievements, all rising gradually over the decades.

**Rise-Plateau-Crash Change:** In criminal justice, specific technologies have appeared, become popular (rising), then become commonplace (the plateau), only to be replaced by new technologies and thus vanish (the crash). This **rise-plateau-crash change** has been evident especially in the applications of communications technologies (the call box, one-way radio, two-way radio, and in-car computer) and in suspect and offender identification (the Bertillon system, inked fingerprints, scanner prints, and DNA identification). Correctional innovations also have followed this pattern (the Pennsylvania silent penitentiary movement, the Auburn congregate system, the rehabilitation movement, correctional boot camps, and, more recently, three-strikes legislation and career-offender long-term incarceration programs. Media attention to spectacular criminal cases also follows this pattern (Marsh, 1991).

**Cyclic Change:** The most predictable events undergo **cyclic change** or follow an **oscillating change pattern**, in which frequencies of some feature will rise, then fall, only to rise again. This cyclic change is obvious in the long-term history of criminal justice; consider issues such as brutality complaints, corruption scandals , and the bias against minorities.

## Issues Criminal Justice Managers Will Face in the Future

**Brutality and Excessive Force Issues:** Police and correctional officers are obliged to use force in the performance of their duties. Several hundred people are killed each year by police and correctional officers, far more than are lawfully executed. This use of force, whether *deadly force* or *nonlethal force*, can be used wrongfully. When serious abuse of force occurs, there will be protests, lawsuits, and changes made in criminal justice training standards to present future abuses. Criminal justice managers also are looking to new nonlethal force devices to reduce the number of police-caused homicides and to reduce cases of **excessive force**. The *crisis-planner* manager will respond in reaction to such cases; the manager who is a *purposeful planner* will anticipate such problems and prepare for them before they occur.

In 1985, a change in case law (*Garner v. Tennessee*) altered the standards by which police could use deadly force. Even before the U.S. Supreme Court made its ruling, though, the IACP (1981) was anticipating what the future would bring to police deadly force practices. Police managers were preparing to apply more restrictive shooting standards. When the court rendered its decision, these managers' agencies were prepared to accept the new standards. These progressive police managers used a process like that described by Kurt Lewin (1890–1947), who wrote that the process of effecting change involves a three-step procedure (Lewin, 1989: 546–547; Souryal, 1995: 128–129):

*Unfreezing:* to "[ … ] break open the shell of complacency and self-righteousness, it is sometimes necessary to bring about deliberately an emotional stir-up."

*Moving or Changing:* make the change-oriented decisions and begin the process of implementation.

*Refreezing:* allow the new ways to become established as the replacement habits.

By the time the court decision was made, most progressive police departments already were training their officers in the procedures recommended by the IACP that were to be expressed in the court ruling. Old procedures, especially the outdated "fleeing felon" rule, already had been discredited (unfreezing). When the new standard was promulgated, police all over the country were anticipating it (changing), and most were ready to apply it (refreeze).

**General Ethical Failures and Shortcomings:** Periodically new scandals arise in which various criminal justice officials engage in corrupt or immoral activities. There are seven recurring ethical problems facing all those who take on responsibilities in the name of justice: (1) wrongful pursuit of personal gain, (2) favoritism and bias, (3) abuses of power, (4) a flawed personal life, (5) deceitfulness, (6) denial of due process to those involved with criminal justice, and (7) neglect of duties (Kania and Dial, 2008: 169).

*Personal Gain:* The criminal justice manager must avoid unlawful personal gain from the position, and similarly must be aware that such misconduct is prevented, detected, investigated, and punished when it occurs within the organization. The criminal justice manager must enforce the prohibitions, both in law and in ethical guidelines, against using public service for personal enrichment, profit, pleasure, or benefits not specifically authorized by law, the work contract, or the rules. Included in this category are the rules against:

## Box 1. • Seven Recurring Ethical Problems in Criminal Justice

1. Wrongful Pursuit of Personal Gain
2. Favoritism and Bias
3. Abuse of Power
4. Flawed Personal Life
5. Deceitfulness
6. Denial of Due Process
7. Neglect of Duties

- taking bribes and extorting pay-offs
- accepting gratuities and unauthorized benefits

- receiving excessive compensation and benefits
- using the office to promote personal aims
- harboring and advancing excessive ambition (Kania and Dial, 2008: 170)

*Favoritism and Bias:* Because it is unethical to use one's office to aid those whom we like or to interfere with those whom we dislike, a criminal justice manager must be attentive to this perpetual threat to agency integrity. These biases often arise from divided and mixed loyalties, holding one's obligation to the public interest below that of oneself (egoism), family (paternalism, nepotism), friends, personal associates, co-workers and peers (peer bias), one's political party and programs (patronage, ideological bias), or church and spiritual faith (theological bias). Included in this category are rules against:

- political and ideological patronage
- racial, ethnic, and religious bias (favorable and unfavorable)
- nepotism and other family favoritism
- overt and covert discrimination (racial, ethnic, sexual, political, etc.) (Kania and Dial, 2008: 170)

*The Abuse of Power:* The prohibitions against public officials using their offices to place their values, desires, needs, or preferences above those of the public they serve, and over the rules and laws they must uphold, are sometimes broken, leading to abuses of power. Criminal justice managers must be alert to such abuses. These need not involve personal material gain. These violations include such activities as:

- authoritarianism, coercion, and harassment
- arranging or condoning unjustified arrests
- seeking to deny opportunities for reasonable bail
- denial of liberty by lengthy detention prior to trial (Kania and Dial, 2008: 170)

*The Flawed Personal Life:* Criminal justice managers must maintain socially respectable private lives and also must enforce the prohibitions against personal activities outside the workplace that serve to bring discredit upon the public servant and the servant's agency or profession among their employees and subordinates. These include private violations of the criminal law and moral violations that are not necessarily illegal but are generally frowned upon by the public. These include:

- criminal wrongdoing by criminal justice officials
- financial improprieties and tax evasion by criminal justice officials
- sexual misconduct, deviance, or unconventionality by criminal justice officials
- civil illegality (tax, regulatory, and civil law violations)
- questionable associations and membership in controversial organizations
- private prejudicial expressions and actions (Kania and Dial, 2008: 171)

*Deceitfulness:* Deceitfulness includes violations that run counter to the expectation that our public officials will be honest and forthright with the public on matters involving their work. Criminal justice managers must set an example for honesty and truthfulness for their agencies to emulate. When they do not, managers must take action to root out dishonesty and restore truthfulness within their agencies. The rules against deceitfulness include the rules against:

- overt lying, duplicity, loop-holing, and evasions
- covering up misdeeds
- unwarranted secrecy in the conduct of the public business
- fraud, trickery, and hypocrisy (Kania and Dial, 2008: 171)

*The Denial of Due Process:* Due process comprises the rules for procedural correctness in dealing with all administrative matters, both within the justice system and in all public service bureaucratic activities. Criminal justice agents are required to follow the policies set out for them, and should not invent personal solutions to the situations they encounter. Criminal justice managers have the responsibility to train staff, monitor their conduct, and take disciplinary action when due process is not followed properly. Citizens have the right to expect that their cases will be dealt with fairly, in accordance with the rules for such cases. Failures include:

- ignoring the civil rights and constitutional guarantees
- not following the rules and procedures
- failing to comply with internal bureaucratic rules
- ignoring regulatory and statutory guarantees (Kania and Dial, 2008: 171)

*Neglect of Duties:* All criminal justice occupations and positions have associated duties and obligations that must be fulfilled. A criminal justice official who does not fulfill these duties is violating that mandate, and sometimes even will be violating laws against:

- malfeasance
- nonfeasance
- misfeasance

## Box 2. • Neglect of One's Duties

Both the law and ethical standards obligate public office holders to be faithful to their lawful duties. Three common failures are:

**nonfeasance**—the failure to perform one's duty by oversight or omission, usually inadvertent (willful nonfeasance typically will be considered malfeasance)

**misfeasance**—the wrongful performance of one's duties, usually in the form of making mistakes, not following procedures correctly, or other unintentional blunders

**malfeasance**—the intentional performance of an official act or use of one's official powers to achieve an end that is circumstantially illegal, harmful, and/or unjustified

- disobeying lawful orders
- abuse of discretion
- failing to comply with regulations and standing orders (Kania and Dial, 2008: 172)

Actual ethical failures in practice have often overlapped two or more of these categories. A criminal justice manager must anticipate that each and every one of these failures will occur. They may be reduced, minimized, or mitigated, but the wise criminal justice manager must be aware and prepared for these failings to recur.

**Ethnic, Race, and Community Relations:** Implicit in the discussion of the failures above, under the categories of bias, abuses of power, and due process especially, are the seeds of public dissatisfaction with the performance of criminal justice agencies. These result in poor criminal justice–community relations. In the 1950s, progressive leaders in criminal justice began the effort to reeducate criminal justice agencies, especially the police, in better community relations efforts. Many programs were developed and experiments attempted. Community-oriented policing and other programs have been tried to improve the image of the police and the justice system, yet problems in race and ethic relations continue to recur.

Sometimes it is not the criminal justice agency that is the source of the problem. Some members of racial and ethic groups engage in behaviors that clash with the customs and laws of the United States. The criminal justice system must maintain a balancing act in trying to enforce the law and also trying to respect the customs and behaviors of such groups. To add to the problems managers will face, leaders of these groups will occasionally seek to confront the laws of the United States and hope to create an us-versus-them conflict. A good criminal justice manager will stay ahead of the conflict, anticipating the reasonable and lawful demands of minority groups, striving to meet those by training agency employees, hiring people able to communicate effectively with minority groups, and creating programs to achieve cooperation and harmony.

When examples of bias, prejudice, or injustice occur, the criminal justice manager has an obligation to address these promptly and judiciously. To suppose that good relations existing today will last indefinitely is naïve. Communities are forever in flux. Good relationships with adults of the minority communities will not guarantee good relationships with their offspring, and new groups will enter into the community or the client population. The future-oriented criminal justice manager must prepare for new challenges.

**Applying New Technologies to Criminal Justice:** What will the new technologies of 2025 and 2050 be? Certainly we cannot do more than guess, but if we have learned from the past and present, we can be sure that new technologies will emerge that will apply to criminal justice.

Existing technologies certainly will be improved upon. Communications, computers, video, transportation, criminalistics, nonlethal weapons, and emergency medical technologies have been improving so dramatically in the past 35 years that criminal justice practice is far different from what it was when the LEAA was helping agencies acquire their first computer systems, upgrade their telecommunications, and add nonlethal controls to supplement the use of firearms.

Foresighted criminal justice managers will stay informed about new technologies and think of ways that they can be applied to criminal justice roles. More than one hundred years ago, August Vollmer and his peers applied the new inventions of their age to police applications, including the patrol car, the police radio, fingerprint identification, and ballistics. In the 1960s, progressive criminal justice managers were exploring ways to use computers to enhance criminal justice operations. Using the unique features of DNA for identification was a new idea just two decades ago. The criminal justice managers who conceived of using it to solve crimes were highly original thinkers (Wambaugh, 1989). What new technology might you apply to criminal justice if you come to hold a managerial position? You might be the change agent who brings about a major improvement in criminal justice practices in the future.

**Media Attention:** A criminal justice manager cannot necessarily predict when a major case within his or her jurisdiction will grab the attention of the mass communications media (Mannion, 1993). When "the big one" hits, the prudent criminal justice manager will have a plan in place to handle the media onslaught. Otherwise there is a great risk of conflict between the media and the agency (Mozee, 1987). There are 12 lessons that a criminal justice manager can learn from the past to anticipate the future:

1.  A major disaster or crisis can happen anywhere, anytime. Even the smallest criminal justice agency in the smallest of communities must be prepared to face this reality (Mannion, 1993).
2.  The criminal justice manager must prepare for two aspects of the crisis: the major crime or disaster case itself, and the media onslaught that will follow it (Mannion, 1993).
3.  The media will be invasive and lack respect for the people involved. For them, the story always takes precedence (Skolnick and McCoy, 1985: 114; Wilson and Fuqua, 1975: 124). The criminal justice manager must be prepared to thwart the media's desires to invade the crime scene and exploit morbid curiosity, while still giving the media opportunities to get key visuals to support their stories (Mozee, 1987: 143).
4.  Such a case invariably will have a long-term impact on relationships among and within the criminal justice agency, the community, and the news media (Mannion, 1992).
5.  The media are a criminal justice agency's most direct link with the public, and can be helpful to the police, the prosecutor, the courts, or corrections if the right lessons are learned and the proper steps are taken to prepare for such a catastrophic event (Garner 1987: 15–16; Graber, 1980; Skolnick and McCoy, 1985: 132).
6.  The media will cooperate with criminal justice agencies when given useful information, sensible direction, and assistance (Jones, 1987; Mannion, 1993; Skolnick and McCoy, 1985: 132).
7.  The media will not go away, but if ignored by official sources, it will seek out less well-informed and less reliable ones to get a story (Jones 1987: 164).
8.  Criminal justice agencies need to know the variety and informational requirements of the news and entertainment media organizations and freelancers that now exist (Mannion, 1993).
9.  The criminal justice manager must have advanced knowledge about how various media organizations operate and their technology and facility requirements (Garner, 1987: 110–113), organization, and ethics.
10. The criminal justice manager must be aware of the capabilities, possible consequences, and hazards of instantaneous live broadcasting (Jones, 1987: 160).
11. Criminal justice agencies need knowledge of the objectives, rivalries, ideologies, and hidden agendas of media organizations (Mozee, 1987: 144–145; Sherizen, 1978).
12. The "media" are not limited to the traditional local and national news-gathering organizations. Criminal justice agencies should expect movie producers, book writers, tabloid newspapers, and television and radio talk shows to join the "feeding frenzy" at the crime scene, and all will likely claim full First Amendment rights and freedoms (Mannion, 1993).

**Educational and Training Standards:** When criminal justice managers were recruiting staff a century or more ago, a high school diploma was considered an advanced educational standard. By the beginning of this century, this has become a minimal standard for most criminal justice occupations. A law degree was not even required to practice law when Abraham Lincoln hung out his shingle as an attorney. Today no one in the United States can practice law without a legal education and having passed the bar examination. A century ago, most police departments and correctional agencies provided no training to their employees. Now in-service training is an essential part of personnel practices in most agencies.

What will the future bring in criminal justice education in the next several decades? What initial training will be required? How much more in-service training will be provided? Straight-line change predicts that all of these will increase gradually over time.

Criminal justice managers will have to revise their recruiting requirements and budget for more training to prepare for the future. Higher entry educational standards and specific educational curricula may need to be specified. In-service training will have to prepare their agencies to deal with each of the future challenges anticipated above. Flexibility and intellectual agility will be needed to deal with these and any other challenges not anticipated in the preceding pages.

## Summary: Using the Future for the Better

Criminal justice needs to be future-oriented. The past is behind us and cannot be redone. We may try to correct past errors and injustices, but they never will go away completely. Some old wounds will last forever. However, the future holds out hope to our society, to the justice system, and to criminal justice agencies. There can be progress. Old mistakes need not be repeated. New technologies can be added. Ineffectual methods can be improved upon. Our objectives can be better met. Moreover, the best of the past can be preserved. The values of our society are worthy of respect. A future criminal justice manager will be responsible for upholding and preserving our constitutional protections and the political values that are associated with them.

We began this book by stating the job of the criminal justice manager may be summed up by the mnemonic "LODESTAR." In fact, though, this is not enough. The criminal justice manager has other important tasks and responsibilities. Maintaining high standards of ethics is an important aspect of criminal justice for managers, for individual criminal justice employees, and for each criminal justice organization. Maintaining good community relations also is important. Acting in a manner to reduce the level of ethnic, racial, class, and social strife will benefit the entire society as well as the criminal justice agencies serving it. Achieving community harmony and public consensus is a goal that can be attained through effective criminal justice performance and a sensitivity to public needs and concerns. Good media relations are important as well. It is via our public information media that the public learns of the activities of our criminal justice agencies, decides how well they are doing their jobs, and either supports or turns against them. An ethical, educated, community-oriented, well-trained, and wisely

## Learning Objectives

Upon finishing this chapter you should be able to do the following:

1. Name and describe three patterns for change.
2. Identify the seven most common patterns of ethical failures occurring across the criminal justice system.
3. Discuss the 12 principles for dealing with the mass communications media that a criminal justice manager should consider.
4. Discuss what future challenges you predict for criminal justice.

supervised workforce can be a very powerful tool in the kit of an effective criminal justice manager. It is, therefore, the additional task of the criminal justice manager to create such a workforce, to build for a better future.

## Important Terms and Names

- *change agents*
- *cyclic change*
- *excessive force*
- *futurists*
- *futuristics*

- *futurologists*
- *oscillating change pattern*
- *rise-plateau-crash change*
- *straight-line change*

## Discussion

This article lays a foundation for the study of what the future holds for the criminal justice manager. People who follow leaders need to commit to giving one hundred percent of their time and talent to help the organization excel. The leader makes the same commitment with one added feature. The leaders must balance the needs of the organization with the needs of their employees.

Innovative leaders are ethical visionaries who, like ship's captains look out to the horizon through the clouds of uncertainty and still accomplish their mission. Risk is the enemy but risk can be conquered if the leader correctly evaluates the risk against the gain. As a leader you must SELL the mission to your troops.

One day you might be the CEO of your CJ management organization. The organization will be looking to you to establish your vision for the future and to take the organization in the right direction to achieve your objectives. Dr. Martin Luther King Jr. established a "strategic vision" when he envisioned a brighter future in the civil rights movement where a person would not be judged by their color but by their character (Salacuse, 2006, p. 68).

As change agents, leaders need to effectively communicate with their employees and their customers. You will need to lead effectively in times of relative calm and disaster. Failure is not an option. Leaders earn their mettle when they are forced to prove themselves under corporate gunfire!

Law enforcement managers learn the tools they need early on in their careers working the streets and applying tactics. As they gain experience in leading their cops during uncertain and ambiguous circumstances, they learn to apply the same leadership models when faced with corporate emergencies. While they might learn leadership styles in the classroom, they eventually learn how to manage more efficiently in real-life situations. At some point they learn that effective communication is the key to all success or all failure. I can assuredly state that correctional personnel use the same methodology in the prison and jail systems.

In addition to leading as a futurist the leader needs to also dwell in the present. It is easy to get ahead of yourself and not see sharks swimming around you. Leaders need to rally their troops to infect them with the motivation to help the organization meet strategic goals. John F. Kennedy inspired the youth of my generation by issuing a challenge. JKF said: "Ask not what your country can do for you ask what you can do for your country" (Salacuse, 2006, p. 23).

I, and many of my generation answered President Kennedy's call for service. Many in my generation served in the military, in the Peace Corps, and in law enforcement, the courts and corrections. Many also served others by volunteering in causes they believed in.

One of the best practices discussed in the article is the relationship with the media. The media can be a friend or foe. However, it is incumbent on the CEO to embrace the media. The media can do much good for the organization by helping to disseminate information to the public and in turn get their story. Never overlook their power. The media can help make you shine or bury you.

Leaders sometimes are thrust into greatness by events of history. Police managers know this concept very well. At any time, the press could descend on your organization because of a historic event such as the 2013 Boston Marathon bombing. Manager must be vigilant and prepared for such an event striking their jurisdiction at any moment. Winston Churchill was a not a successful politician but he was an experienced soldier. By his resolve he was able to pull the English people out of near defeat by the Germans in World War II and led them to victory as member of the Allied Coalition (Salacuse, 2006, p. 23).

To look forward into the future you need to embrace technology. We all have to learn how to operate technology to function effectively. YOU need to learn how to manage technology. As a change agent you need to seek out technology and find ways to fund it to survive; and you need to convince your employees to embrace future technologies. Plus, you need to train them to utilize new technologies or you will fail as a leader.

Jeff Cannon and Jon Cannon in their book, *Leadership Lessons of the Navy SEALS*, suggest "PLAN AHEAD_PREPARE FOR A SITUATION THAT HAS NOT YET BEEN IDENTIFIED." The authors state that organizations must anticipate continued chaos and anticipate continued technological advancements (Cannon, and Cannon, 2003, p. 24).

In 2003, when the Cannons wrote their book, law enforcement and correctional agencies were doing well financially. Today, the public sector is in a serious economic downturn. Police departments are closing their doors and correctional institutions are downsizing and releasing felons to the county jails and eventually to the community. To make things worse public sector workers are facing layoff, reductions in pay and compensation, and pension reform. Department programs that improved quality of life in neighborhoods are gone, but service delivery requirements remain at the same level or have increased.

In your corporate future how will you create a culture to transform your agency into a learning organization? You are the boss so what do you do next? In this rapidly changing criminal justice environment how do you retool and rethink so you can move your organization away from tradition to futuristic thinking (Salacuse, 2006, p. 132)?

How do you stay in front of conflict? Conflict, like a Kung Fu master, can attack from all sides at once. Police chiefs and sheriffs deal constantly with conflict from employees, politicians, and the public. Additionally they have to balance the needs of their employees and the demands of the public. Are you ready for that challenge? So earn your college degree, embrace technology, and move into the future committed to the ideal of change management. You need to evolve into a visionary for change to stay alive in your corporate world.

I close my comments with education. After all the majority of you are reading this book as part of a college course. My father Wallace once told me that you can be stripped of everything except your education. He told me those words in my youth and I have never forgotten them. The important part of your college or university education is to apply what you have learned to improve yourself, your organization, your employees, and other stakeholders. So, my final best practice is for you to mentor others to lead in your place when you are gone.

## Questions for Class Discussion

1. How can you customize services to meet specific needs of your organization and the public?
2. Compare and contrast straight-line change, rise-plateau-crash change and cyclic change. Be prepared to provide specific examples for each concept.
3. How can you improve yourself to become a change agent?
4. Compare and contrast technologies currently used in your workplace. What do you think lies ahead in your technology needs?

## Class Activities for the Professor

1. Utilize the questions for class discussions or on-line chats
2. Managers/Leaders research issues, prepare Power Points and give presentations. Assign the students to find another journal article on future trends and have them design a Power Point presentation on their findings.
3. Recruiting, hiring and retaining qualified personnel will become more challenging in CJ organizations. Select an entry-level position in your organization. List the current requirements and attributes. Design and write a new set of requirements and attributes for the position in 2025. Defend your findings in an academic paper or presentation.

## Works Cited

Jeff Cannon and Lt. Cmdr. John Cannon (2003). "Leadership Lessons of the U.S. Navy SEALS: Battle Tested Strategies for Creating Successful Organizations and Inspiring Extraordinary Results", New York, McGraw-Hill

Salacuse, Jeswald M., (2006), "Leading Leaders", New York: American Management Association.

# References and Supplemental Sources

Bell, Wendell (2000). "Futures Studies and the Problem of Evil," *Future Studies*, 5(2) (November).

Bell, Wendell (1996; 1997). *Foundations of Futures Studies*, 2 volumes. Edison, NJ: Transaction.

Bennett, Georgette (1989). *Crimewarps: The Future of Crime in America*, revised edition. New York: Anchor Books.

Blumstein, Al (1995). *Youth Violence, Guns, and the Illicit-Drug Industry*. Available at http://www.drugtext.org/library/articles/blumstein.htm

Blumstein, Al, and Richard Rosenfeld (1998). "Exploring Recent Trends in U.S. Homicide Rates," *Journal of Criminal Law and Criminology*, 88(4): 1175–1216.

Blumstein, Al, and Joel Wallman, eds. (2000). *The Crime Drop in America*. New York: Cambridge University Press.

Blumstein, Al, and Joel Wallman, eds. (2006). *The Crime Drop in America*, 2nd ed. New York: Cambridge University Press.

Garner, Gerald (1987). *"Chief, the Reporters Are Here."* Springfield, IL: Charles C Thomas.

Inayatullah, Sohail (1990). "Deconstructing and Reconstructing the Future: Predictive, Cultural and Critical Methodologies," *Futures* (March 1990).

Inayatullah, Sohail (1992). "Linking the Future with the Present in Judicial Bureaucracies: Learning From the Hawaii Judiciary Case," in Proceedings of the XI World Futures Studies Federation Conference, edited by Mika Mannermaa. Turku, Finland: World Futures Studies Federation and Hungarian Academy of Sciences.

Inayatullah, Sohail, and James Monma (1989). "A Decade of Forecasting: Some Perspectives on Futures Research in the Hawaii Judiciary," *Futures Research Quarterly* (Spring 1989).

International Association of Chiefs of Police (IACP) (1981). "A Balance of Forces: A Study of Justifiable Homicide by the Police." *IACP Newsletter*. Gaithersburg, MD: IACP.

Jones, Ronald B. (1987). "The Press at the Emergency Scene: Issues and Answers," pages 159–167 in *Police and the Media: Bridging Troubled Waters*, edited by Patricia A. Kelly. Springfield, IL: Charles C Thomas.

Kania, Richard R.E., and Ardie Dial (2008). "Prosecutor Misconduct," pages 165–182 in *Justice, Crime and Ethics*, 6th ed., edited by Michael C. Braswell, Belinda R. McCarthy, and Bernard J. McCarthy. Newark, NJ: LexisNexis Matthew Bender.

Lewin, Kurt (1989). "Group Decision and Social Change," pages 543–548 in *Classic Readings in Organizational Behavior*, edited by J. Steven Ott. Pacific Grove, CA: Brooks/Cole.

Mannion, Marea (1993). "Handling the Fallout When the "Big One" Arrives," *The Justice Professional*, 8(1): 123–145.

Marsh, Harry L. (1991). "A Comparative Analysis of Crime Coverage in Newspapers in the United States and Other Countries from 1960–1989: A Review of the Literature," *Journal of Criminal Justice*, 19(1): 67–79.

Mozee, David M. (1987). "Police/Media Conflict," pp. 141–145 in *Police and the Media: Bridging Troubled Waters*, edited by Patricia A. Kelly. Springfield, IL: Charles C Thomas.

Muraskin, Roslyn, and Albert Roberts, eds. (2009). *Visions for Change: Crime and Justice in the Twenty-First Century*, 5th ed. Upper Saddle River, NJ: Pearson/Prentice Hall.

Sherizen, Sanford (1978). "Social Creation of Crime News: All the News Fitted to Print," pp. 203–222 in *Deviance and Mass Media*, edited by Charles Winick, Beverly Hills, CA: Sage.

Skolnick, Jerome H., and Candace McCoy (1985). "Police Accountability and the Media," pp. 102–135 in *Police Leadership in America*, edited by William A. Geller. New York: Praeger.

Souryal, Sam S. (1995). *Police Organization and Administration*, 2nd ed. Cincinnati: Anderson.

Stephens, Gene (2005). "Policing the Future: Law Enforcement's New Challenges," *The Futurist* (March-April 2005).

Tafoya, William (1998). "How CyberCops Fight Terrorism," 7 August 1998 Online Chat with William Tafoya, for *The Washington Post*. Available at http://www. washingtonpost.com/wp-srv/zforum/national/tafoya080798.htm

Wambaugh, Joseph (1989). *The Blooding*. New York: William Morrow.

Wilson, Jerry V., and Paul Q. Fuqua (1975). *The Police and the Media*. Boston: Little, Brown.

# Chapter 2: Contemporary Trends and Impacts in Police Administration

*The test of police efficiency is the absence of crime and disorder,*
*not the visible police action when dealing with it.*
Sir Robert Peel, 1829

## Student Objectives

1. Evaluate the four major themes of the chapter; community engagement, collaboration, globalization, and leaner and greener.
2. Evaluate the impacts of civil liberties, cybercrime, the media, and new advancements in technology on law enforcement organizations
3. Analyze modern perspectives on management and that apply those concepts to police management.
4. Evaluate the concept of emotional intelligence and its role in law enforcement management.

I selected the article you are about to read because it provides a pivotal foundation in management for the criminal justice student, practitioner, supervisor and manager. All the issues in the article impact policing today and will likely impact law enforcement management well into the future. The management issues presented in the chapter will ground the reader in globalization issues confronting policing as an industry and criminal justice as a whole.

# Contemporary Issues in Police Administration

By Gary Cordner

## Learning Objectives

- Identify several community policing activities that have become commonplace among U.S. police departments.
- Explain why interorganizational collaboration is important for American policing.
- Explain the term "transnational crime" and why it is an increasingly important consideration in modern policing.
- Identify the most promising scenario for addressing the issue of racial profiling and racially biased policing.
- Identify several varieties of mass media that affect police and police administration.
- Identify three categories of computer involvement in criminal activity.
- Identify several of the most critical needs facing local law enforcement in combating computer crime.
- Identify five categories of technology utilization in law enforcement.

This chapter presents information on several important themes and issues in contemporary police administration. These themes and issues attempt to capture present-day trends as well as future considerations affecting the police field. Four themes are highlighted: community engagement, collaboration, globalization, and pressures to operate "leaner and greener." Together, these themes emphasize the growing interdependence of modern policing—police are increasingly more connected to communities, other agencies, and even to events around the world. Four contemporary issues are then discussed: civil liberties (including racial profiling), cybercrime, media, and technology. These issues present serious challenges to police departments today and promise to remain prominent issues well into the future. Finally, we discuss several modern approaches to management as they apply to police organizations.

## Four Contemporary Themes

### Community Engagement

It is generally accepted that many police departments had grown far too isolated from their communities by the 1960s and 1970s. Most officers patrolled in cars and had limited informal contact with the public. Calls for service and reported crimes were handled as quickly as possible; the "just the facts" approach was preferred. Police departments emphasized their crime-fighting role and advised the public to leave crime control to the police. The police expected to achieve crime control with the three-part strategy of preventive patrol, rapid response, and follow-up investigations.

Although we now realize that this model of "stranger policing" and the police-centered approach to crime control was fatally flawed, it developed for understandable reasons. Limiting police-public contact was expected to reduce police corruption and other abuses of authority. The professional model was also a method for administering the same level and quality of policing throughout the community—it showed no favorites. In addition, prior to research in the 1970s, preventive patrol, rapid response, and follow-up investigations were believed to be effective, especially in comparison to such antiquated techniques as the posse, the citizens' protective association, and foot patrol.

Police began to rediscover the value of community involvement in the 1980s. The forms of community involvement that have developed vary widely, from relatively passive participation in neighborhood watch groups to more aggressive action, such as confronting drug dealers and prostitutes, and from individual-level efforts to more organized activities, such as citizen patrols. Community crime prevention programs have become commonplace, as has community policing. One survey conducted in 2002 found that each of the following 12 activities had been implemented by at least 75 percent of the responding police agencies:

- Citizens attend police-community meetings
- Citizens participate in Neighborhood Watch
- Citizens help police identify and resolve problems
- Citizens serve as volunteers within the police agency
- Citizens attend citizen police academies
- Police hold regularly scheduled meetings with community groups
- Police have youth programs
- Police have victim assistance programs
- Agencies use fixed assignments to specific beats or areas
- Agencies give special recognition for good community policing work by employees
- Agencies do geographically based crime analysis
- Agencies use permanent neighborhood-based offices or stations[1]

More important than any particular programs, however, has been a fundamental change in policing philosophy and strategy. Individual police departments may or may not support foot patrol, citizens on patrol, or citizen review boards, but it is now universally recognized that police and citizens need to work together to be successful. Both police chiefs and beat patrol officers recognize this.

Community engagement in policing and crime control takes many forms at several different levels. For example, the Seattle Police Department conducted a community-wide survey in 2003 to identify "friction points" between the police department and the community.[2] The department then worked with the community to address the issues of greatest concern to Seattle's citizens. This is an example of seeking community-wide input in order to improve police-community relations.

Many police agencies today utilize some form of civilian review of complaints against the police.[3] Appointed citizens may simply review the police department's internal investigations and decisions, they may serve as an appeals body, or they may even serve as the actual decision makers in meting out discipline to police officers. Many agencies also utilize community representatives on interview boards in the police officer hiring and promotion processes. These are examples of community involvement in the actual administration of the police agency.

Direct citizen participation in policing has also become more common. Some cities, such as Ft. Worth, Texas, have extensive citizen patrol programs.[4] Many jurisdictions also utilize police auxiliaries or reserves—these are generally citizens who have other jobs but who donate some of their spare time to the police or sheriff's department. In some places these reserves are sworn and armed and perform regular police duties; in others they are non-sworn and assist in traffic control, youth programs, school programs, and similar supporting roles. These are examples of community involvement in police field operations.

Citizen participation in crime prevention activities is also quite common today. Perhaps the most powerful trend in this respect is toward community-based problem solving. When police officers and neighborhood residents work together to identify, analyze, and resolve persistent crime and disorder problems, stunning improvements are possible.[5] Clearly, citizens are in the best position to identify the chronic problems that really affect their lives—police are often surprised that abandoned cars and rowdy kids are of greater concern to neighborhood residents than burglaries and thefts. Engaging citizens in the problem-solving stages beyond problem identification (i.e., analysis and response) is more challenging but very rewarding.[6] This is the ultimate form of community involvement because it engages ordinary citizens in tackling the most serious problems in the neighborhoods where they live and work.

The importance of citizen involvement and community engagement for public safety has been reinforced in the aftermath of the events of September 11, 2001. Police, firefighters, and emergency medical service (EMS) personnel were assisted in their response to the World Trade Center by numerous citizen volunteers. Subsequently, law enforcement officials have recognized that they need the public's help in identifying suspicious activity that might be connected to terrorism. Although the U.S. Attorney General's "Operation TIPS" program was abandoned because it seemed too heavy-handed, there is no doubt that vigilant and engaged citizens are crucial to homeland security.

The underlying principle to all this is that ours is supposed to be a government of the people, by the people, and for the people. Because we the people are very busy these days, there are limits on our willingness and ability to participate in policing, crime prevention, and homeland security. Then too, we have professionals who are trained and paid to perform much of the work associated with public safety. It should also not be forgotten that our history teaches us that citizens will sometimes go too far and want to take the law into their own hands.[7] Thus, there must be limits on the public's role in policing, and we must be careful to strike the proper balance between the roles of paid professionals and volunteer citizens. Nevertheless, what we have learned is that it is essential for effective policing, and for the control of crime and disorder, that the police truly engage the community as partners. It is important that this fundamental principle not be forgotten.

## Collaboration

The importance and necessity of collaboration has similarly become evident in recent years. Just as police departments are more effective when they work closely with the community, so too are they more effective when they collaborate with other public and private organizations.

Interorganizational collaboration is particularly crucial for American policing because of the extreme fragmentation of government resources and authority. Within a typical local community, the police department and fire department are separate agencies, and the ambulance service may also be a separate entity. Emergency communications (the 911 center) may be operated by the county or by a regional board. The county sheriff's department is a separate agency that usually has jurisdiction within the local community, as do the state police. Probation and parole may be one agency or two and may be operated by the county or the state. The same is true of juvenile services. Prosecutors may be employed locally, although it is more common for them to be county or state officials. Then there is the entire additional layer of federal law enforcement, federal probation, and U.S. attorneys arrayed on top of the local and state systems. In times of serious emergency, the National Guard and the military may also be deployed.

Because of the existence of all of these local, state, and federal public safety and criminal justice agencies with overlapping jurisdictions, coordination and cooperation are essential to avoid waste, interference, and conflict. The need goes even further today. Actual collaboration—working together to be more successful—is necessary. This involves sharing resources, expertise, and authority. Evidence of collaboration can often be found in everyday investigations and problem solving, in the formation of multijurisdictional task forces, and in joint training exercises.

Good examples of collaboration can be found today in the investigation of computer crime. Few departments have the necessary in-house expertise to address cybercrime at this point, so it is often provided by state or federal agencies or by a multiagency task force. If a local agency becomes aware of a computer crime or seizes computing equipment that might contain digital evidence, it may request assistance from one of these sources or just "hand off" the case to an agency that is better equipped to deal with the case.

Some effective problem-solving collaboration has recently begun to take place between police and probation, parole, and juvenile services agencies.[8] For too long, many police departments and individual police officers did not work closely with these agencies. Police have found, however, that adult and juvenile probation officers, for example, have detailed information about their clients, as well as authority over them that, in many instances, exceeds police authority. Thus, police and probation officers working together may be able to address a gang problem, an after-hours nightclub problem, or a drug house problem more effectively than either group working alone.

An excellent example of collaboration to improve police and public safety response was recently implemented in a 40-county region in Eastern Kentucky.[9] More than 100 local law enforcement agencies, plus the state police and other state law enforcement agencies, worked together to implement a wireless data and voice communication system. Fire, ambulance, and other public safety agencies will be added to the system in later phases.

This project is designed to address what is referred to as the "interoperability" problem. This is the problem caused by different agencies having separate communications and data systems that cannot "talk" to each other. Lack of communications interoperability among public safety agencies was demonstrated most dramatically in New York and at the Pentagon on September 11, 2001, when responding agencies could not communicate effectively with each other. Lack of data interoperability was uncovered in the subsequent investigation into how the terrorists were able to enter the United States to plan and carry out their attacks—different federal agencies had pieces of information, but no one had the whole picture. It is now obvious that communications and data interoperability are essential prerequisites to effective collaboration to combat both crime and terrorism.

This discussion has centered on collaboration among police, public safety, and criminal justice agencies, but of course the police also need to collaborate with many other public and private agencies in order to address crime and disorder problems. Police departments have demonstrated the value of collaboration with schools, social services, mental health agencies, private security, and a wide variety of other activities over the past decade. The 2002 survey cited earlier in this chapter found that more than 75 percent of agencies had implemented three specific forms of collaboration:

- Police have interagency involvement in problem solving
- Police use regulatory codes in problem solving
- Police work with building code enforcement[10]

Similarly, a study of problem solving by individual patrol officers in San Diego found that it was common for officers to draw on resources from outside the department when responding to specific problems. Also, the types of collaborations that were developed varied substantially from one problem to another, as they should, because problem-oriented policing aims to apply tailor-made responses to each particular problem. The figures below indicate how often officers reported using different resources in the 227 problem-solving projects that were identified:

- 26% private sector
- 18% other city agencies
- 17% code compliance
- 6% other police including federal
- 6% county, state, or federal agencies (nonpolice)
- 4% social services[11]

It makes good sense for police agencies to engage in widespread collaboration with other public and private organizations.[12] Collaboration can help the police be more effective in addressing crime and disorder problems. It can also contribute greatly to efficiency, through coordination of effort and elimination of redundancy and duplication. Collaboration is particularly crucial in a situation as fragmented as the American governmental system.

## Globalization

The third theme that increasingly runs through modern policing is globalization. Trends in business, finance, trade, travel, communications, and computers really have "shrunk the world" in the last decade or two. It is far more likely now than 20 years ago that a local criminal investigation might involve international transactions and foreign individuals. These foreign individuals might have traveled to the local jurisdiction, or they might have played their roles (as witnesses, victims, or suspects) from afar.

Many traditional crimes such as drug distribution and theft can have international features today. Much has also been made in recent years of international organized crime involving Russians, Nigerians, and others. Crimes committed with computers, including fraud, theft, vandalism, and hacking, know no boundaries. Then there are newer crimes (or perhaps crimes that are simply receiving more attention today) such as human trafficking of women and children and illegal trafficking of immigrants, weapons, and even nuclear material. The term *transnational crime* has been coined to describe the increasingly international nature of crime.

International terrorism has become a huge concern for local, state, and federal law enforcement since the events of September 11, 2001. Americans and people all around the world witnessed the death and destruction that could be caused by a relatively small group of terrorists. These were far from the first acts of international terrorism committed against the United States, of course, and in fact other countries had for a long time been more seriously plagued by these kinds of attacks than had the United States. The attacks of 9/11 galvanized national and world attention, however, and drove home the new reality that crime and terrorism emanating from halfway around the globe could threaten American communities and American citizens.

Another aspect of globalization that has affected American policing has been the participation of local and state police in international policing missions in places like Haiti, Bosnia, and Kosovo.[13] As the United States, the United Nations, the European Union, and other bodies have accepted peacekeeping roles in war-torn countries around the world, it has become evident that a key element in the restoration of order and civil society is effective policing. Typically, police and military forces in these countries were previously aligned with repressive regimes. Once the initial military phase of peacekeeping has been accomplished, the country needs reliable, professional policing to maintain order and reassure the citizenry of their safety. While a policing system is being rebuilt along democratic lines, police officers are brought in from around the world to provide police service and help train the country's new police.

Many American police officers have now had the experience of serving in such international missions, and many American police departments believe that part of their responsibility is to support the development of more professional and democratic policing in other countries. This is a relatively new awareness for American police and contributes to their sense of being part of a global police community. It is also a fairly new realization for those in the U.S. government responsible for foreign relations "that security is important to the development of democracy and police are important to the character of that security. Assisting in the democratic reform of foreign police systems has become a front-burner issue in American foreign policy."[14]

It is difficult to predict all the future ramifications for policing of this trend toward globalization. Clearly, international issues and considerations that were once thought to be irrelevant for local American policing have become relevant and even significant. This trend can only continue.

## Leaner and Greener Police Departments

The maxim to "do more with less" is not particularly new. Government agencies, including police departments, have faced regular cycles of budget belt-tightening over the past few decades. In some states, such as California, Oregon, and Florida, tax limitation ballot initiatives and state laws have added extra pressure to the normal level of fiscal conservatism in America. Nationally, however, the recession that began in 2008 has forced additional reductions of services, hiring freezes, and even layoffs in many state and local government agencies, including police departments.[15]

These kinds of fiscal conditions certainly present headaches and challenges to police executives. Police chiefs have a harder time arguing for their annual budgets before mayors and city councils. The need for federal grants to supplement an agency's budget grows greater, but so does the competition for those grants from other police agencies in equally desperate straits. Many police agencies have had to trim their overtime budgets, which reduces operational flexibility and also hurts individual officers' pocketbooks. Popular programs such as McGruff and DARE have been cut back or eliminated in some departments. A few police agencies have closed mini-stations, storefront offices, and other components of their community policing strategies. Police departments have examined the services they provide and, in some cases, opted to eliminate services such as funeral escorts, taking reports at minor traffic accidents, and responding to residential burglar alarms (unless there is verification that it is not a false alarm). In a few extreme cases, smaller agencies have simply given up and gone out of business for lack of adequate funding to continue in operation.[16]

Another economic issue that arose in 2008 that had financial repercussions for police was the sudden increase in the price of gasoline. Quite a few police agencies expended their entire annual gasoline budgets before the year was half over. Fortunately, gasoline prices came down almost as quickly as they went up, and have stayed well below their 2008 peak. In the meantime, police interest in more fuel-efficient vehicles surged. Some police departments also adapted to higher gas prices by putting two officers together in cars, and by increasing their use of foot patrol and bicycle patrol. Time will tell whether these were just temporary adaptations or leading indicators of long-term trends. It seems likely that fiscal pressures will inevitably force police to reduce their traditional reliance on heavy, full-size automobiles for patrol and other purposes.

In conjunction with gas prices, concern about dependence on foreign oil, and worries about global warming, local governments seem to be increasingly committed to adopting "greener" methods of operation.[17] Moreover, in 2009 the Obama administration made environmental jobs and technology a cornerstone of its national economic recovery strategy. In this context, police departments are currently exploring ways in which they can reduce their energy consumption and their "carbon footprint" other than just improved automobile efficiency. Possibilities might include more energy-efficient police buildings, use of alternative fuels for vehicles and heating/cooling of buildings, increased recycling, provision of more police services by telephone and Internet, and increased opportunities for telecommuting by police employees. Police executives may as well get accustomed to the idea that energy efficiency and eco-friendliness are liable to be added to the criteria by which their performance will be judged in the not too distant future.

# Four Contemporary Issues

## Civil Liberties

Our world has changed since September 11, 2001, and the changes have caused us to rethink how we feel about extra security measures. Many citizens think that these measures are necessary precautions that will prevent another devastating occurrence that could once again shatter our perceptions of the "safe" nation in which we live. Others think, however, that our rights are in danger of being taken from us or compromised in some other way. "Some believe that civil liberties have become a casualty in that process; others insist that the exigencies of national security demand restrictions on liberties"[18] or even that "the age-old dichotomy between security and liberty is false and ... that liberty cannot exist without order."[19]

Some Americans are not concerned that the National Security Agency has been given expanded authority to monitor potential terrorist communications, including phone calls and e-mails originating within the United States. Others argue that intelligence and law enforcement agencies already have sufficient authority and simply need to follow established procedures that worked well in the past. This kind of debate has been going on throughout American history, but has become more heated and intense since 9/11.

Our long-standing debates about civil liberties and proper use of government authority have frequently centered on the police. For example, racial profiling, or "driving while black," emerged in the 1990s as perhaps the most serious and sensitive issue facing police departments in the United States.[20] It was the subject of lawsuits, civil rights investigations, and consent decrees. It was discussed and debated in the U.S. Congress and in the 2000 presidential election. Many states mandated new police policies and data collection systems, and even more local communities did so. Only the events of 9/11 deflected attention away from racial profiling, and when the issue reemerged, it was focused more on profiling of potential terrorists and the effects this might have on the rights of Middle Eastern and Islamic persons.

Two aspects of the racial profiling phenomenon merit its identification as one of the most important contemporary issues in American policing, despite its lower profile immediately following the terrorist attacks against the United States. One is that it underscores the continued salience of race for policing. Given the emphasis on community policing throughout the 1980s and 1990s, with its focus on community engagement and the improvement of police-community relations, it might have been expected that police-minority relations would have been greatly improved. During the same period, however, three well-publicized abuses of police use of force—the Rodney King incident in Los Angeles and the Amadou Diallo and Abner Louima incidents in New York—and many other instances of questioned police use of force against people of color occurred in the United States. Understandably, uneasiness and suspicion continue to characterize the relationship between race and policing, as illustrated by the recent nationally publicized incident involving Harvard University professor Henry Louis Gates, Jr. and Cambridge police sergeant James Crowley.

The racial profiling issue clearly strikes a strong chord in minority communities and among those most concerned about civil rights and civil liberties in America.[21] While most police have ardently denied that they use, or support the use of, any such profiles, 40 percent of African Americans believe they have been profiled by police, and even a majority of whites believe the problem is widespread.[22] It seems likely that the term "racial profiling" has gradually expanded in the public mind and come to signify larger issues of racial bias and discrimination by police. Largely for this reason, the Police Executive Research Forum has encouraged police departments to address "racially biased policing," not just the narrower problem of racial profiling.[23]

As racial profiling-inspired data collection has continued around the country, it has frequently been discovered that minority drivers are overrepresented, in comparison to the total population, in vehicle stops by the police.[24] They are also typically more likely to have their persons and vehicles searched subsequent to vehicle stops.[25] Whether this overrepresentation of minorities in stops and searches is the result of police profiling (discrimination), or alternatively, a reflection of police deployment in lower-income neighborhoods, police efforts to address crime- and gang-related problems, or even differential driving habits, is currently not empirically known.[26] It is the subject of much discussion and debate, however. In the most promising scenario, police and citizens will work together to collect and analyze these data, interpret the results, discuss implications, and fashion appropriate responses.[27] This approach employs the themes of community engagement and collaboration within the framework of community policing to encourage open conversation about a thorny and complex issue—something that has not happened often enough with respect to race and policing in America.

The other aspect of the racial profiling phenomenon that makes it a particularly salient contemporary issue is that it reflects the larger and even more endemic issue of police accountability. As discussed in Chapters 1 and 2, one of the most distinguishing features of policing is that ordinary police officers exercise substantial low-visibility discretion. Historically, officers have not been held to strict accountability in their use of this discretion. During the 1970s and 1980s some accountability began to be exacted for particularly serious police officer decisions, such as whether to use force against a person, to engage in a high-speed pursuit, and to make an arrest in a domestic violence situation. Despite these developments, however, most police decision making remained highly discretionary and not particularly accountable.

The racial profiling issue arises over concern about whether police officers make good and fair decisions when stopping people and cars and conducting searches. The common response of collecting and analyzing data on each stop creates conditions under which greater accountability can be established, especially if data collection includes information on each officer's identity. The types of cars and people that each officer stops can be scrutinized; patterns of discrimination and abuse can be identified. This represents a degree of supervision and accountability over everyday, ordinary police officer decision making that has not previously been available or even anticipated. It might well be the harbinger of other forms of ever closer supervision over the actions of police officers, perhaps aided by modern technology (e.g., in-car video systems, tiny cameras worn by officers, vehicle location systems, police car black boxes, etc.).

Will closer supervision lead to more effective and more just police work? Only time will tell us the answer to this question. Certainly, police have not always used their authority justly. It should be the case that greater supervision and accountability over police decision making will reduce unnecessary use of force, improper searches, unjustified stops, and other forms of abuse of authority. If the net effect of such accountability measures is to reduce police discretion, however, it is possible that officer decision making will become more legalistic (just following the law) and bureaucratic (just following the rules), which might or might not make policing more effective or just, as illustrated in 2009 in Dallas when police delayed NFL football player Ryan Moats on his way to pay his last respects to his gravely ill mother-in-law.[28] If not properly implemented, such supervision could also greatly inhibit police officer initiative. The issue of accountability is one that we will surely wrestle with as long as we give some government employees police power and authority over the rest of us.

## Mass Media

The mass media, both news and entertainment, have changed substantially over the last few decades. The media, and through them the public, seem to be increasingly interested in police work and crime. With more channels competing for the public's attention (thanks to cable and satellite TV), and the new medium of the Internet with unlimited "channels," it is easy to feel overwhelmed. At the very least, the attention of the mass media can definitely overwhelm a police agency that happens to find itself in the spotlight.

One example of the effect of the mass media was illustrated during a series of sniper slayings in the Washington, D.C., area in the autumn of 2002.[29] For several weeks, area police departments had to contend with an army of news reporters representing local, national, and international news organizations. Some of these organizations, especially those providing 24-hour news programming, seemed to have unquenchable appetites for information. Such organizations need something new every few hours, whether the police have any "real" news to report or not. In addition, these news organizations compete vigorously (some would say viciously) with each other for readers, listeners, watchers and, ultimately, advertisers (i.e., money). Consequently, hundreds of reporters were constantly pestering witnesses, victims, families, Montgomery County Police Chief Charles Moose, and other police officials for new information. This led to leaks from the investigation team and the release of both inaccurate information and information that the police had hoped would be kept confidential while the investigation was underway.

Intense news attention can be beneficial as well. In the case of the sniper slayings, it is unlikely that an old acquaintance of the eventual suspects, who lived 2,500 miles away in Tacoma, Washington, would have known about the D.C.-area crimes, put two and two together, and notified the authorities about his suspicions, if not for the intense, nationwide news coverage of the crimes. Similarly, it was an unauthorized leak about the suspect vehicle, broadcast over commercial radio, that led a trucker and another citizen to locate the suspects at an interstate rest stop in western Maryland within a few hours of the broadcast.

Another example of mass media effects was evident in Los Angeles at the end of 2002. New LAPD Chief William Bratton focused on the phenomenon of police pursuits. Such pursuits are a serious consideration in most jurisdictions. In Los Angeles, however, and a few other cities, it is common for police pursuits to be televised live through the use of TV helicopters and airplanes. The chief expressed concern that such live television coverage, often carried on several stations, emboldens those who are being chased, giving them the means to achieve their 15 minutes (or two hours) of fame. Giving chase on live television may also lead to poor police decision making if officers feel pressure to perform bravely and capture their suspect at all costs.

"Reality TV" cop shows have joined 24-hour news and live TV coverage as means of presenting non-fictional accounts of policing to mass audiences.[30] These shows, from *Cops* to *Real Stories of the Highway Patrol*, are typically filmed by riding along with police officers for hundreds of hours and then editing the film down to a 30-minute or 60-minute program. Thus, although the footage is realistic, the condensed form of presentation gives audiences an unrealistic sense of the pace of police work and an unrepresentative sample of police activity. These shows stand in contrast to the many fictional TV dramas based on police work, which audiences presumably understand to be fiction and not news or documentary.

A different application of the mass media is represented by the television show *America's Most Wanted*. This network TV show is specifically designed to help police solve actual crimes and capture real suspects. It is essentially a bigger-budget, national version of Crimestopper shows that run regularly on many local TV stations. Unsolved crimes are dramatized in order to solicit the public's assistance in identifying and/or locating persons involved in the crimes.

As these examples illustrate, the entertainment and news media have complicated and complex effects on policing and police administration. These media, especially 24-hour television and Internet news, create demands for information that are difficult to satisfy. They present a combination of live, edited, realistic, and fictional accounts of police work to millions of viewers that influence the public's perceptions and expectations. This in turn affects police officers, who are aware that the public (including victims, offenders, journalists, lawyers, and politicians) watches these shows, forms opinions about the police, and develops expectations that are often unrealistic.[31] The police sometimes then find themselves playing to roles defined by *Cops*, *Law and Order*, or *CSI* instead of to roles defined by their agency's values, policies, and training.

For police administrators, the mass media are both a blessing and a curse; regardless, they are a reality. One hundred years ago, most police executives only had to deal with a local newspaper or two. Once television came onto the scene, most police chiefs still only had to deal with local TV news and reporters. This could be challenging, of course, but relationships could be developed, and the parameters were fairly well understood. As television matured, the LAPD and the FBI were early pioneers in working with Hollywood to influence fictional portrayals of their agencies, and a few other large police departments began to attract attention from national news organizations. Gradually, mass media began to affect policing through more intense news coverage and a seemingly endless array of TV shows and movies.

Only in the last 20 years or so, however, have the mass media really become a factor that the average police executive might actually have to work with and respond to. The Fox Network could show up at any time to film a reality show. Alternatively, following a significant crime or police shooting, a fleet of satellite TV trucks can be expected to park across the street from police headquarters. Any chief's worst nightmare would be to have an officer's questionable actions replayed every half hour on CNN or available continuously on YouTube. That scenario becomes increasingly more likely with the proliferation of mini-cams, surveillance cameras, cell phone cameras, and police car video systems. This all represents a revolutionary shift in the police-media relationship that is still developing. The effects that it will have on police-public relations, and on police officer behavior, are uncertain. What is certain is that police executives will have to become more sophisticated and savvy in their relationships with the mass media.

## Cybercrime

Cybercrime is computer-mediated activity that is illegal or illicit and that can be performed through global electronic networks.[32] It can best be understood by examining the potential roles of the computer in criminal activity. Three useful categories are (1) the computer as a *target*, (2) the computer as a *tool* for the commission of a crime, and (3) the computer as incidental to the crime itself, or simply put, as *evidence*. Crimes in which the computer is the target involve individuals breaking into or attacking a victim's system and may include activities such as hacking, cracking, or sabotage. Crimes in which the computer is used as a tool for the commission of a crime typically involve traditional crimes, such as fraud, being committed in ways to which we are less accustomed. For example, theft, forgery, embezzlement, and even stalking are familiar crimes to us. However, any of these crimes may be committed today using a computer, consequently complicating the investigation. Finally, crimes in which the computer is incidental to the criminal activity could include using a computer to keep financial records of illegal business activities or perhaps sending a threatening e-mail message to someone.[33]

Although numerous efforts have been undertaken to give us a better description of the incidence and prevalence of cybercrime, what we know is limited. Long-term initiatives are viewed as key in obtaining a valid assessment of cybercrime. For example, the National Crime Victimization Survey has recently added questions to examine fraud, identify theft, and stalking victimization. The FBI has also included a question in the National Incident-Based Reporting System to indicate whether an offender used a computer in the commission of a crime. In other efforts, a Bureau of Justice Statistics national survey of state prosecutors found that 42 percent of these offices prosecute computer-related crimes under their state's computer statutes. As one might expect, in larger cities, prosecution of these crimes was even more likely, with 97 percent of full-time large offices indicating that they prosecute computer-related crimes. The most frequently prosecuted type of computer-related crime is child pornography, with three in 10 offices reporting prosecuting this type of offense. Credit card and bank card fraud represented the next most frequently prosecuted cases.[34]

The National Institute of Justice (NIJ) also conducted an assessment of the needs of state and local law enforcement in combating electronic crime and cyberterrorism. In this survey, respondents indicated what they perceived as being the 10 most critical needs:

- public awareness
- adequate data and reporting
- uniform training and certification courses
- onsite management assistance for electronic crime units and task forces
- updated laws
- cooperation with the high-tech industry
- special research and publications
- management awareness and support
- investigative and forensic tools
- structured computer crime units[35]

In response to some of the findings of this survey, the NIJ developed the Electronic Crime Program, which was designed to address any type of crime involving digital technology. The goal of the program is to help the criminal justice community build capacity for addressing electronic crime through collaboration among federal, state, and local law enforcement; industry; and academia.[36]

When addressing cybercrime, community engagement and community education are important. Citizens must know the extent of cybercrime so they will be less likely to become a victim. Anecdotal evidence indicates that a complicating factor about cybercrime is that oftentimes its victims go for long periods without knowing they are a victim. This is unlike most of the crimes with which law enforcement is familiar and accustomed to investigating. Collaborative efforts for dealing with cybercrime will require more partnerships among the private and public sector, specifically law enforcement and security. This may come in the form of assistance with investigations, training, and/or education. With increased and extensive Internet use, globalization has become a significant component of cybercrime. Today, we know no jurisdictional boundaries, which makes dealing with cybercrime an even greater challenge.

## Technology

Technological advancement in the last decade has dramatically changed the way we work and the kind of work we do. This holds true for most occupations and certainly for law enforcement. While one might argue that technology makes our jobs easier, it also makes our jobs more challenging. It is true that technology can enable us to perform activities more efficiently and effectively, but that is assuming that we have the technology, understand its application, and have been trained to use it. Another complicating factor is that criminals have access to technology as well, so this enables them to commit crimes using means they have not had in the past, or commit crimes they have not considered in the past.

The RAND Science and Policy Institute categorized technology by its uses for law enforcement in an effort to assess current needs and capabilities and hopefully identify future directions in maximizing appropriate technologies and finding technological gaps that must be filled. Law enforcement uses technology in the following areas, some of which might overlap:

- first response
- investigation and apprehension
- forensic analysis
- administration and management
- crime prevention

Examples of first-responder technology applications include those used for situation reporting, officer safety, officer deployment, and tactical communications. Tasers, digital crime scene photography, and remote case filings are technologies that are used for criminal investigation and apprehension of suspects. Forensic analysis technologies deal primarily with the identification and analysis of physical evidence and include, for example, explosive residue analysis and ballistics analysis with the National Integrated Ballistics Information Network (NIBIN). Administration and management have broad-ranging technology applications in areas such as information processing, planning, training, and accountability.[37]

Technology can be a valuable asset, but it can also cause problems if used inappropriately or inadequately. Potential barriers to effective technology use include real costs, potential costs, technology risk, and human risk. Real costs include initial procurement costs and opportunity costs, as compared to the cost of other resources. Potential costs are those that are unanticipated and usually involve unintended consequences of the use of a technology. Technology risk is the risk that the technology will not work, either in its application to a problem or as it is intended to be used. Human risk typically deals with resistance to technology by personnel or their inability to use it appropriately. Occasionally, human risk may include potential danger with the use of a technology.

Technology certainly affects modern life in many ways. Technology may make community engagement and collaboration easier or harder. If people spend all their time playing video games and surfing the Internet, their social skills and social interaction might wither. On the other hand, a lot of modern social interaction occurs via technology. In this regard, police agencies are currently beginning to use their web pages and various social networking services in order to send out crime alerts and other information to the public.[38] E-mail, text messages, blogs, twittering, and social networks have quickly become key methods by which some police departments are communicating with the public—and not just by sending out information to citizens, but also by soliciting tips, videos, and other evidence, and by actually engaging the public in dialogue about crime and disorder issues in the community. As more and more social interaction and social life occurs electronically, police are finding it necessary to join their community online.

## Modern Perspectives on Management

The organization as we know it today is much different from the organization of 1950, when the traditional perspective on police administration reigned supreme. This is understandable. The fact that organizations are open systems means that they are affected by changing environmental influences. Organizations must necessarily change if they are to be responsive to changing societal demands.

In the 1970s many observers believed that the organizational turmoil and loss of respect for authority then evident were indicators of social and organizational disintegration that threatened the very foundations of society. Other observers saw these conditions as temporary aberrations of a society in a state of cultural lag, changing so rapidly that its institutions were unable to keep up with the change and respond to it meaningfully. Still others saw these trends producing an administrative revolution that would increase personal freedom as the organization became a "shelter without walls."[39]

In recent years, however, with less fear of social and organizational disintegration, organizational life has become more humane and, indeed, more considerate of the needs and concerns of employees. In addition, the tenor of the times has changed. Foreign competition and the trade imbalance have forced the United States into a more pragmatic posture, with emphasis on quality workmanship. Everyone now recognizes the necessity for improving their productivity in order to make their goods and services more competitive in the world market. In similar fashion, government agencies have begun to see the need to improve their productivity in order to provide more and better services at reduced cost to the taxpayer.

In this chapter we will briefly discuss some organizational improvement methodologies and applications that have been advanced in recent years and that apply to police management. Some of these approaches to improvement are embodied in specific police programs, while others are adapted from general management practices. Four approaches are presented: strategic management, command accountability, emotional intelligence, and the learning organization approach.

### Strategic Management

Part 4 of this text, with chapters on information systems, evaluating performance, and police strategies and tactics, presented many of the latest developments in the strategic management approach to police organizational improvement. Today, the police field has reached a stage of maturity in which we now recognize that police departments have some basic choices open to them in deciding how best to achieve their goals and objectives, serve their communities, and improve their efficiency and effectiveness. This represents a big step forward from a time when few options seemed to be available. It also signals perhaps the major responsibility of top police executives—choosing and then implementing their agencies' basic strategies.

In Chapter 1 we presented a simple outline of police history based on the evolution of police strategy from political through professional to community eras.[40] This picture of police history has the virtue of simplicity, but it has been criticized for oversimplifying the 150-plus years of American policing.[41] It has also given rise to endless arguments about which of the three models is best and, in particular, whether the community model should replace the professional model.

In our view, this latter debate is naive and once again overly simplistic. The choice between the community and professional models is not an either/or decision, but rather is a matter of degree and emphasis. Moreover, there are more choices than just these two. For example, in the series that offered the three-stage vision of the evolution of policing, a later paper identified four contemporary "corporate" strategies of policing: professional crime fighting, strategic crime fighting, problem-solving policing, and community policing.[42] A brief description of each of these strategies will help illustrate the choices now open to police executives and their departments.

The *professional crime-fighting* approach heavily emphasizes the crime control function of policing, the law and professional standards as sources of police legitimacy, and the traditional tactics of motorized patrol, rapid response, and follow-up investigations. Under this model the police seek and accept the primary responsibility for crime control. Police officers are seen as professionals, with the attendant reliance on training and technology. Police executives seek maximum independence in running their departments.

The *strategic crime-fighting* approach accepts most of the tenets of the professional model outlined above, except for two modifications: the effectiveness of traditional police tactics is questioned, and more focus is placed on types of crime other than common street crime. The strategic model emphasizes such targeted techniques as directed patrol, case screening, differential responses, and repeat offender programs. This model also gives greater attention than the professional model to organized crime, white-collar crime, drug trafficking, and other specialized types of criminal activity.

The *problem-solving* approach varies from both the professional and strategic models in several respects. It recognizes the importance of the crime control function but also stresses other important functions of the police, such as fear reduction, dispute resolution, and control of disorder. It also emphasizes that law enforcement is but one method available to the police for controlling crime, fear, and disorder; other methods include prevention, mediation, education, and referral, to name just a few. The problem-solving approach urges police to reconceptualize their business away from incident handling and law enforcement and toward problem solving and prevention. This model gives the greatest importance to gathering and analyzing information as the bases for identifying and solving problems.

The *community policing model*, more than the others, insists on giving citizens a greater role in policing and police administration. The idea that the police can effectively assume the primary responsibility for crime control is rejected. Instead, police must work closely with citizens and communities in identifying problems, setting priorities, and solving problems. Community policing argues that policing must become more customer-oriented and that in the end the customer is always right. This model urges departments to assign police officers and commanders to geographic areas on a more permanent basis so that they will come to identify more strongly with communities and so that those communities can influence them more effectively. Ultimately, under community policing, community norms and values join the law as sources of police legitimacy. Creating positive police-community relations is seen as a valid and important objective of policing.

To these four major police strategies we can now add a fifth option, *intelligence-led policing*,[43] discussed in Chapter 14. The basic premise of this strategy is that police resources and tactics should be deployed based on systematic and continuous analysis of information and intelligence. The use of the term "intelligence" tends to suggest that this is a strategy solely aimed at terrorism, organized crime, gangs, and drugs, but in fact its reach is much broader. In principle, all police resources, including patrol, traffic, and investigations, could be targeted and deployed based on up-to-the-moment information about crime, disorder, vulnerabilities, threats, and other problems confronting the community.

Many police executives, upon reading these descriptions, are inclined to say that they support all five strategies and that their agencies are guided by each one. This response is commendable in the sense that these executives recognize the merits of each strategy and want to avoid unnecessary either/or choices. However, any police agency will tend to emphasize some features of these strategies over others. In today's tight financial circumstances, most police agencies cannot afford to be all things to all people. In fact, whether by design or by default, police departments will adhere more to one or two of these strategies than to the others. The job of the police executive is to choose the organization's strategy consciously and carefully instead of letting it drift or emerge by default.

Which strategy is best? It all depends. The police executive should make every effort to adopt the strategy or combination of strategies that best fits the needs of his or her community and police organization. Just as critically, police executives must continually monitor developments within the field of policing, within their organizations, and within their communities in order to make strategic adjustments and changes when they are needed. For, as noted by Kenneth Andrews, "the highest function of the executive is … leading the continuous process of determining the nature of the enterprise, and setting, revising, and achieving its goals."[44]

## Command Accountability

Just as police supervisors have long found it difficult to hold police officers truly accountable, police chief executives have often wrestled with the task of holding their commanders accountable. In recent years, owing largely to the popularity of the *Compstat* system developed in the New York Police Department,[45] *command accountability* has received renewed attention. The Compstat process is based on four principles: (1) accurate and timely intelligence, (2) effective tactics, (3) rapid deployment of personnel and resources, and (4) relentless follow-up and assessment.[46] In the Compstat process, area commanders (e.g., precinct captains) are regularly "put on the hot seat" in front of their peers, presented with the latest crime analysis information from their command areas, and expected to demonstrate intimate familiarity with ongoing problems and present solutions already undertaken to resolve those problems. The commander who is caught unaware or unprepared is not only embarrassed, but also may be looking at a different assignment if the performance is repeated.

Although this Compstat system sometimes seems to be rather harsh in its implementation, and although it may sometimes be more about "the numbers" than actual community conditions, it addresses a real problem of police administration. Perhaps its greatest potential contribution is that it shifts the focus of command accountability away from merely internal administrative issues (the budget, personnel, etc.) toward what really matters the most—substantive problems in the community. Any process that can successfully redirect police management's attention and accountability away from internal concerns and toward community problems is probably beneficial.[47]

## Emotional Intelligence

Daniel Goleman proposes that while technical skills and high IQ are important qualities in leaders, emotional intelligence (EQ) is imperative for quality leadership.[48] His research indicates that most effective leaders have high degrees of emotional intelligence. In related research, David McClellan found that a correlation exists between EQ and high performance.[49] In other words, leaders who had high degrees of emotional intelligence outperformed others who were similarly situated.

Emotional intelligence consists of five components that culminate in the keystone of the concept, which is "awareness of one's own feelings as they occur."[50] The five components that make up EQ are self-awareness, self-regulation, motivation, empathy, and social skill. Self-awareness is a critical awareness of one's emotions, strengths, weaknesses, needs, and drives, with an acute understanding of how these affect self-perception, others' perceptions, and their job performance. Self-regulation is being in control of one's feelings and impulses—those who are masters of their emotions. Motivation is the want and desire to achieve for simply the satisfaction of achievement versus some external reward such as notoriety. Empathy, often easily recognized, is the thoughtful consideration of others' feelings in decision making. Finally, social skill is "friendliness with a purpose" that enables leaders to direct people in ways they desire.[51]

Can emotional intelligence be learned? Goleman indicates that while research indicates that there is a genetic component to EQ, nurture plays a significant role as well. He also contends that EQ increases with age and maturity. He proposes that traditional methods of increasing characteristics such as emotional intelligence are not sufficient alone, but that an individual's sincere desire and concerted effort are more important. While EQ may have not been considered a crucial element of police leadership to date, it is worthy of consideration for managers not only for their own self-improvement, but also for developing leadership skills in their employees.

In a later work, *Primal Leadership*, Goleman and colleagues describe what they call a "resonant leader."[52] A resonant leader is one who has not only acute self-awareness and social awareness, but also the ability to use these in dealing with his or her employees. Empathy, which is achieved through self-awareness and social awareness, is of extreme importance to the leader in dealing with his or her employees. By being empathetic, leaders are able to motivate people and spread enthusiasm about the work of the organization. According to the authors, leaders who exhibit empathy can be especially effective in service occupations or those that require extensive dealings with the public, such as policing.

Goleman et al. also stress the importance of a leader letting employees see who he or she really is—letting emotions show. For example, they advocate the use of humor in the workplace under certain circumstances, to engage people and to contribute to a calming work environment. In policing, gallows humor has long been a common device for relieving stress, but humor has not been widely recognized as a leadership technique. Nor has "letting emotions show." While the macho nature of the traditional police culture may have worked against open displays of emotion and humor by leaders and managers, it seems highly likely that police leader effectiveness has always been enhanced by EQ. Finding better ways to incorporate EQ into police promotional testing and leadership training should probably be a high priority.

## The Learning Organization

The learning organization approach was popularized by Peter Senge in his book *The Fifth Discipline*.[53] In this approach, you will see concepts that have been previously discussed throughout this text and have been developed into a contemporary multifaceted perspective by Senge. Learning organizations are those "where people continually expand their capacity to create the results they truly desire, where new and expansive patterns of thinking are nurtured, where collective aspiration is set free, and where people are continually learning how to learn together."[54] The fifth discipline that is necessary for the creation of learning organizations is *systems thinking*. Only when systems thinking is accompanied by building shared vision, mental models, team learning, and personal mastery, however, will it work to create a learning organization.

As we discussed earlier, systems thinking, or the systems approach, emphasizes the interrelatedness among different parts of the organization in working toward the unified goals and objectives of the organization. As Senge maintains, systems thinking (the fifth discipline) is the framework for the learning organization. Shared vision is necessary for people to work toward common goals and objectives while learning and excelling at what they do. Mental models are deeply ingrained assumptions and generalizations through which individuals develop perspective and consequently view the world. Team learning is necessary because these are the fundamental learning units in organizations; without them, nothing can be accomplished. Finally, personal mastery is the cornerstone of the learning organization. It is the process of continually clarifying personal vision by maintaining patience and focusing one's energies in order to see reality objectively.

William Geller (1997) suggests that applying the learning organization model to policing would be no easy task. Among obstacles he identifies are skepticism about research, unwillingness to encourage critical thinking among all members of the organization, and the belief that too much "thinking" prevents action. However, he maintains that while obstacles do exist, benefits from adopting a learning organization model may outweigh the costs. Geller identified 13 suggestions for fostering a learning police organization:

1. Create a Research and Development Unit that is well supported, actually does research, and is run by someone who actually understands policing.
2. Use geographical crime analysis that spans work units.
3. Involve senior police administrators in the process so as not to create turf battles; encourage collaboration.
4. Inventory the wealth of talent of all sworn and civilian employees.
5. Inventory the wealth of talent of citizens and groups in the community.
6. Use the SARA model for problem solving.
7. Encourage critical thinking and discourage groupthink.
8. Use middle managers to facilitate critical thinking.
9. Hold units accountable, measured against industry (CALEA) standards.
10. Institutionalize bottom-up evaluation of organizational performance.
11. Demonstrate practical results of previous police research.
12. Expand police-researcher partnerships.
13. Hire a "research broker" to enable the organization to become a better consumer of research.[55]

Of course, not all of these suggestions would be practical in every police organization. Additionally, resources may dictate the extent to which a police administrator can employ some of these suggestions.

Those that present little or no cost to the organization are easier to implement. The size of an organization is a characteristic that may affect the applicability of any of the suggestions. For example, in a small police organization there may be little need or few resources to create a research and development unit. However, encouragement of critical thinking of all personnel seems reasonable and would probably be very useful.

In a review of Chris Argyris's work, Leanne Alarid examined the applicability of the learning organization to police agencies implementing community-oriented policing.[56] She maintains that because an essential element of community policing is organizational change, the learning organization framework could support the sometimes monumental changes involved in community-policing implementation. Going from a traditional law enforcement organizational structure to one that embodies tenets such as decentralization and individual empowerment can be quite overwhelming for a manager. By employing some of the principles of the learning organization, such as shared vision and personal mastery, managers may find the task of organizational change not quite so daunting.

## Summary

Four themes that run through modern policing at the start of the twenty-first century were discussed in this chapter. The community engagement theme refers to the importance of police working closely with individual citizens and neighborhood groups. The collaboration theme is similar—police need to collaborate with other organizations and agencies. These two themes, community engagement and collaboration, are not simply feel-good programs, nor are they important merely because they tend to enhance public satisfaction with the police. Rather, research and the experience of recent decades demonstrates that they are central to effective policing—to controlling crime and disorder and solving community problems.

The third theme is globalization. While most policing is still local, the rest of the world is slowly creeping into local police work, thanks to immigration, travel, free trade, modern telecommunications, computers, and related social and economic trends. Today's police executives must become more knowledgeable about global issues and international relations than their predecessors ever had to be. The fourth theme is related to efficiency—fiscal and environmental. Police departments are constantly fighting the budget battle while learning to do more with less. In the age of global warming, that means doing with less energy too. Police agencies are not exempt from the government-wide and economy-wide need to become more fuel efficient and "greener" in the way they operate.

Four contemporary issues were also discussed: civil liberties (including racial profiling), mass media, cybercrime, and technology. The diversity of these issues illustrates the growing complexity of police administration. While extremely challenging, this diversity also serves to keep the study and practice of police administration dynamic and vibrant. Because of these contemporary issues as well as the endemic issues discussed throughout the text, modern police administration continues to need and deserve the best efforts of the best and brightest women and men who can be attracted to such an honorable calling.

This final chapter also discussed strategic management, command accountability, emotional intelligence, and the learning organization. These are among the most important developments in modern police administration and modern management. Serious students of police administration should be familiar with these concepts and should continue to scan police and organizational literature for similar developments that are likely to arise in coming years.

## Discussion Questions

1. What role do you think the United States, and U.S. police, should play in international police missions in places such as Bosnia, Kosovo, and East Timor?

2. When vehicle stop data are analyzed in a jurisdiction and it is found that African American and Hispanic drivers are overrepresented in stops and searches, what steps do you think should be taken?

3. As a police chief, what would you do if the Fox Network approached you about filming a *Cops*-style television show in your department?

4. A lot of modern technology has been introduced into policing in the past decade or two. Which new technologies do you think have had the biggest impact on police work? On the effectiveness of police? Which do you think have had the least impact?

5. What methods can you think of to make police agencies "greener"? Do you think modern police will be able to reduce their reliance on heavy, full-size automobiles? At what cost?

## Discussion

The article you just read provided a comprehensive look at four major themes impacting police administration and four vital contemporary issues facing criminal justice organizations. However, the chapter provided a thumbnail sketch of globalization and the impact transnational crime has on the criminal justice field. Therefore, my discussion will address globalization in more detail.

Globalization can be defined as the manifold process of increasing transnational interconnectedness of societies (Aas, 2011, p. 25). Globalization has been in large part driven by the information age. Legal businesses and governments utilize the Internet to communicate with people and connect with markets. The global economy has benefited greatly from utilizing the communication platform provided by the Internet. Criminal justice agencies have adopted business models and integrated new technology systems to connect more efficiently with the public. The result has in many instances increased public satisfaction and trust.

For example, in 1996, Megan's Law made available information on high-risk and convicted pedophiles. Identifying information, photographs, and addresses were viewable on the California Department of Justice website (Department of Justice [DOJ], 2013).

The data base contained 47,000 registered sex offenders. At that time, the public did not have direct access so law enforcement agencies were required to release information to the public after a screening process.

At the same time, the Monrovia Police Department discovered that parole agents had transferred a high-risk convicted child molester to live at a Monrovia address. According to prevailing law, the department notified residents in the area. The result was a firestorm of fear from the neighborhood and Monrovia found itself thrust into a media frenzy.

The police department eventually convinced the convicted felon to move back to Sacramento. The department installed a computer in the lobby of the police station to allow the general public to view the Megan's Law files, saving hundreds of hours of police time and in return gained the community's trust.

The other option was to assign patrol officers from the field to search the information for the public (Emett, personal communication, October 14, 2013). In 2004, the Megan Law database was made available to the general public without a screening process. The data base currently houses information on 88,000 registered sex offenders (DOJ, 2013).

Organized crime groups have used the same information and communication systems to reach new markets and supply their customers with drugs, vice, and firearms. Criminals use these platforms to steal identities for economic gain or to supply fraudulent passports to terrorists.

A new term has emerged to identify enterprising criminals who utilize the information highway to market their products. The term is "transnational organized crime." Groups who fall under this definition conduct their activities by crossing national borders and exploiting communication technology to deliver illegal products or services (Aas, 2011).

A new trend has emerged that illustrates the new breed of transnational criminals. Many traditional organized crime groups who practice "turf warfare" and have a hierarchical structures have been weakened by law enforcement interdiction (United Nations Office of Drugs and Crime, 2010 [UNODC]).

These new transnational group are loosely structured and tend to gravitate to their own families, clans, and tribes, making it impossible for law enforcement to infiltrate their ranks. Their composition is very similar to the cell structure utilized by terrorist groups. These agile and low profile groups have the connections to step in and replace a more structured group dismantled by law enforcement (UNODC, 2010, pp. 27–28).

An example of traditional crime revolutionized by global communication is child pornography. A recent study by the United Nations revealed that out of 187 countries surveyed 93 countries have not outlawed the practice (UNODC, 2010, p. 31).

Child pornographers outside the United States are rarely prosecuted. Mailing print photographs and films has been replaced with cheap, instant and anonymous websites that charge fees to download images. These groups also use the web to collect their fees from customers. Men, women and children are filmed being raped, tortured and molested in countries where the likelihood of arrest is unlikely (UNODC, 2010, p. 31).

Thailand is a prime example of the problem. The culture does not view the sex trade as illegal or immoral. The country is a source and destination for women and children who ply their sexual favors for money (Central Intelligence Agency, [CIA] 2013).

As a matter of fact, the sex tourism industry is an integral part of the economic prosperity of the country. It is dominated by foreign nationals who enter the country to prostitute themselves. Corrupt law enforcement plays a role: they are bribed by the pimps and in turn protect the sex workers. The country has built a very successful sex tourism industry where foreigners can book tours that include sex with men, women or children (Aas, 2011, p. 31).

## Questions for Class Discussion

1. Discuss the four major themes presented in the article. What impacts and challenges do law enforcement face from those trends?
2. Compare and contrast the four contemporary issues presented in the reading.
3. Do you think that the studies in emotional intelligence are valid? Do you see any evidence of emotional intelligence in your personality? Why or why not?
4. Compare and contrast the concepts of globalization and transnational organized crime. Research two transnational organized crime groups and evaluate the factors on why they qualify for such classification.

## Class Activities for the Professor

1. Assign the discussion questions in the classroom or as on-line posts.
2. Assign the students to write a ten-page research paper on any of the themes or contemporary issues listed in the reading
3. Assign a research paper using the *CIA World Fact Book* (available on the CIA website). The student will select a country that poses either a transnational organized crime threat to the United States or other countries. Evaluate a specific transnational organized crime group. For example if the student selected Somalia they could analyze maritime piracy.

## Works Cited

Aas, K.F, (2011), "Globalization and Crime", Los Angeles, SAGE Books.

United Nations Office on Drugs and Crime, (2010), "The Globalization of Crime: A Transnational Organized Crime Threat Analysis", Vienna.Cases

Cases 3 through 5 at the back of the text all describe efforts to implement organizational change and improvement in police departments. You should analyze these three cases from the perspective of the contemporary management models presented in Chapter 15 as well as other approaches to police organizational improvement presented throughout the text. You should draw upon everything you have learned to (1) analyze and explain the events and practices described in the cases and (2) make recommendations about how these organizations could be managed even more effectively.

## Notes

1. L. Fridell and M.A. Wycoff, *The Future of Community Policing* (Washington, DC: Police Executive Research Forum, 2003).

2. Request for Proposal: Police-Public Contact Survey. City of Seattle, WA: Office of Policy and Management, 2002. Available online at http://www.cityofseattle.net/mayor/docs/rfp.doc.

3. P. Finn, *Citizen Review of Police: Approaches and Implementation* (Washington, DC: National Institute of Justice, 2001).

4. See http://www.fortworthpd.com/communit.htm.

5. R. Sampson and M. Scott, *Tackling Crime and Other Public-Safety Problems: Case Studies in Problem-Solving* (Washington, DC: Office of Community Oriented Policing Services, 2000).

6. W.G. Skogan and S.M. Hartnett, *Community Policing, Chicago Style* (New York: Oxford University Press, 1997); M.E. Correia, *Citizen Involvement: How Community Factors Affect Progressive Policing* (Washington, DC: Police Executive Research Forum, 2000).

7. P. Walters, "Philly Case Rekindles Debate on Vigilante Justice," *Associated Press* (June 10, 2009). Available online at: http://www.msnbc.msn.com/id/31214450/.

8. D. Presman, R. Chapman, and L. Rosen, *Creative Partnerships: Supporting Youth, Building Communities* (Washington, DC: Office of Community Oriented Policing Services, 2002).

9. G. Cordner and A. Cordner, "Law Enforcement Technology Program: Evaluation Report" (Richmond, KY: Justice & Safety Center, 2008). Report submitted to the National Institute of Justice, Office of Science and Technology.

10. Fridell and Wycoff, *Future of Community Policing.*

11. G. Cordner and E.P. Biebel, "Problem-Oriented Policing in Practice." *Criminology & Public Policy* 4,2 (2005): 155–180.

12. M.S. Scott and H. Goldstein, *Shifting and Sharing Responsibility for Public Safety Problems* (Washington, DC: Office of Community Oriented Policing Services, 2005); S. Chamard, *Partnering with Businesses to Address Public Safety Problems* (Washington, DC: Office of Community Oriented Policing Services, 2006).

13. R.M. Perito, *The American Experience with Police in Peace Operations* (Clementsport, Nova Scotia: Canadian Peacekeeping Press, 2002).

14. D.H. Bayley, *Democratizing the Police Abroad: What to Do and How to Do It* (Washington, DC: National Institute of Justice, 2001), p. 5.

15. *Violent Crime and the Economic Crisis: Police Chiefs Face a New Challenge, Part II* (Washington, DC: Police Executive Research Forum, 2009).

16. 16. A. Greenblatt, "Squeezing the Cops: You Thought Police Were Safe From Budget Cuts? So Did They," *Governing* (June 2009), available online at: http://www.governing.com/node/1767; K. Johnson, "Economy Limiting Services of Local Police," *USA Today* (May 18, 2009), available online at: http://www.usatoday.com/news/nation/2009-05-17-police-closure_N.htm.

17. D. Parsons, "Board Chairman Wants James City to Go Green," *WTKR News Channel 3* (June 5, 2009). Available online at: http://www.wtkr.com/news/dp-local_greenbuilding_0605jun05,0,6652626.story.

18. K.B. Darmer, "Introduction." In K.B. Darmer, R.M. Baird, and S.E. Rosenbaum (eds.), *Civil Liberties vs. National Security in a Post-9/11 World* (Amherst, NY: Prometheus Books, 2004), p. 11–19.

19. V. D. Dinh, "Freedom and Security after September 11." In K.B. Darmer, R.M. Baird, and S.E. Rosenbaum (eds.), *Civil Liberties vs. National Security in a Post-9/11 World* (Amherst, NY: Prometheus Books, 2004), p. 105–113.

20. M. Buerger and A. Farrell, "The Evidence of Racial Profiling: Interpreting Documented and Unofficial Sources." *Police Quarterly* 5, no. 3 (September 2002): 272–305.

21. M. Alexander et al., *Driving While Black or Brown: The California DWB Report* (San Francisco: American Civil Liberties Union Foundation of California, 2002).

22. 22. F. Newport, "Racial Profiling is Seen as Widespread, Particularly Among Young Black Men." (Princeton, NJ: The Gallup Organization, 1999).

23. L. Fridell, R. Lurney, D. Diamond, and B. Kubu, *Racially Biased Policing: A Principled Response* (Washington, DC: Police Executive Research Forum, 2001).

24. See, for example, G. Cordner, B. Williams, and A. Velasco, "Vehicle Stops in San Diego: 2001." Report to the San Diego Police Department, 2002.

25. E.L. Schmitt, P.A. Langan, and M.R. Durose, "Characteristics of Drivers Stopped by Police, 1999." (Washington, DC: Bureau of Justice Statistics, 2002).

26. R.S. Engel, J.M. Calnon, and T.J. Bernard, "Theory and Racial Profiling: Shortcomings and Future Directions in Research." *Justice Quarterly* 19, no. 2 (June 2002): 249–273.

27. A. Farrell, J. McDevitt, and M. Buerger, "Moving Police and Community Dialogues Forward through Data Collection Task Forces." *Police Quarterly* 5, no. 3 (September 2002): 359–379.

28. S. Thompson and T. Eiserer, "Dallas Police Chief Apologizes for Conduct of Officer Who Drew Gun on NFL Player Outside Hospital," *The Dallas Morning News* (March 27, 2009). Available online at: http://www.dallasnews.com/shared-content/dws/dn/latestnews/stories/032609dnmetcopstop.3e9c080.html.

29. G.R. Murphy and C. Wexler, *Managing a Multijurisdictional Case: Identifying the Lessons Learned from the Sniper Investigation* (Washington, DC: Police Executive Research Forum, 2004).

30. J.L. Worrall, "Constitutional Issues in Reality-Based Police Television Shows: Media Ride-Alongs." *American Journal of Criminal Justice* 25, no. 1 (Fall 2000): 41–64.

31. D.D. Perlmutter, *Policing the Media: Street Cops and Public Perceptions of Law Enforcement* (Thousand Oaks, CA: Sage, 2000).

32. D. Thomas and B.D. Loader, "Introduction: Cybercrime: Law Enforcement, Security and Surveillance in the Information Age." In D. Thomas and B.D. Loader (eds.), *Cybercrime: Law Enforcement, Security, and Surveillance in the Information Age* (London, England: Routledge, 2000), pp. 1–13.

33. S.W. Brenner, "Defining Cybercrime: A Review of State and Federal Law." In R.D. Clifford (ed.), *Cybercrime, The Investigation, Prosecution, and Defense of a Computer-Related Crime* (Durham, NC: Carolina Academic Press, 2001), pp. 11–69.

34. C.J. DeFrance, *Prosecutors in State Courts, 2001* (Washington, DC: Bureau of Justice Statistics, 2002).

35. H. Stambaugh, D.S. Beupre, D.J. Icove, R. Baker, W. Cassaday, and W.P. Williams, *Electronic Crime Needs Assessment for State and Local Law Enforcement* (Washington, DC: National Institute of Justice, 2001).

36. National Institute of Justice Electronic Crime Program, http://www.ojp.usdoj.gov/nij/sciencetech/ecrime.htm.

37. W. Schwabe, L.M. Davis, and B.A. Jackson, *Challenges and Choices for Crime-Fighting Technology: Federal Support of State and Local Law Enforcement* (Santa Monica, CA: RAND, 2001).

38. "Social Networking Sites Help Combat Crime," *CBS Evening News* (March 13, 2009). Available online at: http://www.cbsnews.com/stories/2009/03/13/eveningnews/main4864837.shtml.

39. G.E. Berkley, *The Administrative Revolution: Notes on the Passing of Organization Man* (Englewood Cliffs, NJ: Prentice-Hall, 1971).

40. G.L. Kelling and M.H. Moore, "The Evolving Strategy of Policing." *Perspectives on Policing* No. 4 (Washington, DC: National Institute of Justice, 1988).

41. F.X. Hartmann, ed., "Debating the Evolution of American Policing." *Perspectives on Policing* No. 5 (Washington, DC: National Institute of Justice, 1988); S. Walker, "Broken Windows and Fractured History: The Use and Misuse of History in Recent Police Patrol Analysis." *Justice Quarterly* 1, no. 1 (1984): 75–90; V.G. Strecher, "Histories and Futures of Policing: Readings and Misreadings of a Pivotal Present." *Police Forum* 1, no. 1 (1991): 1–9.

42. M.H. Moore and R.C. Trojanowicz, "Corporate Strategies for Policing," *Perspectives on Policing* No. 6 (Washington, DC: National Institute of Justice, 1988).

43. J.H. Ratcliffe, *Intelligence-Led Policing* (Devon, UK: Willan Publishing, 2008).

44. K.R. Andrews, *The Concept of Corporate Strategy* (Homewood, IL: Richard D. Irwin, 1980), p. iii.

45. D. Anderson, "Why Crime Is Down." *New York Times Magazine* (February 1997): 47–62.

46. J.M. Shane, *What Every Chief Executive Should Know: Using Data to Measure Police Performance* (Flushing, NY: Looseleaf Publishing, 2007), pp. 196–205.

47. H. Goldstein, *Problem-Oriented Policing* (New York, NY: McGraw-Hill, 1990).

48. D. Goleman, *Emotional Intelligence* (New York, NY: Bantam, 1995).

49. D. Goleman, "What Makes a Leader?" *Harvard Business Review* (November–December 1998): 93–102.

50. Goleman, *Emotional Intelligence*, p. 46.

51. Goleman, "What Makes a Leader?" p. 101.

52. D. Goleman, R. Boyatzis, and A. McKee, *Primal Leadership: Realizing the Power of Emotional Intelligence* (Boston, MA: Harvard Business School Press, 2002).

53. P. M. Senge, *The Fifth Discipline: The Art and Practice of The Learning Organization* (New York: Doubleday, 1990).

54. *Ibid.*, p. 3.

55. W.A. Geller, "Suppose We Were Really Serious about Police Departments Becoming Learning Organizations?" *National Institute of Justice Journal* (Washington, DC: December 1997).

56. L. Alarid, "Law Enforcement Departments as Learning Organizations: Argyris's Theory as a Framework for Implementing Community-Oriented Policing." *Police Quarterly* 2, no. 3 (September 1999): 321–337.

## Suggested Reading

Andreas, Peter and Ethan Nadelman. *Policing the Globe: Criminalization and Crime Control in International Relations*. Oxford: Oxford University Press, 2006.

Bayley, David H. *Changing the Guard: Developing Democratic Police Abroad*. Oxford: Oxford University Press, 2006.

Deflem, Mathieu. *Policing World Society: Historical Foundations of International Police Cooperation*. Oxford: Oxford University Press, 2002.

Neyroud, Peter and Alan Beckley. *Policing, Ethics and Human Rights*. Devon, UK: Willan Publishing, 2001.

O'Hara, Patrick. *Why Law Enforcement Organizations Fail: Mapping the Organizational Fault Lines in Policing*. Durham, NC: Carolina Academic Press, 2005.

# Chapter 3: Doing More with Less

## Economic Impacts on American Policing

*We pass bills authorizing improvements and grants. But when it comes time to pay for these programs, we'd rather put the money toward tax breaks for the wealthy than for police officers who are protecting our communities.*

David Price

## Student Objectives

1. Analyze the economic conditions that have impacted law enforcement budgeting
2. Examine best practices utilized by law enforcement organizations to be more efficient in responses to downsizing
3. Explore technologies that law enforcement agencies are using to maximize people power
4. Examine how increased civilianization may help to free up police officers for crime-fighting operations

As Chair of the Union Institute and University's Criminal Justice Management program, I have the opportunity to talk to chiefs of police and county sheriffs on a regular basis. Every conversation eventually turns to budget and resource allocation. The downturn in the U.S. economy has hit law enforcement and correctional agencies like Thor's hammer. All public sector agencies are feeling the crunch, including law enforcement, the courts, corrections, fire fighters, paramedics, and other first responders. I selected the article you are about to read because it is the most current and comprehensive reading I could find on this topic. I believe it will be worth your effort and perhaps will help your agency to efficiently do more with less.

# The Impact of the Economic Downturn on American Police Agencies

By U.S. Department of Justice-COPS

## Cops

Dear Colleagues,

*As law enforcement agencies throughout the nation continue to face challenges brought about by the current economic changes, it is increasingly important that law enforcement practitioners and our communities work together to ensure the safety of the public. The core mission of the United States Department of Justice (USDOJ) is the protection of the American people, and the law enforcement community plays an integral role in the advancement of this mission. As a component of the Justice Department, the COPS Office is committed to acting as the voice for state and local law enforcement agencies within the federal government. We believe that the changes that have been occurring across the country are going to continue to have a serious impact on the way American police agencies operate in the years to come.*

*Central to the philosophy of community policing is the achievement and advancement of public safety by building relationships and solving problems on a local, neighborhood level. As police departments across the nation face budget cuts, and are therefore limited in resources and staffing levels, community policing strategies are essential to maintaining effective public safety services within this changing economy.*

*The Department of Justice is determined to help build the framework necessary to enable our law enforcement partners to make the most of these limited resources and to promote promising and effective public safety efforts. In advancing these goals, the COPS Office recently awarded more than $240 million in new grants that supported the hiring and retention of more than 1,000 officers in 238 agencies and municipalities across the country. These funding opportunities helped support local departments to increase the total number of staff; enhance their relationship with the community; and directly address the public safety concerns facing their communities.*

*This report also reflects our commitment to assisting local law enforcement agencies thrive in the current economy. To date, it is also the first federal analysis that examines the impact the economy has had on the law enforcement community. It is our goal to continue to examine these issues so that we may provide the best available resources, information, and guidance to the field to assist police in the development of sustainable policies and procedures that will help shape the new reality in American policing.*

*Sincerely,*

*Bernard K. Melekian, Director*

*Office of Community Oriented Policing Services*

## About the COPS Office

**The Office of Community Oriented Policing Services** (the COPS Office) is the component of the U.S. Department of Justice responsible for advancing the practice of community policing by the nation's state, local, and tribal law enforcement agencies through information and grant resources. The community policing philosophy promotes organizational strategies that support the systematic use of partnerships and problem-solving techniques to proactively address the immediate conditions that give rise to public safety issues such as crime, social disorder, and fear of crime. In its simplest form, community policing is about building relationships and solving problems.

The COPS Office awards grants to state, local, and tribal law enforcement agencies to hire and train community policing professionals, acquire and deploy cutting-edge crime-fighting technologies, and develop and test innovative policing strategies. The COPS Office funding also provides training and technical assistance to community members and local government leaders and all levels of law enforcement.

Since 1994, the COPS Office has invested more than $16 billion to add community policing officers to the nation's streets, enhance crime fighting technology, support crime prevention initiatives, and provide training and technical assistance to help advance community policing. More than 500,000 law enforcement personnel, community members, and government leaders have been trained through COPS Office-funded training organizations.

The COPS Office has produced more than 1,000 information products—and distributed more than 2 million publications—including Problem Oriented Policing Guides, Grant Owner's Manuals, fact sheets, best practices, and curricula. And in 2010, the COPS Office participated in 45 law enforcement and public-safety conferences in 25 states in order to maximize the exposure and distribution of these knowledge products.

More than 500 of those products, along with other products covering a wide area of community policing topics—from school and campus safety to gang violence—are currently available, at no cost, through its online Resource Information Center at www.cops.usdoj.gov. More than 2 million copies have been downloaded in FY2010 alone. The easy to navigate and up to date website is also the grant application portal, providing access to online application forms.

## Acknowledgments

This report was developed by the Research & Development Division, in the Community Policing Advancement Directorate—specifically through the efforts of Jessica Mansourian, John Markovic, Deborah Spence, and Mora Fiedler.

U.S. Department of Justice Office of Community Oriented Policing Services (the COPS Office) Community Policing Advancement Directorate Research & Development Division

# Introduction

The economic downturn of the past several years has been devastating to local economies and, by extension, their local law enforcement agencies. According to a report by the National Institute of Justice, the United States is currently experiencing the 10th economic decline since World War II (Wiseman 2011). The impact of this downturn will result in a change of how law enforcement services are delivered. As has been discussed by the COPS Office Director, Bernard Melekian, in a series of recent articles published in the *Community Policing Dispatch*, expectations will not be lowered just because an agency now has fewer officers, or because the budget is limited. Simply doing less while waiting for local budgets to recover to pre-2008 levels is not a viable option. Faced with a dramatic budget contraction, law enforcement leaders need to start identifying different ways to deliver police services and, perhaps more importantly, articulate what the new public safety models will look like to their communities (Melekian 2011a). The effects of the economic downturn on law enforcement agencies may be felt for the next 5–10 years, or worse, permanently. The permanence of this change will be driven not just by the economy, but by the local government officials determining that allocating 30–50 percent of their general fund budgets for public safety costs is no longer a fiscal possibility (Melekian 2011b).

While some people see signs that the economy is beginning to recover on the national level, most economists agree that local jurisdictions are still in decline and will continue to be so, at least in the short term. County and municipal budgets tend to lag behind the general economy and continuing foreclosures are slowing the recovery of property tax revenues, which are the backbone of local agency funding. Faced with these budget realities, the current model for service delivery—which has been with us for the last 50 years—is already starting to change, and will be forced to continue to change dramatically and rapidly in the next 3–5 years. As articulated in the June edition of the *Community Policing Dispatch*, Director Melekian discusses the need for a change in delivery of police services from a mid-20th century model to a more forward-looking 21st century model. He explains:

> *Police service delivery can be categorized into three tiers. The first tier, emergency response, is not going to change. Tier two is non-emergency response; where officers respond to calls after the fact, primarily to collect the information and statements necessary to produce reports. These calls, while an important service, do not require rapid response—the business has already been vandalized, the bike already stolen. Tier three deals with quality of life issues, such as crime prevention efforts or traffic management duties. They help make our communities better places to live, but they are proactive and ongoing activities. The second and third tiers of police service delivery have always competed for staffing and financial resources, but as local budgets constrict, that competition becomes fiercer. The public expects that both tiers are addressed, and agencies with shrinking payrolls are faced with finding new ways to make sure that can happen (Melekian 2011c).*

Faced with these dramatic budget contractions, law enforcement leaders have begun identifying the most cost conscious ways to deliver police services, and developing a new model of policing that will ensure that communities continue to receive the quality police protection they are entitled to. In a 2011 survey of police chiefs conducted by the International Association of Chiefs of Police (IACP), 94 percent of respondents agreed that they were seeing "a new reality in American policing developing" (IACP 2011).

Police agencies are some of the hardest hit by the current economic climate. Curtailing revenues nationwide have forced local governments to make cuts in spending across the board, which includes public safety operating budgets. While budget cuts threaten the jobs of law enforcement officers, the duties and responsibilities to ensure public safety remain.

However, to date, there has been no systematic way of measuring the impact the economic downturn has had on police agencies across the country. This report intends to delve into the existing information, research the ways in which law enforcement agencies have been affected, and examine the ways they have responded.

The following surveys, publications, and data sets were used in this report in order to analyze how the economic downturn has affected staffing at police agencies, delivery of services, and organizational management.

### The Recession Continues: An Economic Status Survey of Counties

In February 2011 the National Association of Counties (NACo) published a report titled, *The Recession Continues: An Economic Status Survey of Counties*, which outlined the results of a survey of 500 counties (across population size) as a means to determine the impact that the declining economy was having on county budgets, and the ways in which these counties were reacting to the challenge of lower revenues. The results of the study showed that counties were cutting services and personnel, as well as making across-the-board cuts to budgets, in order to address shortfalls. The data are different than what was found from previous surveys, where counties indicated they were using pay and hiring freezes to deal with the economic downturn. As the shape of the economy has gradually worsened, more counties have turned to furloughs and layoffs, with 53 percent of counties working with fewer staff in FY2011 than in FY2010 (Byers 2011).

### National Survey of County Elected Officials—Looking for the Light at the End of the Tunnel: A National Survey of County Elected Officials on the Economy, Budgets, and Politics

In 2011 a survey developed by the Carl Vinson Institute of Government, in partnership with NACo, polled a random sample of 508 county officials on issues related to the economy, budgets, and politics. Overall, the study found that while many elected county officials still rate the national economy as poor, there appears to be a slightly more optimistic opinion than what was found in the 2010 study (Clark 2011).

### Policing in the 21st Century: Preliminary Survey Results

As a part of President Mark A. Marshall's Policing in the 21st Century Initiative, IACP conducted a number of surveys and held roundtable discussions with over 400 law enforcement leaders to discuss the impact that the new economy is having on the field. These efforts were spearheaded by IACP's Research Division, working in partnership with IACP's Division of State Associations of Chiefs of Police, Division of State and Provincial Police, the Indian Country Section, and Mid-Size Cities Section (IACP 2011). Results of the study provide insight into ways in which national police agencies are responding to the effects of the economic climate on their agency operations.

### Major Cities Chiefs Association (MCCA) Survey

In 2011 the Major Cities Chiefs Association surveyed 23 major city departments to discuss the economic challenges they faced in light of the current economy (MCCA 2011). The results demonstrate some of the trends that are being experienced in police agencies across the nation as a result of reductions to operating budgets.

### Is the Economic Downturn Fundamentally Changing How We Police?

This is the 16th report in the "Critical Issues in Policing Series" that the Police Executive Research Forum (PERF) has developed in order to provide timely information and guidance on a number of difficult issues that police agencies have faced over the years. The report highlights findings from a survey conducted in

2010 of 608 police agencies focusing on the current economic challenges their departments are facing, and what the agencies have done in order to confront such challenges (PERF 2010).

### State of America's Cities Survey on Jobs and the Economy

The *State of America's Cities* is an annual survey of municipal officials that has been conducted for almost 25 years by The National League of Cities (NLC). The 2010 survey yielded 349 respondents consisting of local officials from various cities nationwide. The data from the survey provide insight into the effects of declining fiscal and economic conditions on American cities (McFarland 2010).

### City Fiscal Conditions in 2010

The *City Fiscal Conditions Survey* is a national survey of city financial officers throughout the United States. The survey yielded 338 respondents from cities of different population sizes, and produced information on the current fiscal state of the nation's cities and the struggles cities face while managing rapidly declining revenues (Hoene and Pagano 2010).

### Law Enforcement Management and Administrative Statistics (LEMAS)

The Department of Justice Bureau of Justice Statistics (BJS) is the United States' primary source of criminal justice statistics. Every "3 to 4 years, LEMAS collects data from over 3,000 state and local law enforcement agencies, including all those that employ 100 or more sworn officers" as well as "a nationally representative sample of smaller agencies. Data are obtained on the organization and administration of police and sheriffs' departments, including agency responsibilities, operating expenditures, job functions of sworn and civilian employees, officer salaries and special pay, demographic characteristics of officers, weapons and armor policies, education and training requirements, computers and information systems, vehicles, special units, and community policing activities" (LEMAS 2011).

### Census of State and Local Law Enforcement Agencies (CSLLEA)

In conjunction with the LEMAS data discussed above, BJS also conducts a census every 4 years of publicly funded law enforcement agencies with one or more full-time-equivalent sworn staff. This master list of law enforcement agencies is compiled from the previous CSLLEA census; lists provided by Peace Officer Standards and Training offices and other state agencies; and a list of agencies requesting new FBI-ORI identifiers since the previous CSLLEA. The latest CSLLEA was conducted in 2008 and included 17,985 state and local law enforcement agencies employing at least one full-time officer or the equivalent in part-time officers. The CSLLEA represents the sampling universe from which the LEMAS survey is drawn. Data collected as part of the CSLLEA include number of sworn personnel, number of civilian personnel, and agency-type category (CSLLEA 2011). CSLLEA data are recognized as the most definitive counts of law enforcement agency personnel operating with local, state, and tribal funding.

### COPS Hiring Program (CHP)—Office of Community Oriented Policing Services, U.S. Department of Justice

For the last 3 years, the Department of Justice, Office of Community Oriented Policing Services (the COPS Office) has collected data from its Hiring Program applicants, including data on agency operating budgets, officer and civilian layoffs, furloughs, hiring freezes, service populations, and authorized and actual sworn force strengths. With thousands of applicants each year, the data set represents a sizeable sample of all the state, local, and tribal law enforcement agencies in this country, although it is not a random sample. For the analysis in this report, two subsets of data were used. The first subset is all the agencies that submitted a hiring program application in 2011 and who are currently staffed with at least 10 full-time officers. The second subset is those agencies that applied both in 2009 and 2011, as well as having at least 10 full-time officers. The significance of the 10 officer threshold is that while agencies of at least that size account for just 51 percent of all law enforcement agencies in this country, they employ more than 95 percent of all sworn officers. In addition, those agencies can generally be presumed to be full-service departments offering 24/7 patrol and response coverage.

Some of the CHP data used in this report will evaluate the total sample of applicants regardless of sworn force levels. These samples will be indicated as such.

### News Media

Current news articles offer a way to capture the effects of the economic downturn that police agencies throughout the country are experiencing and highlight the ways in which agencies are mitigating the adverse effects of cuts to operating budgets. Within each section of this report, information from numerous media outlets helps to paint a more personal picture of how law enforcement agencies are dealing with today's challenges.

### A New Method of Data Collection is Pertinent to Successful Resource Allocation

The lack of an annual and systematic data collection of law enforcement agencies nationwide poses serious challenges for the development of aggressive and productive problem-solving strategies. In order to successfully develop effective techniques to combat challenges resulting from the economic climate, it is important to have an accurate understanding of the problems that are facing police agencies as they occur. While the BJS census (CSLEAA) and survey (LEMAS) provide representative and systematic data about U.S. law enforcement agencies and staffing, they were last administered prior to the current recession. It is likely that by the time the next cycle of BJS data is available much of the economic turbulence that has occurred over the past three years will have changed yet again.

The BJS census and surveys of law enforcement agencies are methodologically robust and have enormous intrinsic value. However, the cycle by which the census and survey data are collected (every 3–4 years), as well the time lag between when the data are collected and when they are made publicly available are not ideal for the types of analysis we believe are necessary for keeping on top of important trends as they emerge. The usefulness of these data sources for assessments of economic impact would be enhanced if the data were collected more often and made available in a shorter time frame. The next census and survey data for law enforcement agencies, to be conducted in 2011, will likely reveal a new reality in policing that is fundamentally different to what we have seen to date. Moreover, by the time the data is readily available (typically several years after collection) the entire state of the American economy will have changed and the immediate impacts of the recession on police agencies will have already occurred. Given the historic importance of state, local, and tribal law enforcement and their impact on the quality of life, the COPS Office feels the law enforcement community and the Department of Justice could benefit by enhancing these efforts of data collection and release by determining whether annual reports would be feasible. Even if the urgency of data collection was not underscored by the current economic crisis, a more timely collection and dissemination of data would be warranted by the new responsibilities law enforcement agencies have taken on in the last decade (i.e., homeland security, cyber crime, and greater cooperation necessitated in a more globalized society). Indeed, never has the need been more important for immediate and proactive data analysis of this kind. Federal, state, and local governments can collaboratively and effectively refocus and realign their resources to ensure the successful preservation of public safety, but their efforts will be compromised significantly if they lack up-to-date data and metrics on which to base their efforts. In summation, we encourage our colleagues at the Department of Justice to support ongoing efforts at BJS, as well as consider more frequent and timely censuses and surveys of law enforcement agencies.

# The World of Policing Prior to the Great Recession

To properly assess the changes that have occurred among police agencies as a result of the economic downturn, it is important to get an idea of what police agencies looked like before.

## Law Enforcement Trends Prior to the Economic Downturn

Periodically, BJS conducts two major data collection efforts. One is a census of state, local, county, and tribal law enforcement agencies (CSLLEA) and the other is a more detailed survey of approximately 3,000 state and local law enforcement agencies, including all those that employ 100 or more sworn officers and a nationally representative sample of smaller agencies (LEMAS). The most recent data are from 2008, prior to the current economic downturn (see Figure 1). The data provide an overview of the staffing numbers police agencies nationwide have maintained in the years prior to the economic downturn Figure 2 (on page 8) indicates that since 1986 the number of general purpose law enforcement agencies (publicly funded law enforcement agencies with the full-time equivalent of at least one sworn officer with arrest powers) fluctuated between about 14,000 and 17,000. (This graph excludes special purpose police agencies that are included in the analysis of the BJS census, e.g., the 17,985 total agencies in 2008.)

Note: Most of the fluctuation in agencies is accounted for by smaller agencies that tend to come in and out of existence, but some may be reflective of newly formed agencies or consolidations. There is no systematic effort to track newly formed or consolidated agencies.

***The Number of Law Enforcement Officers Was on a Steady Upward Climb Through 2008*** As indicated in Figure 3 (on page 8), there was a steady increase in the number of full-time equivalent sworn officers employed by general purpose state and local law enforcement agencies between 1986 (N = 514,494) and 2008 (N = 724,413). This represents a 41 percent increase in sworn personnel over the entire period, although the growth was slower from 1997 on.

**Full-Time, Part-Time, and Full-Time Equivalent Sworn Officers, LEMAS and LE Census, 1986–2008**

|  | CSLLEA 1986 | LEMAS 1987 | LEMAS 1990 | CSLLEA 1992 | LEMAS 1993 | CSLLEA 1996 | LEMAS 1997 | CSLLEA 2000 | LEMAS 2000 | LEMAS 2003 | CSLLEA 2004 | LEMAS 2007 | CSLLEA 2008 |
|---|---|---|---|---|---|---|---|---|---|---|---|---|---|
| FT Sworn | 496,845 | 510,422 | 547,740 | 562,583 | 581,216 | 618,465 | 648,688 | 661,979 | 656,645 | 683,599 | 680,182 | 700,259 | 704,814 |
| PT Sworn | 35,298 | 25,306 | 32,978 | 35,934 | 39,427 | 41,953 | 41,779 | 37,718 | 38,511 | 35,152 | 40,533 | 34,132 | 39,198 |
| 1/2 PT Sworn | 17,649 | 12,653 | 16,489 | 17,967 | 19,714 | 20,977 | 20,889 | 18,859 | 19,256 | 17,576 | 20,267 | 17,066 | 19,599 |
| FTE Sworn | 514,494 | 523,075 | 564,229 | 580,550 | 600,930 | 639,441 | 669,577 | 680,838 | 675,901 | 701,175 | 700,449 | 717,325 | 724,413 |
| Agencies | 15,641 | 14,081 | 15,148 | 15,637 | 15,494 | 16,715 | 16,700 | 15,785 | 15,798 | 15,766 | 15,882 | 15,636 | 15,614 |

**Figure 1.** Full-Time, Part-Time, and Full-Time Equivalent sworn officers data from 1986–2008

*Source*: Bureau of Justice Statistics

State and Local General Purpose
Law Enforcement Agencies, 1986–2008

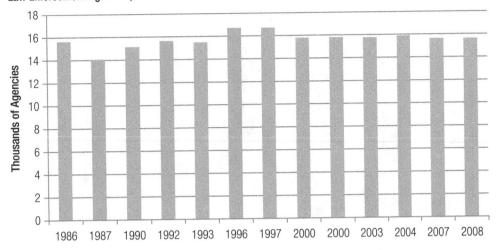

**Figure 2.** General purpose state and local law enforcement agencies identified by BJS Census

*Source*: Bureau of Justice Statistics

### *Civilian Personnel Also Increased Steadily Prior to 2008*

As Figure 4 indicates (based only on census years), the increase in sworn personnel was paralleled with an increase in civilian personnel. The increase in civilian personnel between 1986 and 2008 (91 percent) actually outpaced the increase in sworn personnel (41 percent). This historic data indicate a general increase in civilianization. In 2008, civilians accounted for about one-third (32.5 percent) of full-time employees in general purpose law enforcement agencies. In 1986, civilians had accounted for just over one-fourth (26.5 percent).

The preceding analysis of BJS data indicates there had been steady increase in law enforcement personnel, both sworn and civilian, between 1986 and 2008. No BJS census or survey data for law enforcement agencies have been collected since the current economic downturn. New data that are

Full-Time Equivalent Sworn Officers in State & Local
General Purpose Law Enforcement Agencies, 1986–2008

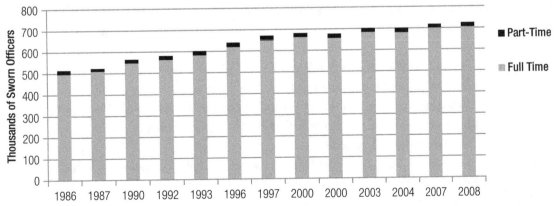

**Figure 3.** Full-Time Equivalent sworn officers in state and local general purpose agencies

*Source*: Bureau of Justice Statistics

**Sworn and Nonsworn Full-Time Employees in State & Local General Purpose Law Enforcement Agencies, 1986–2008** (Census Years Only)

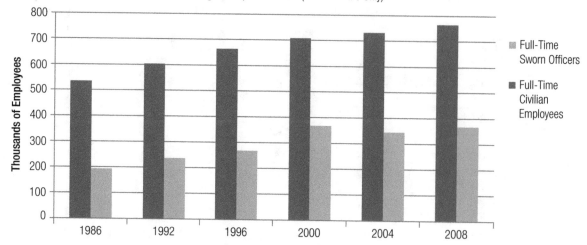

**Figure 4.** Full-Time Equivalent sworn officers and civilian employees in state and local general purpose agencies

*Source*: Bureau of Justice Statistics

scheduled to be collected by BJS in 2011 should prove to be revealing. It will likely reveal the first ever decrease in national, state, local, and tribal law enforcement personnel since BJS began collecting data in 1986. This trend is clearly linked to the economic downturn, but what makes it more adverse is that the national population continues to grow and police have to take on new responsibilities related to homeland security, cybercrime, and modern challenges.

## The Great Recession Has Changed the Face of American Policing

The economic crisis that began in 2008 has changed America in many ways. Unemployment rates have increased sharply, the stability of the housing market has collapsed, consumer spending has slowed, city revenues have lessened, and the federal deficit has reached a record level. As the fiscal conditions worsen and costs continue to escalate, many have articulated that America must learn how to "do more with less." However, when it comes to public safety, scholars and practitioners have noted that this motto is simply not a viable option. Instead, law enforcement agencies must develop ways to do things *differently*, and use the resources that are available in the most efficient and effective ways possible.

In the 2010 NLC study of the nation's city finance officers, data showed the largest downturn in revenues and cutbacks in spending in the history of the survey, with revenues declining for the fourth year in a row. Further, since city budgets tend to lag behind the national economic conditions by anywhere between 18 months to several years, the belief is that 2011 will likely result in further revenue declines and cuts in spending (Hoene and Pagano 2010).

Similar findings resulted from the 2010 NLC survey of municipal officials, in which 75 percent reported that the overall economic and fiscal conditions within their cities had worsened over the past year. Nearly a quarter of cities (22 percent) indicated that they had made cuts to public safety, which were likely to impact activities essential to the quality of life and safety of their cities, such as crime prevention and service response times (McFarland 2010).

In particular, the economic decline has severely affected law enforcement agencies' operating budgets across the nation. While there is no systematic data collection method used to gather information on how law enforcement agencies' budgets have been affected in the past few years, using the data from a number of smaller studies provides an idea of the prevalence, scope, and type of budget constraints affecting police across America.

The following data reflect local law enforcement agencies' responses to questions related to reductions in their operating budgets.

### PERF Study

- Over half of the responding agencies (51 percent) reported a decrease in their budgets between fiscal years 2009 and 2010, with an average budget cut of 7 percent.
- Of the departments that experienced budget cuts in 2010, 59 percent were expecting additional cuts in FY2011 (PERF 2010).

### IACP Study

- Over 85 percent of agencies reported that they were forced to reduce their budget over the last year.
- More than half of the respondents reported that they had to reduce their budgets in the prior year by 5 percent or more; a quarter had to reduce their budgets by more than 10 percent.
- These reductions were on top of the cuts that agencies already had to endure over the past several years.
- Most did not anticipate the reductions or the seriousness of the problem to end soon. In fact, 98 percent of respondents stated that they anticipated the economic impact on their agency was going to be at least "somewhat" problematic in the upcoming year.
- Over 40 percent said the coming year presented a serious or severe problem to their agency, with over one-third saying that they would have to further reduce their budgets by 10 percent or more in the coming year (IACP 2011).

### MCCA Study

- Seventy-eight percent of respondents indicated that their department had experienced budget cuts, with an average budget reduction of 5.4 percent.
- Of those who experienced budget reductions, 97 percent said they had experienced flat or reduced budgets over the past 1 to 12 years.
- Forty-three percent of respondents stated they had experienced reduced/flat budgets within the last 3 years (MCCA 2011).

### COPS Hiring Program (CHP)

In analyzing the budget data provided by applicants over the past 3 years (for agencies that applied both in 2009 and 2011 with a sworn staff of 10 or more) from 2009 to 2011, the average change in agency budget was an increase of only 1.75 percent. Despite this slight increase in average budget, it was found that over one third (35.7 percent) of 2011 applicants reported a budget drop of greater than 5 percent between 2009 and 2011. This is based on those 2011 applicants who provided operating budget data for both years (N= 2,701). This proportion is consistent with the findings of the PERF, IACP, and MCAA studies. During that same period, the Consumer Price Index (the generally accepted indicator of inflation) increased 1.09 percent in 2010, and then another 3.57 percent in 2011 (see Figure 5 on page 12). The cost of business rarely gets cheaper, and the costs of police services have escalated in spite of

**Increase in CHP applicant's
budgets compared to CPI**

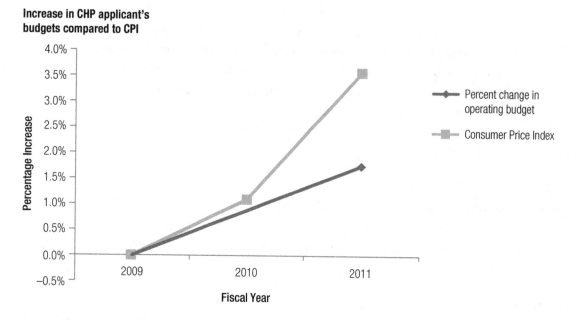

**Figure 5.** Average percent increase in operating budget of COPS Hiring Program applicants from 2009 and 2011 as compared to the increase in Consumer Price Index over that same time period

*Source*: The COPS Office

declining or stagnant operating budgets. Salaries and insurance costs—which can make up 90 percent or more of a police budget—generally increase as employees earn years of experience, making it extremely difficult for agencies to make enough cuts in other areas in order to maintain a balanced budget (Wexler 2010). Further, vehicle fuel costs have also increased dramatically in recent years, with the national average price of gasoline up 45 percent from just 5 years ago, with even higher price spikes experienced in the spring of 2008 and again earlier this year (Department of Energy 2011). All of these factors combine to put added pressure on agency operating budgets

These data indicate that among these agencies, operating budgets that *were* fairly stagnant are now losing spending power as they fail to keep up with the rate of inflation. If operating costs continue to rise, and revenues continue to decline, law enforcement agencies will likely remain challenged to provide policing services at the levels that citizens are accustomed to receiving.

## Effects on Staffing

As agencies have been pressured to make difficult decisions in light of the current fiscal conditions, many are being forced to provide the same services with fewer employees than they have in the past.

- According to a May 2010 survey conducted by the National League of Cities, 71 percent of city officials surveyed reported making cuts to personnel in order to deal with the fiscal implications of the current economic conditions. This number increased to 79 percent of survey respondents by the October report (McFarland 2010).
- A 2011 survey by the National Association of Counties found that counties are cutting services and employees, with 53 percent of counties working with fewer staff today than in FY2010 (Byers 2011).

- Among respondents to the 2010 PERF study, there was a 3 percent decrease in the average number of sworn officers between FY2009 and FY2010 (PERF 2010).
- Agencies have used a number of techniques to reduce their personnel costs. Layoffs, mandatory furloughs, and attrition are often the result of these budget reductions in many police agencies.

## Layoffs

Currently, the data of officer positions laid off are not collected by any one agency. However, the Bureau of Justice Statistics is planning to collect the data in their 2011 LEMAS Survey. Given that the LEMAS Survey uses a stratified random sample,[1] the study should provide a reliable estimate of layoffs using weighted averages (based on the agency size stratification scheme).

So while there is no single database of layoff information, a number of smaller agencies have put together estimates regarding the number of police positions terminated as a result of budget reductions.

- The Fraternal Order of Police can directly document 4,000 layoffs, but estimates relying on less direct measurements suggest a more realistic number would be between 12,000 and 15,000 sworn officer positions lost.
- The International Association of Chiefs of Police estimate the number of law enforcement officer positions lost is 10,000.
- COPS Hiring Program data for the last 18 months estimate that 5,738 state, local, and tribal law enforcement officers have been laid off. The actual number may be as high as 10,000 if one extrapolates beyond the applicant pool to the full universe of U.S. law enforcement agencies.

## Police Layoffs

IN THE NEWS:

**PATERSON, NEW JERSEY POLICE DEPARTMENT** laid off 125 officers on April 18, 2011. This is a quarter of their entire force. In addition, more than 30 lieutenants and sergeants were demoted to patrol. Patterson experienced a 15 percent spike in violent crime in 2010 over the 2009 level (CBS Broadcasting, Inc. 2011; Henry 2011).

**FLINT, MICHIGAN**—The Flint police force has been hurting since being slammed with layoffs. Flint has become one of America's murder capitals. In 2010, with a population of 102,000, there were 66 documented murders in Flint. The murder rate is higher than Newark, St. Louis, and New Orleans, and even Baghdad's. Flint has laid off two-thirds of its police force over the last 3 years and a typical Saturday night has experienced reduced staffing to only six patrolmen on duty (LeDuff 2011).

**CAMDEN, NEW JERSEY POLICE DEPARTMENT**—In January 2011 the Camden Police force was nearly cut in half. One hundred and sixty-three officers were laid off, leaving Camden with only 204 sworn officers—the department's lowest number since 1949 (Goldstein 2011).

- Major Cities Chiefs Association found that 52 percent of agencies surveyed had laid off sworn officers (McFarland 2010).
- According to the PERF survey, 22 percent of respondents indicated they had laid off employees as a result of decreasing budgets (PERF 2010).

### COPS Hiring Program Data Indicate Number of Officers Requested to Refill Positions on the Rise

CHP applicants are eligible to apply for funds in order to a) hire new officers, b) rehire officers who had already been laid off as a result of state, local, or tribal budget cuts, and/or c) rehire officers who are currently scheduled to be laid off on a future date as a result of budget cuts. Additionally, agencies were asked to identify which of these categories they would intend to use the hiring funds toward, if they were to receive an award.

In FY2009, 2.3 percent of applicants applied for funds to rehire at least one officer who had previously been laid off due to budget cuts. These positions made up 1.5 percent of the total number of positions requested. In comparison, in FY2011 4.6 percent of applicants applied for funds to rehire at least one officer who had previously been laid off due to budget cuts, making up 5.3 percent of the total amount of positions requested.

In FY2009, 12 percent of applicants applied for funds to rehire officers who were scheduled to be laid off. These requests made up 13 percent of the total amount of positions requested. Comparatively, in FY2011, 6 percent of applicants applied for funding to rehire officers scheduled for layoffs, making up 7.4 percent of the total positions requested.

So while the percentage of agencies requesting CHP funds in order to prevent future layoffs has decreased, the percentage of agencies requesting funds to rehire officers who have already been laid off has tripled along with the number of 'rehire positions' requests (from 1.5 percent of the total requests in 2009 to 5.3 percent of the total requests in 2011) (see Figure 6 on page 15). This indicates that many agencies had to lay off a number of officers between 2009 and 2011, and therefore are requesting funds in order to reinstate some of their sworn personnel. This is further supported by the data in which 6 percent of total applicants in FY2009 stated that they had laid off a percentage of their sworn staff, while in FY2011 this number increased to 12 percent of total applicants.

### Agency Types—Request for Funds to Rehire Laid Off Officers

In 2011, a total of 125 agencies applied for positions to rehire officers. A total of 478 rehired officer positions were requested. Interestingly, the amount of rehire positions requested was fairly even when categorized by agency size (agencies serving populations of 100,000 or more were considered "large agencies"). One hundred and twelve small agencies applied to rehire a total of 233 officers. The number of positions requested within small agencies ranged from 1 to 14, with an average request of 2 officers per agency. Thirteen large agencies applied to rehire a total of 245 officers. The number of positions requested by large agencies ranged from 1 to 50, with an average request of 19 officers per agency (see Table 1 on page 15).

In 2011, rehiring of layoffs accounted for 14 percent of total requests by municipal agencies. By comparison, the rate for Sheriff Departments was 11 percent.

### Agency Types—Request for Funds to Prevent Scheduled Layoffs

Also in 2011, a total of 172 agencies applied for at least one position in order to prevent a scheduled layoff of a sworn officer (see Table 2 on page 16). A total of 664 positions were applied for, totaling $18,207,013 in requests. One hundred and fifty-four small agencies applied for 313 preventive layoff positions. The number of positions requested ranged from 1 to 6, with an average of 2 positions per

**Table 1.** Total number of agencies and rehire positions requested in 2011 by agency type

| Agency Type | Number of Agencies | Number of Rehire Requests |
|---|---|---|
| **SMALL:** | | |
| Tribal | 1 | 1 |
| Regional Police Department | 1 | 3 |
| School/Universities | 5 | 6 |
| Sheriff Departments | 21 | 41 |
| Municipal Agencies | 84 | 182 |
| **LARGE:** | | |
| Sheriff Departments | 8 | 148 |
| Municipal Agencies | 5 | 97 |

*Source*: The COPS Office

agency. Large agencies made up the majority of the requests for preventive layoff positions. Seventeen agencies applied for 351 positions, ranging from 3 to 50, with an average of 16 positions per agency.

In 2011, preventive layoff requests accounted for 25 percent of total requests by municipal agencies. By comparison the rate for Sheriff Departments was 8 percent.

## Mandatory Furloughs

Many agencies are using furloughs as a method of managing labor costs. According to the PERF survey, 16 percent of responding agencies indicated they had implemented unpaid furloughs (PERF 2010). In

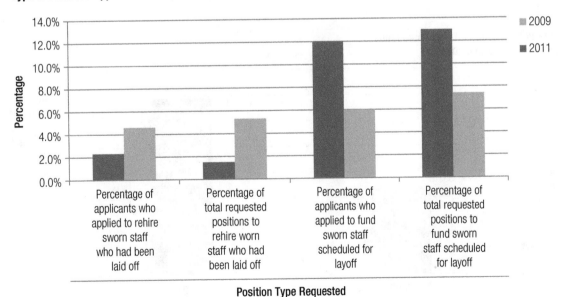

**Type of Positions Applied for in FY2009 and FY2011 COPS Hiring Program Solicitation**

**Figure 6.** Comparison of types of positions requested in the COPS Hiring Program in 2009 and 2011

*Source*: The COPS Office

**Table 2.** Total number of agencies and positions in 2011 requesting funds for preventive layoff positions

| Agency Type | Number of Agencies | Number of Preventative Layoff Requests |
|---|---|---|
| **SMALL:** | | |
| Constable | 1 | 1 |
| County Government | 1 | 1 |
| Tribal | 1 | 1 |
| Schools | 5 | 6 |
| Sheriff Departments | 33 | 64 |
| Municipal Police | 113 | 240 |
| **LARGE:** | | |
| Sheriff Departments | 7 | 78 |
| Municipal Police | 10 | 273 |

*Source*: The COPS Office

the COPS Hiring Application, agencies were asked to report the percentage of their sworn positions that have been furloughed for at least 40 hours in the year of application. In looking at the 1,569 agencies that applied for CHP funding in both FY2009 and again in FY2011:

- In 2009 3.4 percent of these agencies reported that at least some of the sworn officers were furloughed for 40 hours or more that year.
- By 2011 the percentage reporting furloughs had more than doubled to 6.9 percent for those same agencies (see Figure 7 on page 17).

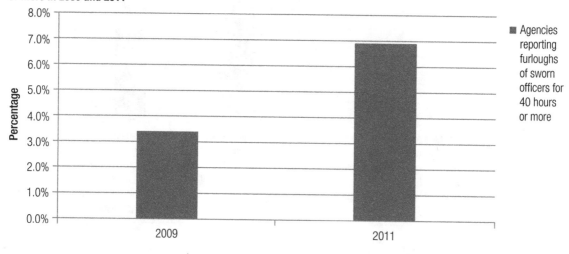

**Furloughs of sworn officers for 40 hours or more in 2009 and 2011**

Legend: ■ Agencies reporting furloughs of sworn officers for 40 hours or more

**Figure 7.** Comparison of agencies reporting furloughs for 40+ hours in 2009 and 2011

*Source*: The COPS Office

**Percentage of officers subject to the furlough within
furlough-affected agencies in 2009 and 2011**

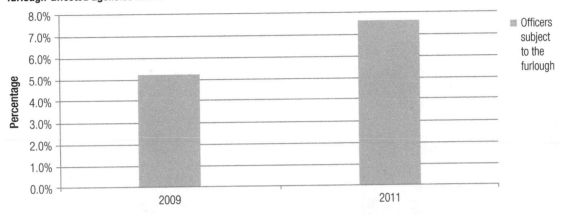

**Figure 8.** Comparison of the percentage of officers subject to furloughs in 2009 and 2011

*Source*: The COPS Office

For those agencies with furloughs in either year, the percentage of staff subject to the furlough also increased dramatically from 2009 to 2011 (see Figure 8 on page 17):

- In 2009 39 percent of the officers in a furlough-affected agency were subject to the furlough.
- By 2011 57 percent of the officers in a furlough-affected agency were subject to the 40+ hour furlough.

Based on the size of our sample, it is possible to estimate that more than 28,000 officers nationwide have been furloughed for at least 40 hours this year, which is equivalent to more than 500 full-time positions.

## Staffing Reductions through Attrition

As agencies are doing all they can to avoid layoffs and furloughs, many are instituting hiring freezes in order to balance operational budgets through voluntary departures.

- In the survey by National League of Cities, the most common reaction regarding personnel-related cuts made in 2010 was hiring freezes (74 percent) (McFarland 2010).
- In the 2011 National Association of Counties survey, 41 percent of responding counties stated they had instituted hiring freezes as a means of adjusting their budgets in light of revenue shortfalls (Byers 2011).
- Thirty-six percent of agencies who responded to the PERF survey stated they had experienced reduced staffing levels through attrition (PERF 2010).
- According to the 2011 CHP data, 43 percent of total applicants indicated they had sworn positions that went unfilled due to budget restraints.

## Shift in Average Number of Officers per Population Served

LEMAS reports from 2004 and 2008 show the average officers per population to be about 250 per 100,000 (see Figure 9) (LEMAS 2011). This can vary dramatically across the country and between types and settings of agencies, but that number did hold steady for the 10 years prior to the recession.

**Officers applying to CHP in 2009 and 2011 experience
lower police to population ratio's than the national average**

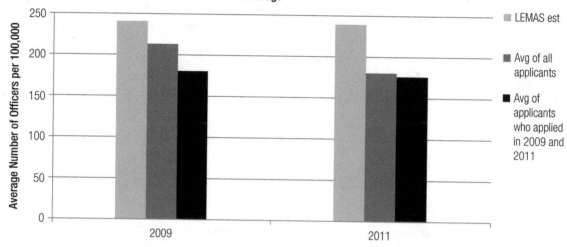

**Figure 9.** The average number of officers per 100,000 among CHP applicants compared to national average

*Sources*: Bureau of Justice Statistics and The COPS Office

In 2009, the CHP applicants had (across all agency sizes) an average of 215 officers per 100,000. In 2011, CHP applicants (across all agency sizes) had an average of only 184 officers per 100,000 (see Figure 9). Again, looking at the sample of applicants who applied in both years with more than 10 officers:

- In 2009 the sample agencies averaged 189 officers per 100,000
- By 2011 that average had dropped to 181 officers per 100,000

## COPS Hiring Program Provides Relief to Agencies Suffering from Personnel Reductions

IN THE NEWS:

*BURTON, MICHIGAN*—The Burton Police Department has used 2010 COPS funding to rehire two officers who were laid off as a result of budget cuts. Police Chief John Benthall said the grant "will help the Burton Police Department to maintain adequate services in the city of Burton." Budget cuts required the department to lay off two officers while losing three to attrition. In rehiring these two officers, Burton is able to "bring our police force back up to a good level," Benthall stated, and they were "ecstatic to get the news" (Acosta 2011).

***FEDERAL WAY, WASHINGTON***—"I'm planning to utilize this grant to maintain officers I'd otherwise have to terminate."—Police Chief Brian Wilson of Federal Way, Washington, said of the $1.03 million award the agency received in 2010 (Howard 2010).

***EGG HARBOR TOWNSHIP, NEW JERSEY***—Five Egg Harbor Township police officers who received layoff notices earlier in the year were able to stay on the job after the township was awarded $1.1 million through the COPS Hiring Program. "This should be a major relief to those young officers who went through the layoff ordeal in the past 2 years, serving the township the best they could while continuously worrying what will occur in 2011," Chief Blaze Catania said in a statement. "I'm very happy for them and what this means to the township and its citizens" (Rose 2010).

***TULSA, OKLAHOMA***—In January 2010 the Tulsa Police Department was forced to lay off 124 officers due to budget cuts. According to Tulsa Deputy Police Chief Daryl Webster, "There probably hasn't been a layoff in this department since the Depression." However, with the help of COPS funding, 18 Tulsa police officers who were laid off were re-hired. "You're talking about [reinstating] almost an entire shift of officers in one of our divisions. … Certainly, it's a blessing," Webster said (Loren 2010).

***BEATRICE, NEBRASKA***—In 2009, the city of Beatrice received COPS funding that allowed them to retain one officer who would have otherwise been laid off. Police Chief Bruce Land said the grant will significantly impact the community. With a police force of only 22 officers—a percentage of only 1.8 officers per 1,000 residents—"To lose even one position would be a great loss," Land said (Masoner 2009).

***PEORIA, ILLINOIS***—The jobs of 10 Peoria police officers were saved through funds from the COPS hiring grant. The news came to the city just days after they had to make the hard decision to lay off 13 officers because of budget reductions. "This is good for the officers, this is good for the community, and this is good for the (City Council)," said Peoria Police Chief Steven Settingsgaard during a 2010 news conference. The department had lost 33 police officers the previous year in order to close a $14.5 million budget deficit. Settingsgaard stated; "The thought of seeing another significant layoff here at the Police Department has been weighing heavy on our minds. The grant could not have come at a better time and it will directly benefit the community by keeping more police officers in the streets" (Oldendorf 2010).

While this may not seem like a dramatic difference, statistical analysis revealed it to be significant, meaning that it is a greater decline than we would expect to see through random chance. In addition, the 1,569 agencies in our sample serve 4.2 million people, so the impact of even small decreases can likely be felt by many. However, this result could also be due to sample bias—meaning agencies with a lower number of officers per thousand are more likely to apply for COPS Office grant funding.

## Effects on Delivery of Services

The effects of such staffing reductions are likely to influence the capacity of law enforcement agencies to provide the same services, in the same ways, as they have in the past. The PERF study revealed that this indeed is the case for many of their respondents. Nearly half (47 percent) of the responding agencies surveyed by PERF indicated that budget cuts had already caused or will cause changes in the services they provide to their communities. Further:

- Eight percent of departments surveyed are no longer responding to all motor vehicle thefts.
- Nine percent of departments are no longer responding to all burglar alarms.
- Fourteen percent of departments are no longer responding to all non-injury motor vehicle accidents (PERF 2010).

The MCCA survey found that 25 percent of their respondents had experienced service reductions as a result of budget cuts. Of those agencies, the following are ways in which the agencies compensated for such budget reductions:

- Seventeen percent of respondents said that their agency had stopped responding to some calls for service.
- Forty-three percent stated they had increased the use of telephone reporting, along with 30 percent who had increased the use of online reporting.
- Twenty-six percent stated there had been a reduction in investigations follow-ups, specifically related to property crimes, fugitive tracking, non-felony domestic assaults, financial crimes, computer crimes, narcotics, and traffic cases (MCCA 2011).

### Changes in Policies and Procedures

Delivery of services is not the only area of law enforcement that is suffering due to budget cuts. Police policies and practices are undergoing a transformation in order to adapt to the economic changes. PERF found that two-thirds of their responding departments reported that they had reduced or discontinued training programs because of their limited budgets. More than half stated that they have cut back or even eliminated plans to obtain new technology (PERF 2010). The various ways departments responding to the survey have felt the impacts on policies can be seen in Table 3 on page 21.

The MCCA survey showed similar responses to questions relating to areas that had been cut as a result of budget reductions, as shown in Table 4.

The IACP Survey further mirrored these trends, as shown in Table 5.

**Table 3.** PERF study respondents indicating impacts of reduced budgets on policies

| Percentage of PERF Study respondents indicating impacts of reduced budgets on policies | |
|---|---|
| Reduced out-of-town travel? | 72% |
| Reduced or discontinued training? | 68% |
| Considered increasing fees for police services? | 60% |
| Cut back or eliminated plans to acquire technology? | 55% |
| Discontinued special units (e.g., gang, traffic enforcement)? | 38% |
| Implemented or considered a tax increase to avoid police service cuts? | 35% |
| Discontinued take-home cars? | 31% |

*Source*: Police Executive Research Forum

**Table 4.** MCCA study respondents indicating impacts of budget cuts

| Respondents of MCCA Study who indicated budget cuts were made in the following areas | |
|---|---|
| Travel | 61% |
| Vehicles | 61% |
| Training | 48% |
| Aviation | 48% |
| Community Policing | 39% |
| Narcotics Enforcement | 35% |
| School Resource Officers | 22% |
| Federal Task Forces | 22% |

*Source*: Major Cities Chiefs Association

**Table 5.** IACP survey respondents indicating impacts of budget cuts (IACP 2011).

| | Yes |
|---|---|
| Has your agency had to cut back on training? | 60% |
| Has your agency had to cut back on buying or upgrading major equipment, such as vehicles in the last year? | 64% |
| Has your agency cut back on buying or upgrading major technology such as In-Car Cameras or LPTs in the past year? | 58% |

*Source*: International Association of Chiefs of Police

# Law Enforcement Service Reductions

IN THE NEWS:

***CAMDEN, NEW JERSEY***—"After the layoffs of 163 police officers, Camden is feeling the impact. Callers to 911 who report things like home burglaries or car break-ins are asked to file a report over the phone or at police headquarters; officers rarely respond in person. 'If it doesn't need a gun and a badge at that location,' officers are not sent, the city's police chief, J. Scott Thomson, said last week" (Goldstein 2011).

***OAKLAND, CALIFORNIA***—"Cutbacks … have forced police to tell residents to file their own reports—either online or in writing—for break-ins and other lesser crimes. 'If you come home to find your house burglarized and you call, we're not coming,' said Oakland Police spokeswoman Holly Joshi. The city laid off 80 officers from its force of 687 [in July] and the department can't respond to burglary, vandalism, and identity theft" (Johnson 2010a).

***PERF***—"For the first time, because of the economy, police departments … may have to change how they do business," says Chuck Wexler, executive director of the Police Executive Research Forum. "People will see a change in basic delivery of services," from longer police response times to a dramatically reduced police presence in some communities (Johnson 2009).

***SACRAMENTO, CALIFORNIA***—"The Sacramento Police Department is dealing with severe budget cuts this year, including fewer officers and task forces. A total of 43 officers lost their jobs, and the narcotics unit and gang unit was cut all together. The police department also does not respond to home burglaries unless they are in progress, and they don't respond to minor traffic accidents unless some type of crime is involved" (Maher 2011).

## Civilianization

Some police agencies have also begun shifting some of the duties typically reserved for sworn staff to civilian employees as a means of cost savings. The term civilianization generally refers to a law enforcement agency's hiring of non-sworn personnel in order to replace or supplement its current sworn staff (Forst 2000). In utilizing civilians to perform duties typically performed by sworn staff, police departments are able to save money primarily through lower pay, reduced training requirements, and smaller overhead requirements. According to a study by American University Professor Brian Forst on *The Privatization and Civilization of Policing*, estimates from New York City indicate the average cost of civilian employees is about one-third to one-half that of a sworn officer, even when they are performing the same functions (Forst 2000).

More and more cities across America have begun to make the shift toward civilianization under the current budget constraints. In fact, 22 percent of respondents in the IACP survey stated their departments had begun shifting sworn responsibilities to non-sworn personnel (IACP 2011).

In BJS's report, *Census of State and Local Law Enforcement Agencies*, 2008, analysis reveals that between 1992 and 2008 the number of sworn full-time personnel in state and local law enforcement

## Police Civilianization

IN THE NEWS:

**MESA, ARIZONA**—The Mesa Police Department has begun using civilians for everything from crime scene processing to fraud investigations. They created a team of nine civilian investigators who make 30 to 40 percent less than an officer. In 2010, the unit handled about 50 percent of all burglary calls (Adams 2011).

**OKLAHOMA CITY, OKLAHOMA**—In Oklahoma City, civilians working as part-time police ambassadors help relieve some of the light duties formally performed by police, such as giving directions or working special events. For $9 an hour, these civilians provide a significant cost savings for the department. Sergeant Baxter of Oklahoma City PD has said, "They do provide what I believe is a vital service. They do help the police departments and officers out on the streets" (Loren 2010).

**SAN FRANSICO, CALIFORNIA**—"In San Francisco, the police department unveiled a test program last year [2010] that uses civilian investigators to respond to nonviolent crimes. They interview victims and witnesses, write reports, take crime scene photos, and collect fingerprint and DNA evidence" (Fenton 2011). "The $1 million pilot program and others like it are being designed to allow dwindling numbers of uniform officers to focus on more serious violent crime. San Francisco Assistant Chief Thomas Shawyer says the civilians will save up to $40,000 per person in training, equipment, and benefit costs required to hire an officer" (Johnson 2010b).

agencies grew by 34 percent, with the growth among civilian personnel (a 54.7 percent increase) outpacing growth among sworn personnel (a 25.9 percent increase). In 2008, civilian employees accounted for 32.5 percent of full-time employees in U.S. law enforcement agencies compared to 28.2 percent in 1992. Based on the 2008 BJS survey, sheriff's departments had a substantially higher proportion of civilian employees (48.2 percent) than local police departments (22.5 percent). The civilianization trend between 1992 and 2008 was much more pronounced in sheriff's departments relative to local police departments. Between 1992 and 2008, the number of civilian employees employed by sheriff's departments grew by 91 percent (relative to 34.0 percent growth in sworn employees). In contrast, the growth of civilian employees among local police was more modest at 26.7 percent (and only slightly above the 23.1 percent growth of sworn employees) (CSLLEA 2008).

### Law Enforcement and Private Security Collaboration

The combination of increased demands and stagnant or declining local law enforcement resources makes it clear that, now more than ever, law enforcement agencies must pursue all reasonable avenues for collaboration with private security. Private Security is defined in the COPS publication *Operation Partnership* as, "both the proprietary (corporate) security and contract security firms across the full spectrum of security services and technology" (Law Enforcement—Private Security Consortium 2009).

At the field level, private security has the potential to reduce the cost of public law enforcement.

- In Las Vegas, Wilmington (DE), Minneapolis, New York, and other cities, law enforcement's ability to view private security closed-circuit television (CCTV) cameras has the potential to save taxpayer money that would have otherwise been spent to buy this same equipment.
- In Durham, North Carolina, and in several counties in Florida, private transit security officers are being used on public transit systems (Law Enforcement—Private Security Consortium 2009).

Data from the 2011 National Survey of County Elected Officials indicate that 23 percent of surveyed officials stated that their county has privatized one or more services once supplied by the county government due to economic conditions (McFarland 2010).

## Using Volunteers

Another technique that is being used by law enforcement agencies to help manage personnel cutbacks is the use of volunteers whenever possible. In the Department of Justice National Institute of Justice report on "Strategic Cutback Management," supplementing staff with volunteers when feasible is highlighted as having significant cost saving potential (Wiseman 2011).

Using volunteers to help supplement sworn staff is a possible way for law enforcement agencies to continue to enhance the safety of the community, through increasing the efficiency of sworn personnel and promoting the partnership of citizens and police in a time when police agencies are losing manpower. The North Miami Beach Police Department Neighborhood Services and Inspections (NSI) Unit has taken volunteerism to a unique level by using police "recruits from local academies to volunteer their time to gain experience in the field." The NSI Community Policing Cadet Program allows "these cadets [to] patrol the city for quality of life issues, offering a valuable service—providing free services to the agency" (Alqadi 2011).

Agencies across the nation have begun to take part in volunteer programs after the creation of the USA Freedom Corps (USAFC) by President Bush in 2002, which resulted from the September 11, 2001 attacks. The national Volunteers in Police Service (VIPS) Program provides access to resources and information for and about law enforcement volunteer programs of all kinds and is one of five Citizen Corps partner programs that developed as part of the USAFC initiative. The program aims to improve the ability of state and local law enforcement to utilize civilian volunteers (Volunteers in Police Services 2011a). IACP manages and implements the VIPS Program in partnership with the White House Office of the USAFC and the U.S. Department of Justice Bureau of Justice Assistance.

In 2009, IACP conducted a survey of 115 law enforcement agencies that had registered VIPS Programs. The data provide a good overview of law enforcement volunteerism from the field's perspective. Of the 115 respondents, the following responses were rated according to perceived importance. The percentages below represent the number of respondents who indicated that the described factor was "important" or "very important"

- Ninety-four percent cited added value to the department
- Ninety-two percent cited the ability for officers to respond to more pressing needs
- Ninety percent cited it increased their ability to provide additional service
- Eighty-five percent cited enhancing citizens understanding of the police (Volunteers in Policing Services 2011b)

IACP has also found a vast increase in the number of volunteers that are being used by law enforcement agencies to perform police duties since 2004 (see Figure 10) (Johnson 2010b).

**Use of citizen volunteers has increased over the years**

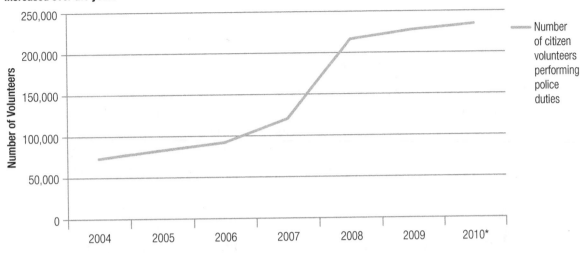

**Figure 10.** Data provided by IACP on the number of citizen volunteers used by police agencies from 2004 to 2010

* Data are through 10/6/2010
*Source*: International Association of Chiefs of Police

## Law Enforcement Agency's Use of Volunteers

IN THE NEWS:

***RICHLAND, WASHINGTON***—"In Richland a group of nearly 40 volunteers is taking on the smaller tasks, lightening the workload so cops can stay focused on more serious threats—all for free. … Richland's Police Volunteers logged more than 600 hours just last month, providing that sense of security to more and more people" (Vedadi 2011).

***DURHAM, NORTH CAROLINA***—"Teams of civilian volunteers help police canvass neighborhoods immediately after murders and other violent crimes, to help responding units and put potential witnesses at ease. Durham Chief Jose Lopez says other volunteers in city-issued cars patrol shopping centers during the busy holiday seasons and conduct property checks for residents who are away from home. 'They are additional eyes and ears for us,' Lopez says. 'It effectively puts more people on the street'" (Johnson 2010b).

***WACO, TEXAS***—"Students from Baylor College, Texas State Technical College, and McClennan Community College can earn college credit in political science while learning about the law enforcement profession first-hand. Citizens on Patrol student volunteers help patrol the Baylor campus and direct traffic during special events. The patrol is especially active during Christmas break and other school holidays, when fewer 'eyes and ears' are typically around to report crimes" (USAonWatch n.d.).

***LOS ANGELES, CALIFORNIA***—Due to a $100 million cut in budget, LAPD will use volunteers to fill the gap. Currently there are 700 unpaid workers in its Reserve Corps—saving the city about $5 million each year (Hillard 2011).

Furthermore, 43 percent of MCCA survey respondents reported that they increased the use of volunteers as a means to compensate for budget reductions (MCCA 2011).

## Technology as a Force Multiplier

Around the country, cash-strapped communities are looking for any way to boost efficiency and cut spending. As indicated in several of the current surveys, many law enforcement agencies have been forced to reduce or entirely cut their budgets for technology (more than half of the PERF study respondents stated they had cut back or eliminated plans to acquire technology) (PERF 2010). However, other police agencies are shifting their operational models to include the use of technology systems that can help agencies

## Police Use of Technology as Force Multiplier

IN THE NEWS:

**ALBUQUERQUE, NEW MEXICO**—Albuquerque police have led the way in utilizing technology and social media to make up for the loss of officers and resources due to budget cuts. Their system provides "real-time investigative information to private business groups on interactive websites to help stop theft rings, locate violent crime suspects, and track fugitives. Police Chief Raymond Schultz has said that the system has helped make up for the loss of about 60 officers over the past 2 ½ years. The Albuquerque model is now being replicated in agencies in Georgia, Minnesota, Washington, and California" (Johnson 2011).

**CAMDEN, NEW JERSEY**—Camden Police use a combination of GPS, gunshot detectors, and CCTVs to identify problem areas and dispatch officers to those places, which is more efficient than waiting for calls for service. "Technology can never fully replace an officer," said Camden Police Chief Scott Thomson, whose department of 250 officers has been nearly cut in half since 2006. "We are just trying to leverage technology ... to appear bigger than we are" (Johnson 2011).

**FULTON COUNTY, GEORGIA**—"Fulton County has received permission from the Board of Supervisors' Public Safety Committee to accept a one-time state grant of $30,000 for teleconferencing equipment ....
The Sheriff's Department currently spends about 6 hours a day [at the courthouse]; 'The video teleconferencing will help reduce transportation costs' by allowing computerized court appearances" (Anich 2011).

**BELMONT COUNTY, OHIO**—"A juvenile court in eastern Ohio has found that instituting video court hearings has decreased costs and increased the delivery of swift services. Juvenile Court Judge Mark Costine who began the program has found that by reducing the number of prisoner transports, the sheriff's office has saved $50,000 year, while the video installation only cost about $7,000. Judge Costine notes; 'All the courts have these issues of transportation of prisoners. ... We have found a way to make the hearings go faster and also save money'" (Long 2011).

to improve outcomes and increase efficiency. Certain technologies such as Closed-Circuit Televisions (CCTVs) and Light-Based Intervention Systems (LBIS) can act as force multipliers through incident intervention and crime prevention, without requiring the immediate presence of an officer (Cordero 2011).

A recent COPS publication, *Evaluating the Use of Public Surveillance Cameras for Crime Control and Prevention*, studied the public surveillance systems in Baltimore, MD, Chicago, IL, and Washington, D.C. A cost-benefit analysis was used to analyze the cost of the surveillance systems with the savings from victim and criminal justice costs. One neighborhood in Chicago alone saw a cost savings of $4.30 for every dollar that was used for the system. Most law enforcement agencies have to balance the cost of implementing, maintaining, and training for a new piece of technology with the savings that this technology will bring, and this study provides some interesting examples (La Vigne et al. 2011).

Some agencies have increased the use of a type of geographical technology called the Tactical Automatic Vehicle Locator (TAC-AVL) which is used to reduce police response times to emergency calls. TAC-AVL provides commanders the locations of patrols cars with a real-time map of the city, allowing them to determine whether the vehicles are in the right place at the right time (Mayer 2009). Efficient management of resources is crucial for agencies with limited manpower. Automated Emergency Dispatch Systems (AEDs) are used in some agencies to automate emergency police dispatch by electronically locating and dispatching the nearest available patrols (Cordero 2011).

A new trend developing in law enforcement agencies today is the use of social media. According to a PERF survey, 86 percent of responding agencies used some form of social media, including Facebook, Twitter, MySpace, YouTube, and Nixle. Social media provides a cost effective avenue for police to communicate directly with their communities, as well as receive information and feedback from those that they serve (Johnson 2011).

The Boca Raton (Florida) Police Department has created a social media project called VIPER (Visibility, Intelligence, Partnerships, Education, and Resources), which provides the community with a forum to share crime tips, view recent mug shots, receive information, or even request emergency services (Madeiros 2011).

Chuck Wexler, the executive director of PERF, has said; "Departments are looking to technology as a force multiplier. They are using this technology to better manage fewer resources, because just saying 'We don't have enough officers' isn't cutting it with the public" (Johnson 2011).

Another example of how technology has been leveraged by police agencies forced to reduce spending, is through the use of video teleconferencing. For judicial proceedings that had previously required inmates to appear in court, and therefore required an official to transport them, videoconferencing provides some agencies with an efficient and resourceful tool to provide services at a reduced cost. Through the use of teleconferencing equipment, court proceedings are able to be held via video as lawyers discuss their cases in front of the judge, instead of having a constable, sheriff, or police officer transport the defendants to court.

A survey conducted by the Administrative Office of Pennsylvania Courts' (AOPC) Office of Judicial Security, on the use of video conferencing as a means of conducting preliminary arraignments and other judicial proceedings, found that utilization of this technology had a cost savings potential of $21 million annually. Results from the study showed that on average, more than 15,700 proceedings are currently being held via video conferencing in Pennsylvania, resulting in a cost savings of about $1.7 million monthly (AOPC 2011).

Eliminating court transports has the potential to save agencies both monetarily and through officer productivity. A typical prisoner transport involves one officer and one car for what can take up to an entire day. The AOPC study found on average it costs $73 to transport a defendant to and from a local facility and an addition $588 to transport to and from a state correctional institution (AOPC 2011). The cost savings realized as a result of implementing this new method of service delivery have been staggering in some places, including annual savings of $30 million in Pennsylvania, $600,000 in Georgia, and $50,000 in Ohio from transportation costs alone (Long 2011).

## Effects on Organizational Management

With agencies nationwide struggling to uphold their levels of service while losing personnel, many have been forced to consolidate efforts with neighboring agencies. The term *consolidation*, as used here, describes a number of concepts related to the pooling of resources between law enforcement agencies. In 2007, the New Jersey State Association of Chiefs of Police published the white paper *Police Department Regionalization, Consolidation, Merger & Shared Services: Important Considerations for Policy Makers*, and defined the different types of consolidation efforts as follows:

*Shared Services:* Is when two or more agencies combine certain function units, such as emergency communications, SWAT, dispatch, or records.

*Local Merger/Consolidation:* When two separate police agencies form a single new unit.

*Regionalization:* When a number of jurisdictions combine efforts to police a geographic area rather than a jurisdictional one. The new entity does not contain elements of any existing agency—either the jurisdictions had no previously-existing police department, or those that existed have been disbanded.

*Contract Services:* Is when a formal contract to pay for law enforcement services is provided by one jurisdiction to one or more other jurisdictions (NJSACOP 2007: 2).

State and local law enforcement agencies throughout the country are finding the need to develop effective methods and strategies in order to compensate for their dwindling resources. In order to keep communities safe in an affordable and cost effective way, some police agencies are combining their efforts to optimize productivity and increase efficiency (Cordero 2011).

### Studies of Law Enforcement Agency Consolidation

- In the 2011 National Survey of County Elected Officials, 26 percent of respondents said that their county had consolidated services with another county government in response to economic conditions. Further, another 31 percent said that their county has participated in discussions regarding the consolidation of services (McFarland 2010).
- One quarter of IACP survey respondents referenced innovative multi-jurisdictional arrangements their department was taking to promote cost-effective service delivery, including:

  - Joint task forces, combinations that include police, sheriffs, state police, and constables.

  - Service/function-specific resource sharing, including crime scene technicians, dispatch, SWAT, Hazmat, laboratories, and training (IACP 2011).

- Seventy-seven percent of IACP survey respondents said that their agency has been asked to increase its support of other agencies (IACP 2011).
- Seventy percent of MCCA survey respondents stated that they had used consolidation of functions as a means to compensate for budget reductions (MCCA 2011).
- In the 2011 National Association of Counties survey, 38 percent of respondents said that they had been approached by other units of the government during FY2010 about consolidating various activities. Of those approached, 23 percent said they have consolidated law enforcement and/or fire protection (Byers 2011).
- In the 2011 National Survey of County Elected Officials, 56 percent of respondents indicated that their county had cooperated regionally to reduce the cost of services (McFarland 2010).
- A study conducted by Cumberland County, New Jersey, found that the cities could collectively save $4.5 million over 5 years through consolidation (Zager 2011).
- Somerville, New Jersey, also conducted a study, which found that regionalizing their municipal police services under one county umbrella could save about $18 million a year (Cooper 2011).

## Regionalization and Consolidation

IN THE NEWS:

*MINNEAPOLIS/SAINT PAUL, MINNESOTA*—In the Twin Cities of Minneapolis/Saint Paul, the Police Authority and the San Anselmo Police Department began taking steps towards consolidation by sharing some dispatch services and officers. The proposed plan would save San Anselmo $51,000 immediately, and another $113,000 in the future (Dunleavy 2011).

*PORTAGE, MICHIGAN*—Portage has consolidated the police and fire departments. The city's police chief has taken the role of public safety director, reporting directly to the deputy city manager, and is responsible for the overall management of both the fire and police departments (Hall 2011).

*NEW JERSEY*—Berlin Township, Berlin Borough, and Waterford Township Police Departments in New Jersey have developed their own approach to sharing public safety services by combining their police detectives in a shared investigative bureau. Further, Berlin's volunteer fire department is being used to staff evening hour shifts in order to save costs (Mast 2011).

*CAMDEN COUNTY, NEW JERSEY*—Camden County is developing alternate plans for regionalized special services, such as a central detective bureau and SWAT (SNJDC 2011).

*MARION COUNTY, OREGON*—"Marion County Board of County Commissioners (Fire Rescue/Public Safety Communications) and the Marion County Sheriff's Office are initiating efforts to combine their dispatch services. County and Sheriff's Office staff determined that consolidating those efforts would create a recurring savings of $370,000 per year" (Bryant 2011).

*LANSING, MICHIGAN*—"A plan to consolidate Lansing's north and south police precincts could save the city $535,380 in rent, utilities, and janitorial services by the 2015 fiscal year" (VanHulle 2011).

*Continued*

## Regionalization and Consolidation (*Continued*)

***GREENFIELD, CALIFORNIA***—The Greenfield City Council approved an agreement to merge its police force with the city of Soledad's. City Manager Brent Slama stated, "'Given the fiscal realities facing our cities, especially the four south Monterey County cities, regionalization is going to be important [in the future].' The Soledad proposal is projected to save Greenfield $158,699 beginning in the 2012–13 fiscal year. David Cariaga [a representative of both Greenfield Police associations] stated, 'It's the best solution to keep the men and women in the department working and … it's creating a savings for the city'" (Vijayan 2011).

***BROWARD COUNTY, FLORIDA***—"Facing an estimated $9 million deficit, mostly for police and fire services, Lauderdale Lakes has asked the Sheriff's Office for help. The solution came in the form of consolidation between Lauderdale Lakes and the unincorporated Central Broward district, which will save a combined $3.4 million. 'Many of our cities ought to look to merge with each other and have economies of scale and save the taxpayers a lot of money,' Broward County Commissioner Dale Holness said at a June County Commission workshop" (East 2011).

## The Importance of Community Policing in Tough Financial Times

Many of the cost saving techniques discussed within this report are directly related to community policing efforts. Community policing is a philosophy that promotes organizational strategies, which support the systematic use of partnerships and problem-solving techniques, to proactively address the immediate conditions that give rise to public safety issues such as crime, social disorder, and fear of crime (COPS Office 2009a). The three tenets of community policing—community partnerships, organizational transformation, and problem solving—are of increased importance when facing budget cuts that reduce the number of officers on the streets.

Collaborative partnerships to develop solutions to problems and increase trust in police can be seen in many of the solutions police agencies are using in light of the economic downturn. Specifically, the use of volunteers, partnerships between the police and private agencies, and the use of social media as a means to communicate effectively with the community in order to meet their needs, are all examples of how collaborative partnerships act as a cost-saving tool.

Organizational transformation exists through the alignment of organizational management, structure, personnel, and information systems to support community partnerships and proactive problem solving. From its inception, community policing's goal is one of forging strong relationships between law enforcement and the communities they serve. It aims to redesign the practice of public safety into a collective, collaborative effort (COPS Office 2009a).

The current economic crisis, which has thwarted many police activities, requires police agencies to place a greater emphasis on problem-solving techniques. By engaging in the proactive and systematic examination of identified problems and developing and rigorously evaluating effective responses, they will be able to best use the limited resources that are available to them.

Unfortunately, when agencies are forced to make widespread budget cuts, some have done so by reducing or eliminating some of their community policing programs. In fact, according to the MCCA survey, 39 percent of respondents who have reduced budgets stated that those budgets cuts were made to their community policing efforts (MCCA 2011).

Herein lies one of the major fallacies as it relates to community policing. Community policing should not be viewed as a particular program within a department, but rather as a department-wide philosophy. Programs are typically initiated as a response to a specific problem, in which only a small portion of the organization is involved and once the problem has been addressed the program is dissolved (Trojanowicz and Bucqueroux 1994). Instead, community policing must be understood as a philosophy that promotes the systematic use of partnerships and problem-solving techniques to proactively address the conditions within a community that are cause for public concerns over crime and social disorder issues (Melekian 2011d).

Community policing is an organizational strategy. It can be used to govern the way police services are delivered, recognizing the police officer as an organizer of resources in pursuit of public safety rather than someone designated to perform specific tasks (Trojanowicz and Bucqueroux 1994).

In an article in *The Police Chief*, COPS Office Director Melekian articulates the importance of the community policing philosophy in the face of the current economic climate. He argues that the downturn in the economy has affected the country in ways that could not have been predicted even 5 years

## The Importance of Community Policing in a Recession

IN THE NEWS:

*CONCORD, MASSACHUSETTS*—Deputy Police Chief Barry Neal has utilized the proactive approach of community policing to prevent crime and reduce victimization. "We recognize that we can't solve problems alone, we need to engage the community and work in partnership with them," he said. "It gives us direct daily face-to-face contact between the community and the officers, and also gives us the ability to prevent problems from occurring instead of reacting to them" (Ball 2009).

*ALBUQUERQUE, NEW MEXICO*—Chief Schultz of Albuquerque is having officers develop partnerships with retailers to address shoplifters and boosters. The Police Department has experienced a 20 percent reduction in their workforce and is developing partnerships with retailers with the goal of sharing information in order to link petty crimes together to prosecute larger and stronger cases and get repeat offenders off the street. In addition, they are offering rewards to housekeepers at hotels to report the accumulation of large amounts of merchandise, which can often be found in hotel rooms (Stelter 2011).

*KANSAS CITY, MISSOURI*—"When we talk in Kansas City about 'doing something different,' a mention of community policing usually follows. And surely, the thought of police officers working hand in hand with neighborhood folks is enticing. But successful, citywide community policing would require a culture change for a police department that places more faith in arrest statistics than relationships as a crime-fighting tool. [In looking for a new police chief, Kansas City] believes a chief who finds a way to make it acceptable, indeed desirable, for officers to connect with citizens and help solve problems will be the start of the change that everyone talks about" (Shelly 2011).

ago. The enhancement of community policing and the myriad of social outreach programs that have been employed by local law enforcement were initially brought about in large measure by the combination of federal grant dollars and readily available local funding sources. That financial foundation is now in serious jeopardy in many local jurisdictions.

Melekian further highlights how some have made the argument that these economic challenges may compel us to abandon community policing because we simply cannot afford it (Melekian 2011d). However, experience has shown that community policing is a more cost-effective way of utilizing available resources than simple traditional policing practices, for a number of reasons. Primarily, community participation in crime-prevention amplifies the amount of available resources, while community partnerships used to address problem solving provides a more efficient distribution of combined police and community resources than simply reactive policing program models (Brown 1989).

## Conclusion

In 2008, the entire country was introduced to the largest fiscal crisis since the Great Depression. Many who have worked in the field for decades have never seen an economic situation that has affected law enforcement like the one our country currently faces. As cities and counties across America are experiencing a downturn in local revenues, the effects on public safety budgets have been significant. Americans are faced with a new economic reality, in which they are challenged to develop new and innovative ways to leverage resources and maximize productivity in the face of diminishing financial means. Police agencies have not escaped the effects of shrinking revenues. In fact, the economic challenges facing many Americans are amplified when it comes to public safety.

To compensate for shrinking budgets, many individuals focus on what can be sacrificed from their normal lifestyle in order to offset the reduction in available spending. Families may forego their annual summer vacation, or choose to only shop in discount stores rather than their favorite department stores. However, law enforcement agencies face the more difficult and ever important task of maintaining the same quality of service that they always have provided despite a severe reduction in available resources. Therefore, to successfully deliver the high levels of community protection and emergency responsiveness communities depend on, law enforcement agencies must develop new and innovative techniques to address the needs of their communities in cost-effective and sustainable ways.

The recognition and acceptance of this new economic reality is more important than ever in developing strategic management practices to ensure the effective and efficient delivery of police services. Never before has the law enforcement community experienced such significant cuts to operating budgets and available resources. Rather than continuing to provide services through traditional means in hopes that the economy will return to pre-recession levels, police nationwide are shifting, adapting, and redeveloping the ways in which they do their job—to ensure the highest levels of public safety.

In every corner of the United States, state, local, and tribal police departments are being forced to lay off officers and civilian staff, or modify their operations as a result of budget cuts. Over the last 2 years, many agencies have experienced considerable affects from budget constrictions, including mandatory furloughs and hiring freezes, which have resulted in significant reductions in staffing levels never experienced before. Indeed, American law enforcement is changing, and the effects are likely to last over the next 5 to 10 years, if not longer.

While the exact nature of how these changes will take place is unclear, the data within this report suggest that changes may occur on several fronts. First, there may be greater application of "force-multiplier" technologies such as closed-circuit TVs, automated emergency dispatch systems, video teleconferencing equipment, and social media usage. Utilization of technologies such as these has the ability to provide law enforcement agencies with a way to maximize available information while alleviating the need for an immediate response.

Another fundamental alteration that has been seen in delivery of police services as a result of the changing economy is the increased application of non-sworn individuals—both as employees and as volunteers. More and more police agencies have begun to shift some of the responsibilities that have traditionally been performed by sworn staff to civilian personnel as a means to mitigate payroll costs and maintain staffing levels. Further, some agencies have even engaged citizen volunteers to help alleviate the strain on police work loads. Such approaches can provide sworn staff with more time to focus on pressing and time-sensitive issues that can only be successfully managed by a law enforcement officer.

Some agencies have had to drastically change their methods for handling non-emergency situations and administrative duties. Many police agencies are no longer able to dispatch an officer to every call for service. Instead, more often police managers are forced to direct their resources to focus on situations which pose the most threat to public safety. For example, some agencies are no longer able send officers to collect crime reports for cases that don't involve suspects, or dispatch patrol officers to every non-emergency/non-injury service call. The primary focus on law enforcement is protecting the safety of their communities. Therefore, agencies experiencing limited resources must adjust their approach to focus in on situations that are an immediate threat to public safety.

A more drastic change that is being seen as a result of the economic downturn is the increase in the number of agencies combining efforts and resources through consolidation, shared services, and regionalization. When agencies are faced with maintaining services levels with less and less, collaborating or combining agency's efforts often is the only way to maximize available resources, training, and information.

As this report has shown, the recent economic downturn has placed serious constraints on police budgets and severely diminished the availability of resources. As an additional step to help compensate for declining resources, many departments have also begun collecting and disseminating crime data in real-time via new technology. This has allowed for the effective management and strategic deployment of resources to focus on specific problems as they develop. With the increased use of technology and information-sharing policies being institutionalized throughout many police departments nationwide, it has become essential that the collection of national census data relating to law enforcement agencies be collected with the same urgency.

It is crucial for policy makers to create proactive, aggressive, and productive problem-solving strategies based on relevant and current data. However, the delay in the current methods of data collection and dissemination makes it difficult to present an accurate picture of the state of police agencies as things happen. In turn, a true understanding of the challenges confronting law enforcement agencies as seen through comprehensive analysis takes time and resources. It will be important for federal partners to collaborate on a way to collectively participate in data collection efforts in the future that will increase the availability of up-to-date data, and its analysis and dissemination. By collecting data more frequently and comprehensively, policy makers and government agencies will be able to adjust and realign their strategic goals to provide relevant assistance where law enforcement agencies need it most.

Institutionalization of the community policing philosophy is vital to the ability of law enforcement agencies to succeed and thrive in the current economic climate. Agencies must systematically use partnerships and problem-solving techniques to proactively address the problems that their communities are facing. Development and enhancement of symbiotic relationships between police and the communities they serve is key to ensuring community safety.

It is clear that the challenges facing America as a result of the economic decline that began in 2008 have been significant. Law enforcement communities are facing a new reality in American policing—one that requires a shift in the methods they use to uphold levels of service while dealing with ever shrinking budgets. However, the importance of maintaining and expanding community policing practices during this time of economic hardship is paramount. Research and feedback from the field indicate that community policing is a successful practice in both small and large agencies with significant public safety problems. Thankfully, many of the law enforcement agencies in the United States already practice community policing, and more are coming to recognize the value of community partnerships in this time of limited resources.

## Discussion

I firmly believe that this chapter on the impact of the economic downturn on policing is the most vital chapter in this textbook. Operating without healthy budgets reduces the effectiveness of policing, allows crime to flourish, and stagnates quality-of-life issues at the neighborhood level. America is in its tenth economic decline since World War II. Law enforcement agencies are scrambling to find ways to deliver services differently. New models of policing are being explored to offset the impact of this great economic decline.

Some things will not change. Law enforcement will still respond to emergencies, make arrests, recover evidence, and investigate serious crime. Sworn law enforcement officers will continue to deliver vital services to the public. The two areas that will fundamentally change in policing are responses to non-emergency calls for service and quality-of-life issues in the community.

Many non-emergency calls such as thefts, vandalisms, and traffic accidents require documentation. Departments are thinking of ways to marry technology with volunteers to more efficiently write crime reports. This change in policing will improve response times and allow sworn officers to solve problems in the community more effectively.

Some agencies have replaced detectives with civilians or retired police officers to handle filings with the district attorney and conduct follow-up investigations on non-violent offenses. Properly trained civilians are replacing sworn law enforcement officers in community policing and other problem-solving units. It is my hope that this devastating economic downturn improves for the benefit of those who serve in law enforcement and corrections. After all, for us active in or retired from law enforcement, our career was a CALLING.

## Questions for Class Discussion

1. What are some of the service challenges facing law enforcement budgets today?

2. Discuss some innovative programs utilized by law enforcement agencies to improve efficiency and effectiveness.

3. How might law enforcement organizations utilize their retired officers or volunteers to free up sworn officers for other pressing duties?

## Class Activities for the Professor

1. Discuss the questions in an on-line chat or in the classroom.

2. Assign the students in the role of a police manager and have them design a proposal to reduce a division or unit In their police or correctional organization by 20 percent.

3. Analyze your department, division, or bureau of your law enforcement organization. Prepare a staff study to expand the role of volunteers in your organization.

4. Analyze your department, division, or bureau of your law enforcement organization. Prepare a staff study with a plan to hire part-time retired police officers to take the burden off sworn personnel.

5. Research a technology that your department could afford to increase efficiency in providing service to the community.

## Note

1. Stratification is by agency size with all 100-plus sworn departments sampled.

## References

Acosta, Roberto. 2011. "Burton officials to rehire two laid-off police officers with reworded COPS grant." *Flint Journal* July 18. www.mlive.com/news/flint/index.ssf/2011/07/burton_officials_to_bring_back.html.

Adams, Paul. 2011. "Arizona police force turns to civilian investigators." *BBC News* April 5. www.bbc.co.uk/news/world-us-canada-12754776.

Alqadi, Nazmia. 2011. Building Relationships and Solving Problems in North Miami. *Community Policing Dispatch* vol. 4, no. 10. www.cops.usdoj.gov/html/dispatch/10-2011/North-Miami-Beach.asp.

Anich, Michael. 2011. "County eyes jail teleconferencing." *The Leader Herald* July 26. www.leaderherald.com/page/content.detail/id/539221.html.

AOPC (Administrative Office of Pennsylvania Courts). 2011. "PA Courts Expand Use of Video Conferencing, Saving $21 Million Annually in Defendant Transportation Costs." AOPC press release June 7. www.aopc.org/NR/rdonlyres/36906F45-C993-4844-A3E1-CC3A68B4300B/0/VideoConfExpdsPACts_060711.pdf.

Ball, Patrick. 2009. "Police face budget cuts: Town could scale back Community Policing." *GateHouse News Service* May 21. www.wickedlocal.com/concord/news/x124592912/Police-face-budget-cut-Town-could-scale-back-Community-Policing#axzz1XykF7BhL.

Brown, Lee. 1989. *Community Policing: A Practical Guide for Police Officials.* Washington, D.C.: U.S. Department of Justice, Office of Justice Programs, National Institute of Justice, NCJ118001.

Bryant, Kathy. 2011. "Dispatch consolidation a win-win for public." *Ocala.com* September 4. www.ocala.com/article/20110904/OPINION/110909913/1162/sitemaps.

Byers, Jacqueline. 2011. *The Recession Continues: An Economic Status Survey of Counties.* Washington, D.C.: National Association of Counties.

CBS Broadcasting, Inc. 2010. "Fears Rise as Patterson, N.J. Police Force Lays Off 125 Officers." *CBS Broadcasting, Inc.* April 18. http://newyork.cbslocal.com/2011/04/18/paterson-new-jersey-cuts-125-police-officers/.

Clark, Richard. 2011. *Looking for the Light at the End of the Tunnel: a national survey of county elected officials on the economy, budgets and politics.* Athens, Georgia: Carl Vinson Institute of Government.

Cooper, Warren. 2011. "Somerset County Prosecutor to update public on countywide policing effort." *Somerset Messenger-Gazette* June 2. www.nj.com/messenger-gazette/index.ssf/2011/06/somerset_county_prosecutor_to_update_public_on_countywide_policing_effort.html.

COPS Office (Office of Community Oriented Policing Services). 2009a. *Community Policing Defined.* Washington, D.C.: U.S. Department of Justice, Office of Community Oriented Policing Services.

COPS Office (Office of Community Oriented Policing Services). 2009b. *Operation Partnership: Trends and Practices in Law Enforcement and Private Security Collaborations.* Washington, D.C.: U.S. Department of Justice, Office of Community Oriented Policing Services.

Cordero, Joe. 2011. *Reducing the Cost of Quality of Policing: Making Community Safety Cost Effective and Sustainable,* NJLM Educational Foundation, Friends of Local Government Services, vol. 3, no. 1. Trenton, New Jersey: The Cordero Group.

CSLLEA (Census of State and Local Law Enforcement Agencies), Bureau of Justice Statistics, Office of Justice Programs, U.S. Department of Justice. http://bjs.ojp.usdoj.gov/index.cfm?ty=dcdetail&iid=249.

Dunleavy, Kelly. 2011. "San Anselmo, Twin Cities Move Closer to Police Consolidation." *Patch* June 14. http://sananselmofairfax.patch.com/articles/san-anselmo-twin-cities-move-closer-to-police-consolidation.

Fenton, John. 2011. "Police reports will be taken over phone in city pilot program." *The Baltimore Sun* August 16. http://articles.baltimoresun.com/2011-08-16/news/bs-md-ci-police-report-pilot-20110816_1_crimes-largest-police-district-northeast-baltimore.

Forst, Brian. 2000. "The Privatization and Civilization of Policing." In C. M. Friel (Ed.), *Boundary Changes in Criminal Justice Organizations: Criminal Justice 2000,* Vol. 2:19–79. Washington, D.C.: National Institute of Justice. NCJ 182409.

Friend, Zack, and Rick Martinez. 2010. "Preserving Community-Oriented Policing in a Recession." *ICMA Press* April. http://webapps.icma.org/pm/9203/public/pmplus1.cfm?author=Zach%20Friend%20and%20Rick%20Martinez&title=Preserving%20 Community-Oriented%20Policing%20in%20a%20Recession&subtitle.

Goldstein, Joseph. 2011. "Police Force Nearly Halved, Camden Feels Impact." *The New York Times* March 6. www.nytimes.com/2011/03/07/nyregion/07camden.html?pagewanted=all.

Hall, Rex. 2011. "Portage police and fire administration to be consolidated under one public safety director." *Kalamazoo Gazette* May 13. www.mlive.com/news/kalamazoo/index.ssf/2011/05/portage_police_and_fire_admini.html.

Henry, Samantha. 2011. "Cops protest as Paterson lays off 125 police officers; mayor hopes to hire some back." Associated Press April 18. www.guardianangels.org/pdf/99226.pdf.

Hillard, Gloria. 2011. "In Tight Times, L.A. Forced to Rely on Volunteer Police." *NPR* May 19. www.npr.org/2011/05/19/136436405/in-tight-times-l-a-relies-on-volunteer-police.

Hoene, Christopher, and Michael Pagano. 2010. *City Fiscal Conditions in 2010.* Washington, D.C.: National League of Cities.

Howard, Jacinda. 2010. "Grant will save four police jobs in Federal Way." *Federal Way Mirror* October 5. www. pnwlocalnews.com/south_king/fwm/news/104379438.html.

IACP (International Association of Chiefs of Police). 2010. *Policing in the 21st Century: Preliminary Survey Results.* Alexandria, Virginia: International Association of Chiefs of Police.

Johnson, Kevin. 2009. "Economy limiting services of local police." *USA Today* May 18. www. usatoday.com/news/nation/2009-05-17-police-closure_N.htm.

Johnson, Kevin. 2010a. "Cutbacks force police to curtail calls for some crimes." *USA Today* August 25. www. usatoday.com/news/nation/2010-08-25-1Anresponsecops25_ST_N.htm.

Johnson, Kevin. 2010b. "Tight budgets lead to more civilians used for policing." *USA Today* October 11. www. usatoday.com/news/nation/2010-10-11-1Acitizenpolice11_ST_N.htm.

Johnson, Kevin. 2011. "Police tap technology to compensate for fewer officers." *USA Today* April 25. www.usato-day.com/news/nation/2011-04-24-police-crime-technology-facebook.htm.

La Vigne, Nancy, Samantha S. Lowry, Joshua A. Markman, and Allison M. Dwyer. 2011. *Evaluating the Use of Public Surveillance Cameras for Crime Control and Prevention.* Washington, D.C.: U.S. Department of Justice, Office of Community Oriented Policing Services.

LEMAS (Law Enforcement Management and Administrative Statistics), Bureau of Justice Statistics, Office of Justice Programs, U.S. Department of Justice. http://bjs.ojp.usdoj.gov/index.cfm?ty=dcdetail&iid=248\.

LeDuff, Charlie. 2011. "Riding Along With the Cops in Murdertown, U.S.A." *The New York Times* April 15. www.nytimes.com/2011/04/17/magazine/mag-17YouRhere-t.html.

Long, Colleen. 2011. "Courts nationwide hold hearings with video." *Associated Press* May 8. http://newyork.cbslo-cal.com/2011/05/08/courts-nationwide-hold-hearings-with-video/.

Loren, Jennifer. 2010. "Stimulus Money Used to Save Police Jobs." *WorldNow and KWTV* February 3. www.news9.com/story/11930579/stimulus-money-used-to-save-police-jobs.

Madeiros, James. 2011. "Police Use Social Media to Shape Image, Fight Crime." *Criminal Justice Degree Schools* June 12. www.criminaljusticedegreeschools.com/police-use-social-media-to-fight-crime-0612111/.

Maher, Jeff. 2011. "Sacramento Police handcuffed by budget cuts." *News 10/KXTV* August 29. www.news10.net/news/article/152169/2/Sacramento-police-handcuffed-by-budget-cuts-.

Masoner, Gloria. 2009. "COPS grant saves loss of Beatrice officer." *Beatrice Daily Sun* July 30. www.beatricedaily-sun.com/news/local/article_b452b12c-e05c-5a37-843d-01c9bf047d4c.html.

Mast, George. 2011. "When merged police forces worked in Camden County—and when they didn't." *Courier Post* June 20. http://pqasb.pqarchiver.com/courierpostonline/ access/2379431651.html?FMT=ABS&date=Jun +20%2C+2011.

MCCA (Major Cities Chiefs Association). 2011. *Police Economic Challenges Survey Results.* Sun Valley, Idaho: Major Cities Chiefs Association (unpublished).

McFarland, Christina. 2010. *State of America's Cities Survey on Jobs and the Economy.* Washington, D.C.: National League of Cities, Center for Research and Innovation.

Melekian, Bernard. 2011a. Director's Message. *Community Policing Dispatch* vol. 4, no. 3. http://cops.usdoj.gov/html/dispatch/03-2011/DirectorMessage.asp.

Melekian, Bernard. 2011b. Director's Column: July 2011. *Community Policing Dispatch* vol. 4, no. 7. http://cops.usdoj.gov/html/dispatch/07-2011/DirectorMessage.asp.

Melekian, Bernard. 2011c. Director's Column: June 2011. *Community Policing Dispatch* vol. 4, no. 6. http://cops.usdoj.gov/html/dispatch/06-2011/DirectorMessage.asp.

Melekian, Bernard. 2011d. "The Office of Community Oriented Policing Services, From the Director." *The Police Chief* 78 (March): 14. www.policechiefmagazine.org/magazine/index.cfm?fuseaction=print_display&article_id=2330&issue_id=32011.

Merkle, Dan. 2011. "Data Driven Decision Making: Reducing Operating Costs While Maintaining Mission Excellence." (Presentation at the 2011 COPS Conference, Washington, D.C., August 1, 2011).

Myer, Allison. 2009. "Geospatial Technology Helps East Orange Crack Down on Crime." *Geography & Public Safety* 1, no. 4 (January):8–9.

NJSACOP (New Jersey State Association of Chiefs of Police). 2007. *Police Department Regionalization, Consolidation, Merger & Shared Services: Important Considerations for Police Makers*: 2. A NAJSACOP White Paper, West Trenton, New Jersey. www.nj.gov/dca/affiliates/luarcc/resources/pdf/WhitePaper-Consolidation.pdf.

Oldendorf, Patrick. 2010. "Grant will save 10 Peoria police officer jobs." *Journal Star* December 21. www.pjstar.com/news/x1882973274/Revised-grant-will-save-jobs-of-10-Peoria-police-officers.

PERF (Police Executive Research Forum). 2010. *Is the Economic Downturn Fundamentally Changing How We Police?* Critical Issues in Policing Series, vol. 16, Washington, D.C.: Police Executive Research Forum.

Rose, Elaine. 2010. "$1.1 million grant helps prevent layoffs for five Egg Harbor Township police officers." *Press of Atlantic City* September 30. www.pressofatlanticcity.com/news/press/atlantic/article_468eb94c-ccf9-11df-af56-001cc4c03286.html.

Shelly, Barbara. 2011. "Next chief has huge tasks waiting, and waiting … ." *The Kansas City Star* September 15. www.kansascity.com/2011/09/15/3145454/next-chief-has-huge-task-waiting.html.

SNJCD (Southern New Jersey Development Council). 2011. "Countywide police force panel reviewing other options for Camden County." www.snjdc.org/2011/08/countywide-police-force-panel-reviewing-other-options-for-camden-county/.

Stelter, Leishen. 2011. "Police chief pushes partnerships: 'Fighting crime is a team sport.'" *United Publications, Inc.* June 21. www.securitydirectornews.com/?p=article&id=sd201106Z0AuM7

Trojanowicz, Robert, and Bonnie Bucqueroux. 1994. *Community Policing: How to Get Started*. Cincinnati, Ohio: Anderson Publishing Company.

USAonWatch. n.d. "Citizens on Patrol Volunteers Boost Texas County's Crime Preventions." www.usaonwatch.org/resource/publication.aspx?PublicationId=98.

VanHulle, Lindsay. 2011. "Lansing looks to merge police precincts." *www.lansingstatejournal.com* August 18. http://pqasb.pqarchiver.com/lansingstatejournal/access/2428604161.html?FMT=ABS&date=Aug+18%2C+2011.

Vedadi, Neena. 2011. "Volunteers Help Lighten the Load for Richland PD." *Fischer Interactive Network* September 12. www.keprtv.com/news/local/129695338.html.

Vijayan, Sunita. 2011. "Greenfield OKs deal to merge police force with Soledad's." *The California.com* September 14. www.thecalifornian.com/apps/pbcs.dll/article?AID=/201109140505/NEWS01/109140314.

Volunteers in Police Services. 2011a. "Origin of the Volunteers in Police Services (VIPS) Program." www.policevolunteers.org/about/.

Volunteers in Police Services. 2011b. "VIPS Registered Program Analysis Results." www.policevolunteers.org/cms/index.cfm?fa=detail&id=670.

Wexler, Chuck. 2010. "Survey Reveals Extent of Police Budget Cuts." PERF press release September 30. www.policeforum.org/dotAsset/36339.pdf

Wiseman, Jane. 2011. *Strategic Cutback Management: Law Enforcement Leadership for Lean Times*. Research for Practice, Washington, D.C.: U.S. Department of Justice, National Institute of Justice, NCJ 232077.

Zager, Matt. 2011. "Consolidations topic of federal budget forum." *The Daily Journal* June 22. www.thedailyjournal.com/article/20110622/NEWS01/106220326.

# Chapter 4: Breaking the Silence on Law Enforcement Suicide

By Donald C. Lacher, MS, Captain-Retired

---

*In the end we will remember not the words of our enemies but the silence of our friends.*

Dr. Martin Luther King Jr.

## Student Objectives

1. Examine personal impacts of police suicide
2. Compare and contrast organizational versus management impacts in police suicide events.
3. Explore police suicide prevention programs

---

**All cops will relate to this statement:**

It has been 38 years since I graduated from the police academy. Like all cops I remember that life-changing experience even to this day. The academy was a rite of passage and passing that hurdle began my professional life in policing.

The first day we reported in suits, dreading the unknown. I was one of the few from outside agencies. I was surrounded by young deputies as we stood on the grinder at the Los Angeles County Sheriff's Department training facility.

So began my immersion into law enforcement culture. The mission of the academy was to teach academics and tactical skill, underpinned by painful physical training. I remember the slogan in the gym: "The More You Sweat Here, The Less You Bleed on the Street." Of course we all dreaded the constant verbal counseling. I vowed to make it through one day at a time.

It all made sense in the end. The staff had only 18 weeks to condition us to function as peace officer recruits. In the third week we were rewarded by wearing our uniforms and Sam Brown belt, absent our firearm and badge. The academy revolved around rewards. Once we passed our first major academic exam, the academy had a ceremony to allow us to pin on our badges.

We were not completely worthy yet. A few weeks later we prepared for range training so we were allowed to wear our unloaded firearms. After successfully qualifying with our handguns and shotgun, we were granted permission to walk the grounds of the academy with loaded firearms; we had finally earned the full trust of the drill instructors. I graduated with the other 88 recruits from Class 187 Los Angeles County Sheriff's Department and went to work at the Monrovia Police Department.

During most of the career, I put on that uniform, badge, and gun. When I worked plainclothes, my gun and badge were on my belt. Working undercover narcotics or vice, I had my firearm secreted in my boot.

Except for being out of the United States, I carried my handgun whether on or off-duty. A cop's firearm is a tool connected to their psyche. It is their survival mechanism. Very few officers will fire their gun in the line of duty. However, the danger of an officer-involved shooting is ever-present. I remember a saying about working patrol: "hours of boredom interpreted by moments of terror."

I would imagine that I removed my gun from the holster several times daily while working patrol. Working patrol, you never knew what the next call or observation had in store for you … one moment things were safe and the next moment you could have to fight for your life.

In those days, the topic of police suicide was not discussed in the academy. When I would hear of a police suicide at other agencies; all reports mentioned that the officer took their life with their firearm. This trend puzzled me because the firearm, a symbol of their protection, was the very tool they used to take their life; WHY?, I wondered.

I decided to write this chapter in the book for a couple of reasons. I discuss this topic in my Contemporary Issues in Criminal Justice Management course at Union Institute & University. Actually, the idea originated from a police chief who believed that there was not enough attention by police managers on this issue. The second reason was to open a dialogue in our industry on this tragic subject. We, in enforcement and corrections must band together to improve the emotional wellness of our personnel with the hope of reducing suicide in our ranks.

I am not an expert on police suicide. I have researched the subject and found that it is not easy to find literature on the topic. So, I sought out the experts in the field and others who can shed a light on this pertinent issue in policing. The victims of police suicide, their families and colleague-survivors deserve to have this issue brought to the forefront of the criminal justice industry.

Ron Clark is the Chairman of the Board of Directors for the Badge of Life. He is a retired sergeant from the Connecticut State Police and a registered nurse. The Badge of Life organization is committed to reducing police suicides by education and prevention. Ron laid the foundation for this chapter in one sentence. He said: *Police chiefs and sheriffs fear two things most; an on-duty death or a suicide by a member of their department* (R. Clark, personal communication. October 21, 2013).

In 2012, O'Hara, Levenson, Violanti, and Clark, completed Phase III of the "National Police Suicide Estimates Web Surveillance" study. The following statistics were gleaned from their journal article comparing 2012 police suicide data with 2008 and 2009 data. The data are narrowed to only police suicide information within the United States and focuses only on peace officers on active duty. According to Ron Clark the International Association of Chiefs of Police (IACP) reports there are 18,000 law enforcement agencies nationally populated by approximately 850,000 peace officers.

The study revealed there were 141 police suicides in 2008, 143 in 2009 and 126 in 2012. The 126 number showed a decline in police suicides by 11.9% (O'Hara, 2012). In comparison, officers feloniously killed in the line of duty by year were:

| | | |
|---|---|---|
| 2008, | Forty-One | (41) |
| 2009 | Forty-Eight | (48) |
| 2010 | Fifty-Six | (56) |
| 2011 | Seventy-Two | (72) |

Note: 2012 statistics for officers felonious killed were not available

Two disturbing trends have been identified when we evaluate these data. The numbers of officers feloniously killed in the line of duty rose significantly increase in 2011. Comparing the 2010, data with 2011, the number of officers slain rose by 16. The number of officers who take their own lives is significantly higher than those who are feloniously killed. Unfortunately, we are more likely to kill ourselves than be murdered by felons.

Other significant trends in the topic are:

- Male and female officer suicides occur at the same rate averaging 92% and 6% respectively in 2012
- Suicides cluster more in the age groups of 40 to 44 years ; more than previous years among officers of lower rank.
- Suicides increased among officers with 15 to 19 years of service
- Gunshots remained the most prevalent means of death across all three years at 91.5%
- Personal problems appeared to be prevalent in 83% of the cases with work and legal problems ranking second at 13%
- Military veterans had the highest suicide rates accounting for 11% of the total police suicides; ten suicides in California and two in New York
- Four murder-suicides were reported in 2012

The O'Hara, Levenson, Violanti, and Clark study revealed that New York led the nation with twelve suicides, followed by federal officers with eleven and California with ten. Reasons for suicides gleaned from the study included personal or legal issues. Some departments reported exposure to work-place trauma to blame while, others reported an unknown cause for the suicide.

In this chapter we will divide the study of police suicide into four broad sections. The sections include personal, operational, organizational and management impacts. We will also explore preventative programs aimed at reducing law enforcement and correctional officer suicides. We will wrap up the chapter with the future endeavors to save the lives of officers who might otherwise kill themselves.

## Personal Impacts

Ron Clark and I agree that policing is more difficult than in times past. Just keeping up with the technology required in law enforcement places a tremendous burden on employees today. In addition, all criminal justice organizations are expecting employees to do more with less because of the economic down turn. Pay and benefits are being reduced for the same reasons. Pile on these stressors with the dangers of police work plus family problems, and post-traumatic stress becomes a national law enforcement issue.

However, there are factors that law enforcement officers have faced for decades. Today, many police officers turn to alcohol or other drugs to numb the emotional pain, stacking more negative issues on their shoulders.

Cops are a sensitive lot. They develop coping mechanisms to mask their feelings and put up an outer façade. How many cops do you know who walk around with that stone face look?

Our subculture conditions both male and female law enforcement officers to build an invisible shield of emotional armor. Just as our body armor is worn around us and shields us from harm, our psyche builds an emotional armor to protect us psychologically.

That emotional armor allows us as a profession to react tactically to danger and to maintain our cool to accomplish the mission. I am not sure if our profession teaches us to do this or if it becomes part of our psyche to deal with the horrors of our job.

There are many times during their deployment that cops have to be tough and show their toughness. They shove their feelings deep down inside them to be able to act as a first responder, to complete the mission without displaying weakness. Across our nation, on a daily basis cops place their lives in danger to rescue fellow officers or members of the public.

Ron Clark estimates the average law enforcement officer will experience 150 to 200 serious traumatic events in their career. Such events are numerous: dead kids, dying kids, tortured kids, molested kids; abused kids; rape victims, fatal traffic accidents, and other mishaps; fatal fires, murders, suicides, drug overdoses; the list is endless. Single-trauma events can cause trouble, too. Just think of the first responders who experienced the terrorist attacks in New York or more recently in Boston.

Professor William Griffin, a retired sheriff's captain said: *We can get officers or deputies past an officer involved-shooting; it is the helpless people we cannot help that takes the toll on all of us* (W. Griffin, personal communication, October 10, 2013).

According to Ron Clark, the underlying issue is that the law enforcement officers are not going to self-report a mental or emotional problem due to fear of being stripped of their firearm, and risking their employment status. Officers who refuse to seek help immediately when subjected to trauma are heading for deep emotional trouble.

## Organizational Issues

Law enforcement organizations have the duty to strike a balance between protecting their employees and the public. This duty extends to protecting the public from officers who can no longer function as a peace officer, due to physical or mental health issues. Depending on the circumstances of the situation, a law enforcement officer may find themselves the subject of a fitness-for-duty examination.

Professor Corina Smith is a retired lieutenant from a major law enforcement organization. She was assigned as the Officer in Charge of a police employment and liability unit. In some cases, employees would file law suits after they were relieved of duty or their firearms were removed from their possession. Professor Smith had oversight of all employment-related lawsuits and sometimes had to deal with officers who were suing the department over their mental health issues. In addition to mental health issues, there were occasions that involved unrelated discipline or misconduct issues that exacerbated the stress the employee may have been suffering.

Professor Smith stated: *It was common to have multiple department entities involved in these workplace issues complicating the situation. For example the commanding officer might believe the employee is a danger to themselves or others and want his firearm taken away. The department psychologist may or may not agree with the commander. Internal affairs might be investigating allegations of misconduct by the officer. The officer's lawyer might argue that the officer is being treated unfairly by the department when the firearm is seized or[the] finding [is that] the employee[is] unfit for duty. The department's legal team would become involved to shield the organization from potential liability. The employee's physician might render an opinion that the employee is not mental capable of continuing working and should be retired. The employee is caught in the middle and often times deteriorates even further due to the stress of the process.*

*The bottom line is that the organization may lose a viable employee in the field. In situations where the employee's doctor renders an opinion that they can no longer function as a peace officer, those records may eventually be used against the employee. The employee has two options. Suicide might be looked as a way out of the situation. Or, the employee may say they have recovered and the process starts over. Unfortunately, the employee may never have their mental health issues addressed. However, once the department is exposed to potential liability the only option for the Department is the fitness for duty hearing so not to risk keeping an officer that could become a risk to themselves or the community.*

*Our department convened a board of two senior command-level officers and one civilian that made the decision to either return the firearm to the employee and assign them back to their duties or initiate administrative proceedings to either terminate their employment or retire them from service.*

*I remember one occasion, where the department made the wrong decision. The firearm was returned to the employee and the employee committed suicide.*

*To understand how deeply an officer may be affected by the removal of their firearm, one must understand the symbolism displayed by the firearm. The firearm is the officer's symbol of protection. It is the tool that in the most extreme of circumstances must protect them and the public they serve. It becomes a part of their identity and the officer rarely is without their firearm even off-duty.* (Smith, personal communication, October 26, 2013).

Officers with mental health issues fall into a different classification than officers with physical injuries. Worker compensation investigations are unique for officers suffering from mental health problems. There is no stigma attached to officers injured while performing their duties. Many times physically injured officers are viewed as heroic while the emotionally or mentally ill officer maybe looked at by their peers or supervision as faking impairment.

Officers are afraid to self-report because of the risk of job loss, being stigmatized as being mentally disturbed, or being viewed as weak. An officer who is contemplating suicide is at risk for being taken into protective custody for a mental evaluation. This is a double-edged sword so it is not surprising officers are resistant to seek help when they are despondent.

In California, section 5150 of the Welfare and Institutions Code, grants peace officers and mental health workers the authority to force people into a designated mental health facility on a 72-hour hold. Persons can be held in protective custody if they are a danger to self, a danger to others, or gravely disabled. So, the reader can understand the reluctance of law enforcement officers to report either thoughts or threats of suicide. If a law enforcement officer is held on 72 hour hold; their career is basically over.

Ron Clark from the Badge of Life summed up organizational impacts when he said: *Look how far law enforcement has progressed with technology. Officer safety is important to the officer and the agency. Our industry issues officers the tools to enhance their physical safety. We need to get them the same assistance for their mental health. Keeping officers mentally safe is an important workers compensation issue that is largely overlooked. It is a heavy price we pay when we lose an officer whether the loss is from death, physical injury, or mental illness. Police unions and associations need to make mental health as much a priority as pay, benefits, equipment, and working conditions. The unions have a duty to take care of the mental health of their members too.*

## Operational Issues

Cases of suicide trigger a law enforcement investigation. A suicide by a law enforcement officer is not different but there is another factor unique to the victim's employment. When a law enforcement officer commits suicide, the event will trigger an administrative investigation by their agency.

Detective Steven Lankford is assigned to the Los Angeles County Sheriff's Department Homicide Bureau. In addition to investigating murders, his unit investigates death investigations to rule out homicides. Detective Lankford personally witnessed a police officer commit suicide. The officer worked for another law enforcement organization but lived in the jurisdiction patrolled by the Los Angeles County Sheriff's Department.

*I was a station detective but I was working patrol because the shift was short deputies. I received a call to meet two supervisors at one of their police officer's home. I learned that the police officer had barricaded himself in his house. I was told by the supervisors that he had been drinking and was the suspected in a felony hit and run. The officer had struck several pedestrians and had fled the scene. After conferring with the supervisors a police helicopter appeared overhead, adding to the confusion.*

*The supervisors thought the helicopter belonged to the sheriff's department and asked me to radio them to leave the scene. I knew it was not one of our helicopters, but it was a police helicopter from their jurisdiction. A few minutes later, the police officer walked outside of his house and shot himself in the head. He died at the scene. Later I was told that the officer's partner had committed suicide years before.*

In this case it was easy to classify as a suicide. However, witnessing suicides is rare. In most police officer suicides the officer kills themselves in private. Also, in the majority of the law enforcement suicides, the victim does not hint that they are planning their own death (R. Clark, personal communication, October 21, 2013).

Detective Lankford continued: *When I joined the homicide bureau I was told that the most difficult part of the assignment was dealing with family members of suicide victims. Ninety percent of family members are in denial when a loved one commits suicide. They want to believe the death was an accident or a homicide.*

*Religion plays a significant role in suicide investigations. This is especially true among those of the Jewish and Moslem faiths because of prohibitions against burials for those who commit suicide.*

Life insurance settlement claims in suicide cases is another important factor to consider. Detective Lankford said: *In Los Angeles County, the Los Angeles County Department of the Coroner determines the exact cause of death. They have investigators who conduct an in-depth forensics investigation. A pathologist conducts an autopsy to determine how the death occurred. The second part of the investigation is the psychological investigation. A coroner investigator conducts a background check into the decedent's life to find out if there was any past evidence of threats of suicide or attempts to commit suicide. In the end a coroner inquest would issue a determination of death* (S. Lankford, personal communication, October 21, 2013)

## Management Issues

The news of a law enforcement suicide sends ripples through the organization. The shock and despair could render a shift unable to perform their duties. Everyone close to the officer is thinking "why did they do it?" Many survivors will ask "why didn't I notice that there was something wrong?"

If the officer left a suicide note survivors might know the reason for the death. In cases where no note is left by the officer, survivors might carry a sense of guilt. If the officer committed suicide due to personal problems such as cancer or a death of a loved one, there may be limited management issues.

However, if the officer committed suicide due to legal or administrative problems there might be significant issues for management. For example if the officer was facing misconduct allegations or had received a notice of termination, his or her friends might blame management for their suicide. If the officer was a member of a protected group, management might be viewed as insensitive to diversity and blamed for the outcome. There is always the possibility that family might file a tort claim against the department.

On the contrary, management is not usually to blame for the suicide, but perceptions of line personnel could polarize the department. In any event, management has much to consider as they design a strategy on how to manage the situation. The most important management question to answer is does the agency conduct a full-honor police funeral? Or, in the case of suicide, does the agency elect to forgo a police funeral? Either decision by management has pitfalls. As you can imagine, management cannot make this decision lightly. Their decision will have a significant impact on employee morale, the media, and future police-union relations.

## Peer Support Programs

Ron Clark stated: *This is not a suicide issue as much as it is a stress issue. Peer support programs are very successful at keeping officers emotionally and mentally healthy. Many agencies across the nation are training officers to be peer counselors. Peer support programs work when both the department head and the union work well together.*

*The goal of peer support programs is to decrease suicide and increase mental health. Fellow law enforcement officers are selected and trained to keep a watchful eye out for peers exhibiting extreme stress or despondency. Peer support officers are trained to intervene when officers suffer emotional trauma. They are also trained in counseling techniques. Officers selected as peer counselors need to be friendly and outgoing. Peer support officers must be approachable and willing to reach out to their troubled officers.*

*Many times, though, officers are reluctant to seek out a peer counselor for fear of being reported to management. Agencies that have successful programs have policies that spell out when a peer counselor must report, such as in the case where an officer is in imminent danger of committing suicide.*

*Some officers might fear if they divulge some violation of policy or a petty crime, they will get a visit from internal affairs. It is imperative that organizations that have peer support programs also write very specific reporting policies to establish trust. It is interesting to note that in Colorado, Wyoming, Hawaii, and Washington, peer support officers by statute have the same confidentially protection as attorneys and the clergy.*

*In addition, agencies need to educate their officers on preventive programs that will help maintain their mental health. Employees need to be educated on warning signs that could lead to serious emotional problems. The same information needs to be taught in law enforcement and correctional academies. Peer support programs have been successful to help reduce police suicide.*

# Employee Wellness Plans

M. E. McDonough in his article entitled: "The Employee Wellness Plan," (2011), remarked that not enough attention has been focused on employee wellness. The risks of not having a wellness program include cynicism, apathy, chemical dependence, unhealthy lifestyle choices, and suicide.

Successful EWP's improves recruitment, and retention, increases job satisfaction and lowers sick time. To be truly successful employee wellness plans should encompass the officer's entire career, beginning in the academy and into retirement (McDonough, 2011).

To maximize employee performance, EWP's need to address protecting officers from repeated exposure to violence and trauma. Police managers should consider collaborating with police chaplains, medical facilities, psychological counseling, and substance abuse professionals, when launching an employee wellness plan. The key to improving law enforcement health is to treat the whole person (McDonough, 2011).

Captain Sarah Creighton is the commanding officer for the San Diego Police Department Wellness Program. She is also a faculty member at the Union Institute and University. One of the courses she teaches is Contemporary Issues in Criminal Justice Management.

The San Diego Police Department made a commitment to improve the physical and emotional health of their officers. To accomplish this goal, they formed a wellness unit.

Captain Creighton said: *Our mission is to treat the employee as a whole person including spiritual, physical, and mental health. The mental health side of the program is to help officers cope with the cumulative effects of trauma. Suicide prevention is one of our main goals.*

*The very next day after an academy graduation, our department hosts a wellness program for the graduates and their families. We devote the entire day to help prepare the new officers and their families to face the emotional and physical dangers of law enforcement. We discuss the impact of violence and trauma that officers are exposed to and how those experiences can lead to serious health issues. We teach the officers and their families how to recognize signs of serious stress and educate them about the services the wellness unit offers them. We also stress the importance of proactivity, monitoring and tending to one's mental health and the importance o continual resilience building.*

*The field training officers are onboard with our program and emphasize wellness while the probationary officer is in the field training phase. Eighteen months later we revisit the program with the academy graduates in on-going in service training. Our unit continues to provide our wellness services as our personnel progress through their careers.*

*The wellness unit is committed to maintain the total health of our personnel. Our goal is to assist in the removal or reduction of interferences to employee wellness to reduce worker compensation filings and early retirement due to health issues. The ultimate payback is a department of well officers who have high work satisfaction and low absenteeism. It is a known fact that satisfied officers provide a higher level of service to the community than unhappy ones.*

*Specifically regarding suicide prevention, we recognize that our first conversation with an employee about their wellness cannot be when we are asking them if they are considering suicide. Developing a rapport with employees requires an investment over time. Our goal is to effectively demonstrate an interest in and genuine care for an employee about smaller issues that impact their wellness. Continually monitoring and educating our employees builds trust so the employee will feel comfortable to contact the wellness unit if they are experiencing serious issues* (S. Creighton, personal communication, October 21, 2013).

Law enforcement and correctional organizations have an obligation to train their personnel to effectively cope with the negative impact of cumulative trauma. Peer support and wellness programs are excellent strategies to reduce stress and improve morale and productivity. The benefit for protecting the mental health of their officers is higher levels of job satisfaction resulting in improved service to the community.

## Breaking the Silence of Police Suicide

Captain Creighton shared her notes with me from the International Association of Chiefs of Police (IACP) Symposium on Law Enforcement Officer Mental Health: Breaking the Silence on Law Enforcement Suicide, held in Washington D.C. on July 11, 2013. The IACP goal is to deploy a nation-wide strategic plan and implement a state-of-the art mental health program across the United States (IACP, 2013).

Realizing agencies are working with limited budgets, IACP hopes to identify existing resources and develop best practices so agencies can adopt effective mental health programs. Part of the plan is to establish a model policy on mental health and suicide prevention. The key elements of the model policy will include best practices in:

- Prevention programs
- Effective intervention programs
- Post-suicide policies to help grieving families and colleagues
- Implementing suicide funeral policies

## Discussion Questions

1. What are the significant factors that cause officers to commit suicide?
2. What steps would you take if a fellow officer told you they were thinking about suicide?
3. Discuss the operational, organizational, and management impacts on the topic.
4. Evaluate peer support programs. Do you think these programs can have a significant impact to reduce the numbers of police suicide? Defend your answer.

## Activities for the Professor

1. Assign the discussion questions to the students either in the classroom or in on-line chats
2. Assign the students to prepare a list of significant factors in personal, operational, organizational, and management issues. Divide them into panels and have them present their findings to the class

3. Assign the students to prepare a Power Point on selected issues and present their Power Points either in class or on-line. In the on-line environment, have the students write abstracts on each presentation and discuss their findings

4. Assign students to prepare a law enforcement funeral policy

5. Assign the students to prepare an executive summary and press release on their organizations new wellness program

## Works Cited

McDonough, M. E. (2011). "The Employee Wellness Plan". FBI Law Enforcement Bulletin, 80 (12), 1–6, Retrieved from http//search.proquest.com/docview/906658198?accountid=14436.

O'Hara, A.F., Levenson, R.L., Violanti, J.M. and Clark, R.G.(2013), "National Police Suicide Estimates: Web Surveillance Study III." International Journal of Emergency Mental Health and Human Resilience. Vol. 15 No. 1, Chevron Publishing.

# Chapter 5: Issues in Community Supervision

## Who Is Watching Them?

*America is the land of the second chance and when the gates of the prison open, the path ahead should lead to a better life.*

George W. Bush

## Student Objectives

1. Explore recent developments in community supervision
2. Examine new trends in financing, technology, and management that improve corrections
3. Debate the AB 109 program in California and examine its impact on policing and corrections

In this reading, the student will examine the question: Does community supervision work? The reading introduces the student to recent developments in the correctional field that improve financing, enhance technology, and increases efficiency in correctional management. The reading also examines the current debate regarding the early release of offenders. Probation, parole, and other early-release programs will be explored.

# Issues in Community Supervision

## By Lawrence Travis

Many important issues in community supervision center around developments in the financing, management, and technology involved in probation and parole. Largely in response to crowded institutions, there is renewed interest in community supervision as an alternative to incarceration. Many recent developments are attempts to improve and enhance the effectiveness and economy of probation and parole. In the past 20 years, however, the central practices of community supervision (probation and parole supervision) have themselves come under attack. This chapter examines the current controversy over community supervision, and discusses specific attempts to improve the efficiency of community corrections.

## Does Community Supervision Work?

In 1978, Andrew von Hirsch and Kathleen Hanrahan published a report to the U.S. Department of Justice titled "Abolish Parole?" In this brief document, they suggested that parole supervision might be useless. On both rational (practical) and philosophical grounds, the authors concluded that there was little reason to continue the practice of parole supervision. They held that a period of supervision under conditions constituted an added penalty. That is, assuming the offender served a prison sentence as punishment, there was no reason to impose conditional release in addition to incarceration. From a practical standpoint, they argued that the research to date did not support parole supervision as a crime-control strategy. The authors also argued that parole officers were not very effective in providing needed services to parolees.

## Box 1. Outcome of Probation Supervision, 1986–89

100 felons tracked through their first 3 years of probation

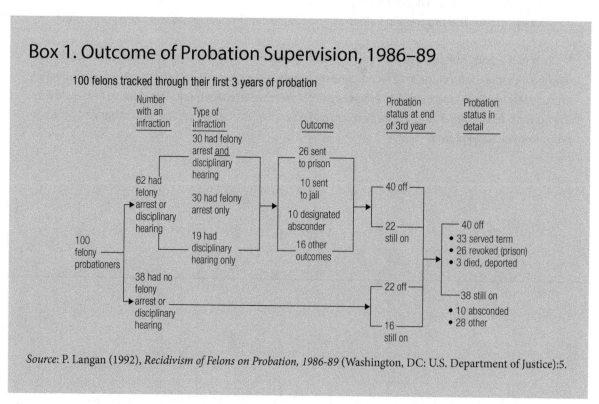

*Source*: P. Langan (1992), *Recidivism of Felons on Probation, 1986-89* (Washington, DC: U.S. Department of Justice):5.

Von Hirsch and Hanrahan were not the first to question parole supervision, but they may have been the most eloquent critics. Later reports (e.g., Gottfredson, Mitchell-Herzfeld & Flanagan, 1982) showed that success of supervision in preventing crimes by parolees often depends on how "new crimes" are defined. If a parolee returned to prison for violating the conditions of release without committing a new crime is counted as a "failure," parole supervision may be less effective in preventing recidivism than no supervision at all. Because parolees must obey the conditions of release, they may be returned to prison for "technical violations." Technical violations are infractions of the rules of supervision that do not involve any new criminality. Examples would include violating curfew, failing to report to a parole officer, and other noncriminal behavior. If returns to prison based on **technical violations** are counted as "failures," parolees have more chances to "fail" than do nonparolees, who must be convicted of new crimes to be incarcerated. The research shows mixed findings. It is difficult, if not impossible, to decide whether parole supervision is an effective crime prevention method (Flanagan, 1985). See Box 1. for a description of outcomes of probation supervision.

Other critics have raised similar concerns about probation supervision. With the increased use of both probation and parole in response to prison crowding, these concerns have grown. Observers believe that not only are more offenders being placed under community supervision, but that probation and parole now include more dangerous offenders (Auerhahn, 2007; Guynes, 1988). Critics are beginning to re-examine the degree to which community supervision protects public safety.

Joan Petersilia (1985) studied probationers convicted of felonies in two large California counties. Her conclusions raised serious questions about the ability of community supervision to control crime. Petersilia and her colleagues concluded that a 65 percent rate of new criminality among their sample showed that granting probation to those convicted of felonies was not in the best interests of public safety. She later summarized the results of this study (1986:2):

> These results would seem to support the contention that routine probation is not an appropriate or effective sanction for convicted felons. It evidently could not provide the kind of supervision that might have prevented the majority of our sample of felony offenders from returning to crime.

The importance of Petersilia's study was exaggerated by news media attention (Goldstein, Burrell & Talty, 1985). In the weeks following the release of her report by the RAND Corporation, newspapers across the country reported the story. They summarized the research, often with forbidding headlines telling of the dangers posed by felony probation. Reactions to the report were quick, but failed to achieve the same level of media coverage.

Vito (1986) replicated the RAND study on a sample of Kentucky probationers. He reported that felons on probation in Kentucky were much less likely to commit new crimes than were those studied by Petersilia. Similarly, McGaha, Fichter, and Hirschburg (1987) replicated the study with probationers in Missouri, finding results similar to those found by Vito. In addition, Goldstein, Burrell, and Talty (1985) concluded that probationers in New Jersey did not pose as great a threat to public safety as those examined in Petersilia's study in California. It is possible that the results of Petersilia's study were unique to California, as they are different from findings in other states. In support of this conclusion, the Bureau of Justice Statistics (Hughes, Wilson & Beck, 2001) notes that national averages of successful completion of parole supervision increase when California's cases are removed from the sample.

In attempting to answer the question of whether community supervision works, we must first determine what we mean by the word "work." In the evaluations of felony probation reported by Petersilia,

Vito, and Goldstein, the criterion was new crime by probationers. That is, probation was considered to "work" if people under supervision did not commit too many new crimes. In general three criteria can be applied to community supervision in order to determine "what works." Alan Harland (1996:2–3) noted that the definition of what works depends on the perspective of the individual asking the question. Elected officials and the public often define "working" as "reducing rates of recidivism." Policy makers may define "working" as "reducing rates of commitment or lengths of stay for prison and jail inmates." Budget officials may define what works by "managing offenders at a lower cost." For retributivists, what works is a system of sanctions that matches the pain of punishment with the harm of the crime and blameworthiness of the offender. In short, probation, parole, and other community supervision practices work to the degree that they (1) can control risk of new crime, (2) reduce incarceration and correctional costs, and/or (3) match punishments with offenders.

Edward Rhine (1997) observed that the entire criminal justice system is facing a crisis of legitimacy resulting from increasing concern about crime, and the perceived inability of the criminal justice system to control crime. This crisis has produced a movement toward more punitive and incapacitative sanctions, with a greater reliance on incarceration. Nonetheless, as Rhine notes, more than two-thirds of convicted offenders are supervised in the community. In response to the call for punitive treatment of offenders and greater emphasis on crime control, community supervision administrators "have adopted a set of practices and a discourse that represent a discernible shift toward risk management and surveillance" (Rhine, 1997:72). The practice of probation and parole supervision, in Rhine's view, is driven more by a desire to increase risk control and surveillance than by an attempt to reform or reintegrate criminal offenders.

## Controlling Risk

Peter Jones (1991) discussed the development of community corrections in Kansas. One of the primary goals of the movement to community correctional alternatives to imprisonment in that state was to protect public safety. As Jones (1991:51) observed, however, "while a public-safety interest was frequently cited, it was usually in the sense of representing an obvious and necessary constraint on how the other goals (reducing prison crowding and developing more appropriate responses for offenders) would be pursued." Thus, protecting public safety was a baseline concern. In the extreme, we could reduce crowding by not sending anyone to prison. If doing so led to a significant increase in crime, however, this policy would be unacceptable.

It seems that much has been made lately of the ability or inability of community correctional programs to control risk. As Bennett (1991:95) noted, "The public is upset, and perhaps rightly so, that people placed on regular probation often do not receive either help or supervision because of large caseloads and inadequate supervision." The critical question is how safe is safe enough? As Jones (1991) describes it, risk control can range from a definition of no new criminality through acceptance of levels of crime no greater than those among persons incarcerated. Harland and Rosen (1987) suggest that minimizing public risk is the primary goal of most intermediate sanctions. Thus, while no new crime would be preferred, achieving similar levels of new crime among a population that is diverted from prison that is less than (or no more than) the level among incarcerated offenders may be "safe enough." There is also the question of what kind of "crime" is being committed.

In an assessment of recidivism among parolees in Tennessee, James Wilson (2005) observed that wide fluctuations in the rate of discretionary parole release were not correlated with changes in revocation rates. This indicates that more offenders could be placed on parole with little or no change in the rate of parole failures. In addition, he observed that a major explanation for the levels of failure had to do with increasingly harsh responses (revocation) for technical violations of parole. This too would indicate that public safety (at least in terms of the threat of new crime) was not endangered by those parolees.

Evaluations of the effectiveness of community supervision use different measures of outcome. The inclusion of violations of technical conditions of supervision, including absconding, with new criminality produces relatively high rates of failure, but may not represent high rates of crime. John Worrall and his associates (2004) studied the link between the size of the probation caseload and the crime rate in California counties. They concluded that the size of the probation caseload is positively associated with the rate of property crime. It is not possible to tell if the crime rate causes probation or the number of probationers causes the crime rate, but there is no evidence that large probation caseloads are associated with any reduction in crime rates. Worrall and colleagues observe that large caseloads are also associated with reduced levels of treatment and reintegration services for probationers. This research suggests that it may be the administration of supervision (large numbers of offenders assigned to too few officers) that explains failure. In contrast, some observers contend that smaller caseloads provide close supervision, which translates into higher rates of technical violations and, thus, higher rates of failure. In a study of "community probation" in Maryland, Nicole Piquero (2003) suggests that the probationers receiving closest supervision were more likely to fail early than those not subjected to such intensive supervision.

Over the past two decades there has been some substantial progress in the development and use of risk assessment devices in both probation and parole. Many classification and prediction instruments have been developed, and several appear to offer valid predictions of the risk of recidivism among correctional populations (Holsinger, Lowenkamp & Latessa, 2006). One problem with these instruments is the incredible diversity of correctional populations. Most risk-assessment devices are not designed for specific subpopulations such as females or racial and ethnic minorities. As a result, the accuracy of risk predictions can vary across different groups. As important is that these general risk-screening instruments are not especially well-suited to the prediction of specific risks, such as the risk that a particular offender will commit a violent offense (Davies & Dedel, 2006). Surely the safest course of action in terms of protecting the community from convicted offenders is to incarcerate the offenders. To do so, however, does not really manage risk, but rather seeks to avoid it. At some point most of these offenders will return to the community, regardless of their level of risk. Attempts to identify and manage risk through probation and parole supervision are necessary, if difficult.

## Reducing Incarceration and Costs

As Jones observed in Kansas, a primary factor motivating the development and spread of community supervision sanctions is a desire to reduce prison crowding and correctional costs. Clear and Byrne (1992:321) flatly say, "The frank bottom line for the intermediate sanction movement must be whether it is able to reduce overcrowding in corrections." The impetus behind the movement to expand community supervision sanctions is our inability to deal with the large numbers of persons whom we believe need or deserve more severe sentences than traditional probation. Our inability emerges, in large part, from the cost of incarceration. Thus, if we had excess prison space, we would simply incarcerate offenders who required tougher punishment than probation. We do not have that excess, and we cannot afford to build enough prisons to house all of these offenders.

The creation of alternative sanctions in the community can have the effect of reducing demand for prison space (Gowdy, 1993). Conversely, the development of more severe community-based sanctions may simply result in **net-widening**. Morris and Tonry (1990) argue that in many cases, the result of alternative sanctions has been to make sentences more severe for those who would not have gone to prison anyway. In this way, the "net" of punishment has been cast wider to catch more people. If they are correct, alternative sanctions as presently developed will not meet the goal of reducing correctional costs and prison crowding. Beck and Mumola (1999), reported that one of the primary reasons for prison population growth in 1998 was the large number of parole violators returned to prison. As Rhine (1997:73) pointed out, the new, risk-centered community supervision strives to identify and arrest probationers and parolees who violate conditions of release. To the extent that this strategy is successful, the "failure" rates for probation and parole increase, and more community supervision violators are sent to prison.

Community supervision can work as an alternative to incarceration and many of the intermediate punishments developed in the past few decades are designed to accomplish just that purpose. The problem arises when, as a result of these more restrictive community punishments, failure rates increase, leading to increased levels of imprisonment. To the extent that offenders originally destined for prison can be placed into community settings, community supervision programs can reduce incarceration costs and prison population sizes.

## Matching Punishments with Offenders

A third goal of the development of intermediate sanctions in the community is to create a range of penalties that can be appropriately applied to the range of offenses and offenders who come before the courts. The traditional choice between probation and incarceration is seen by many as inadequate for responding to the wide array of crimes and criminals that exist. Morris and Tonry (1990:38) argue that, "A variety of intermediate punishments, along with appropriate treatment conditions, should be part of a comprehensive, integrated system of sentencing and punishment."

Community supervision programs and practices have undergone tremendous change in recent times as we struggle to develop this range of punishments. The matching of punishments to offenders includes two dimensions as anticipated by Morris and Tonry. First, the severity of the penalty should be matched more closely to the seriousness of the crime. In this way, there needs to be a range of punishments. Second, the needs of specific offenders should be addressed by the correctional system while the offenders are under sentence. This necessitates a range of appropriate treatment conditions.

Even if Petersilia's findings of risk of future criminality among probationers may not be accurate for the nation, the question that she raised about the ability of probation supervision to provide for community safety remains critical. At a minimum, the perception exists that probation populations are

## Box 2. Felons Having Additional Penalties, 2002

| Additional Penalty | Percent of Felons Receiving |
|---|---|
| Fine | 25% |
| Restitution | 12 |
| Community Service | 4 |
| Treatment | 3 |
| Other | 7 |

Source: M. Durose & P. Langan (2004), *Felony Sentences in State Courts, 2002* (Washington, DC: Bureau of Justice Statistics):10.

more dangerous today than ever before. There is growing concern about the risk posed by offenders placed under community supervision. One result of this perception can be seen in that probation and parole officers, in order to better ensure public safety, are changing the way that they do their jobs. Other changes involve making both probation and parole more punitive, such as the increasing use of "shock incarceration" and "intensive supervision," electronic monitoring, day reporting, and other sanctions that are more severe than traditional probation or parole supervision. Box 2 shows the imposition of selected supervision conditions on adult probationers.

Harris and her colleagues (2001) investigated the use of intermediate sanctions in one county to assess the way in which a range of intermediate sanctions was used. The focus of the research was to determine whether a true "continuum" of sanctions was in place so that the severity of the punishment was linked to the seriousness of the crime. They found that there was a significant relationship between severity of sanction and seriousness of offense, but that the link was relatively weak. They interpreted this to mean that the availability of a range of intermediate sanctions supports efforts to match penalties to crimes. However, other factors still influence the application of penalties in specific cases. They concluded that without the range of intermediate penalties, it would be much more difficult, if even possible, to link crimes and punishments in any meaningful fashion

# Shock Incarceration

Programs of shock incarceration and intensive supervision have affected the operation of traditional probation and parole. They illustrate most clearly how community supervision serves as an alternative to incarceration. In both programs, the attempt is made to use community supervision to meet sentencing goals normally associated with incarceration. Specifically, the desired result is the enhancement of both the deterrent and incapacitation effects of community supervision.

Shock probation and shock parole attempt to deter offenders from continued criminality by imposing a prison sentence that is later "commuted" to a period of supervision. The initial incarceration is expected to "shock" the offender by the severity of the punishment. It also informs offenders what to expect if they continue to break the law (Vito, 1985). Thus, with **shock probation**, the judge might sentence the offender to a long prison term but, within six months, alter the sentence to a probation period. In some states, such as Ohio, the inmate could petition the court for shock probation. In other states, such as Texas, shock probation is solely at the discretion of the judge.

**Shock parole** is similar to shock probation in that it involves an early release from a relatively long prison term. The difference here is that it is the parole authority rather than the judge that grants an early release from incarceration to parole supervision. For example, a convicted forger who receives a 10-year prison sentence could receive shock probation from the judge after four or five months. If shock probation is not granted, in several states the parole authority is empowered to grant early or shock parole to the offender at his or her first hearing before the board. Like shock probation, states differ as to whether inmates must petition the parole board in order to be considered for shock parole.

In practice, the effectiveness of shock programs is unclear. Many of the programs provide no shock value because offenders expect to be released. Ideally, the incarcerated offender is "shocked" when released. In practice, however, the only shock may come if the offender is not granted an early release. Through a combination of a short prison term followed by community supervision, shock programs attempt to gain the benefits of both incarceration and supervision as sanctions. The offender is expected to be deterred. In theory, shock probation and parole provide a stern warning to the inmate.

## Box 3. Prison Boot Camp Programs, June 30, 2000

| | |
|---|---|
| Number of Inmate Participants | 12,751 |
| Number of Prisons with Programs | 95 |
| Security Level of Facility | |
| Maximum | 13 |
| Medium | 31 |
| Minimum | 51 |
| Gender of Inmates | |
| Males Only | 67 |
| Females Only | 11 |
| Both Sexes | 17 |
| Type of Facility Federal | 3 |
| State | 87 |
| Private | 5 |

*Source*: J. Stephan & J. Karberg (2003), *Census of State and Federal Correctional Facilities, 2000* (Washington, DC: Bureau of Justice Statistics):12.

Without the kindness of the judge or parole authority, the offender would be serving a long prison term. In effect, the released inmate is expected to realize that he or she is living "on borrowed time" and will face a long term of incarceration if supervision is unsuccessful. Camp and Camp (1996:163) reported that probation agencies in half of the state and federal jurisdictions operate shock probation programs.

An innovation on the practice of shock probation and parole has been the development of the prison **boot camp** (Anderson, Dyson & Burns, 1999). These programs are sometimes referred to as **"shock incarceration"** because the conditions of incarceration are much more severe but limited in duration. Boot camp programs in prisons subject inmates to austere conditions, including physical conditioning and strict discipline combined with hard labor, akin to the boot camp experience of new recruits in the military. Boot camps were discussed in Chapter 9 as evidence of attempts to make punishment more physically painful for offenders. These camps are also linked to community supervision because they serve to reduce the length of term served by participants. On June 30, 2000, a total of 12,751 inmates were enrolled in boot camp programs operating in 95 correctional facilities across the nation. Many of these programs release their graduates to community supervision as probationers or parolees. Box 3 provides a description of these programs.

Mackenzie and Parent (1991) studied the impact of boot camps on prison crowding in Louisiana. They observed that if careful selection criteria are developed, such camps can reduce the number of inmates admitted to regular prison terms. Further, Mackenzie and Shaw (1990) reported that graduates of boot camps appear to have more socially positive attitudes than other prisoners. They suggest that boot camps may meet offender needs in ways that will improve their chances of avoiding crime in the future. Faith Lutze (1998) surveyed prisoners and found that while boot camp programs provide stricter controls on inmate behavior in prison, they are no more likely to support personal growth and development among inmates than traditional minimum-security incarceration. That is, boot camp participants do not differ from regular prisoners in terms of their learning ways to avoid future problems with the law. In a later study, Lutze (2001) reported that the increased severity of boot camp was associated with negative attitudes and adaptations to prison, when not linked to supporting future improvement for inmates. Being "tough" for the sake of being tough was perhaps seen by the inmates as unnecessary and unfair. As Mackenzie and Parent noted, legislators may support boot camp programs because the conditions in these programs are more punitive than in the typical prison, and thus shorter terms are seen as equally tough on crime. However, the available evidence suggests that boot camps do not reduce rates of new crime (recidivism) by program graduates, and may actually hinder inmates in making a positive adjustment (Mackenzie, 1997). Benda, Toombs, and Peacock (2006) found that boot camp programs appear to have different effects for different kinds of offenders. Like the problem of general risk assessments being applied to diverse populations, boot camp programs seem to help some offenders but be harmful with others. Improvement in boot camps (and other correctional efforts) may depend on our ability to match the right program to the right type of offender.

Another practice that is somewhat akin to shock probation is the imposition of split sentences. A **split sentence** is a penalty that is divided (split) between a period of incarceration and a period of probationary supervision. Because of the great flexibility that judges are allowed in determining the conditions of probation, split sentences are relatively widely used. This is true even in jurisdictions where there is no law that specifically allows the judge to use split sentencing.

Parisi (1980) described four historical methods of imposing split sentences, including shock probation as it is practiced in several states.

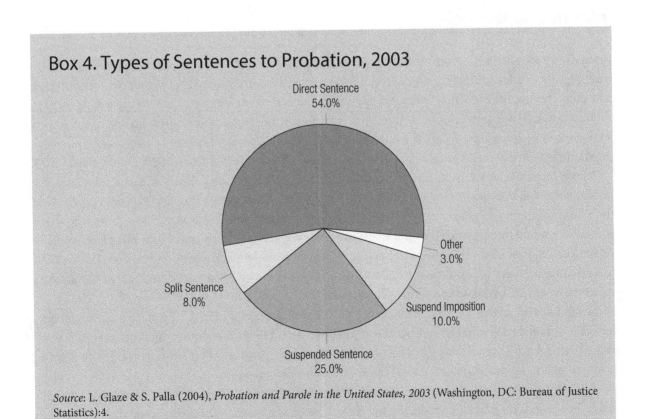

## Box 4. Types of Sentences to Probation, 2003

Direct Sentence 54.0%

Other 3.0%

Suspend Imposition 10.0%

Suspended Sentence 25.0%

Split Sentence 8.0%

*Source*: L. Glaze & S. Palla (2004), *Probation and Parole in the United States, 2003* (Washington, DC: Bureau of Justice Statistics):4.

1. If a defendant is convicted of several offenses or counts, the judge may order incarceration for some offenses and probation for others. Thus, a defendant convicted of two counts of theft may be sentenced to 90 days on the first count and two years of probation on the second.

2. In shock probation, the same offender may receive an initial five-year prison term, and be "shocked" to probation in 90 days.

3. Another way to impose split sentences can be seen in legislation that allows the judge to combine incarceration and probation in one sentence, such as a sentence of 90 days of incarceration followed by two years of probation.

4. Finally, most states have legislation allowing the judge to use incarceration as a condition of probation. In this case, the offender might receive two years probation with the condition that the first 90 days be spent in jail.

Regardless of the method used to impose split sentences, the outcomes are the same. Probation is often seen by judges, offenders, and the general public as a lenient sanction. The use of split or combination sentences allows judges to increase the harshness of the penalty. A judge may not wish to send a minor offender to prison for a long period, but may want the offender to spend some time in jail. Split sentences allow judges to adjust the severity of sanctions. In 2005, 8 percent of persons placed on probation had received a split sentence while more than half were sentenced directly to probation. Of all those on probation in 2003, 22 percent had a sentence combining probation and incarceration, and 6 percent had been placed on probation in some other fashion, before all court proceedings were completed, as is shown in Box 4.

## Intensive Supervision

**Intensive supervision** programs seek to provide more control and service to offenders who otherwise would be incarcerated (Travis, 1984). In practice, these programs rely upon lower client-to-officer ratios, and thus, they assume a higher level of supervision and service delivery (Cullen, Wright & Applegate, 1996; Latessa, 1980). Evaluations of intensive supervision programs show some promise of their effectiveness. However, they do not show that intensive supervision yields better results for the intensive populations than does regular supervision for the regular caseload (Mackenzie, 1997; Fulton et al., 1997).

In the intensive supervision programs in which the level of service delivery actually increased, intensive supervision programs do appear to be modestly effective. Intensive supervision appears to effect the release of many offenders who otherwise would be incarcerated. What is perhaps more important is that the mental picture caused by the label "intensive supervision" may make it politically possible to retain a number of relatively serious or persistent offenders under community supervision, as opposed to incarcerating them (Clear & Shapiro, 1986). This is consistent with the traditional role of community supervision as the "overflow valve" for incarceration.

Several states have implemented intensive supervision programs (ISPs). The state of Georgia, perhaps the leader in ISPs, began a program in 1982 (Erwin, 1986). Evaluations of programs in several states (Petersilia, Turner & Peterson, 1986:41) show that these programs may be successful in preventing criminality among probationers, at least during periods of supervision.

Typically, an intensive supervision program requires the probationer to have more contacts with his or her probation officer. By reducing the size of caseloads, we expect officers to be more vigilant in intensive supervision programs (Byrne, 1986). The net effect of these differences is to make the penalty more painful. The probationer experiences more intrusions by the officer. The penalty is also more incapacitative. The offender is more closely watched, and thus he or she is prevented from relapsing into crime.

Byrne and Pattavina (1992) reviewed evaluations of intensive supervision programs in probation and parole. They reported that by the middle of 1989 there were 40 states operating intensive supervision programs. These programs, they found, were generally effective in meeting the goals of alternative sentencing. Noting limitations of the research, they reported that evaluations of intensive supervision programs report them to be both more cost-effective than imprisonment, and to have achieved true diversion of cases from incarceration. They also found that, in general, intensive programs did not seem to reduce recidivism. Jones (1991) reported similar results in an evaluation of intensive supervision in Kansas. He noted that, while offenders under intensive supervision did not show a decrease in new crime compared to those who were incarcerated, they also did no worse. In an assessment of intensive supervision with juveniles, Sontheimer and Goodstein (1993) suggested that while rates of new offenses may not have decreased, the intensive supervision program was effective in identifying recidivists early and removing them from the community. Thus, while the proportion of offenders under supervision who commit new crimes may not differ, in this program, the number of new crimes committed was fewer for the intensive group than for the nonintensive group. This is probably because offenders under intensive supervision were more likely to be detected and removed from supervision.

Intensive supervision programs that provide increased treatment along with closer supervision may have effects on reducing future crime (Latessa, 1993; Petersilia & Turner, 1993). Fulton and her colleagues (1997:74) concluded a review of intensive supervision programs, writing, "ISP has held its ground as a key element of community corrections programming since its reemergence in 1982. Although the research suggests that ISP has not fulfilled its promise of alleviating prison crowding, it does appear to be serving the important function of providing an intermediate sanction … More importantly, it appears that ISPs that emphasize treatment and services are producing better results than strict surveillance-based ISPs in terms of addressing offender needs and reducing recidivism."

## Electronic Monitoring

In **electronic monitoring** programs, offenders are fitted with transmitting devices that allow correctional staff to monitor their whereabouts. Annesley Schmidt (1989) reported a survey of electronic monitoring usage that showed programs existing in 33 states. Later, Renzema (1992) reported that electronic monitoring programs existed in 47 states by 1990. Estimates of the number of offenders under such monitoring have risen to nearly 100,000 in approximately 1,500 programs (National Institute of Justice, 1999:1). According to Ford and Schmidt (1985), the first operational use of electronic surveillance for monitoring convicted offenders occurred in early 1983.

While the use of surveillance technology to monitor criminal offenders is relatively new, the potential of such technology for crime control has long been recognized. As early as 1966, Ralph Schwitzgebel described a potential telemetric monitoring system for probationers and parolees. In 1968, a prototype of the system was developed and tested. An assessment of the legal ramifications of electronic monitoring was published in the Harvard Law Review in 1966. Later, Robert Schwitzgebel, Ralph's brother, experimented with telemetric monitoring with volunteers in California (Schwitzgebel, 1969). For years, a debate about the acceptability of electronic monitoring continued, and the debate periodically found expression in commentary (Ingraham & Smith, 1972; Szasz, 1975). The debate continues today (Corbett & Marx, 1991; del Carmen & Vaughn, 1986), but the sheer practicality of the technology has meant that, while many important issues remain to be solved, electronic monitoring of criminal offenders is an ongoing practice.

Currently, there are two basic types of radio frequency electronic surveillance systems in use (Ford & Schmidt, 1985; Huskey, 1987; National Institute of Justice, 1999; Schmidt, 1987). These systems can be described as either active or passive surveillance. In an active system, the supervising agency takes positive steps to monitor the offender. Generally, this system involves fitting the offender with a transmitting device. The transmitter sends a tone over the telephone. A computer program randomly calls offenders

## Box 5. Systems for Electronic Monitoring of Offenders

Purpose: to monitor an offender's presence in a given environment where the offender is required to remain.

### *Devices that use a telephone at the monitored location*

| Continuously signaling | Programmed contact |
| --- | --- |
| A miniaturized **transmitter** is strapped to the offender and it broadcasts an encoded signal at regular intervals over a range.<br><br>A **receiver-dialer,** located in the offender's home, detects signals from the transmitter and reports to a central computer when it stops receiving the signal from the transmitter and when it starts receiving the signal again; it also provides periodic checks.<br><br>A central **computer** or **receiver** accepts reports from the receiver-dialer over the telephone lines, compares them with the offender's curfew schedule, and alerts correctional officials to unauthorized absences. | A **computer** is programmed to call the offender during the hours being monitored either randomly or at specifically selected times. It prepares reports on the results of the calls.<br><br>Strapped on the offender's arm is a **wristlet,** a black plastic module.<br><br>When the computer calls, the wristlet is inserted into a **verifier box** connected to the telephone to verify that the call is being answered by the offender being monitored. The computer functions similarly to that described above, calling the offender and preparing reports on the results of the call.<br><br>However, **voice verification** technology assures that the telephone is answered by the offender being monitored. |

### *Devices that do not use a telephone*

| Continuously signaling | Radio signaling |
| --- | --- |
| A **transmitter** is strapped to the offender which sends out a constant signal.<br><br>A **portable receiver,** in the car of the officer who is monitoring the offender, is tuned to receive the signal from the specific transmitter when the officer drives within one block of the offender's home. | The **link** is a small transmitter worn by the offender.<br><br>The **locator unit,** placed in the offender's home or other approved location, receives the signal from the link, records it and relays the information by radio signals to the local area monitor.<br><br>The **local area monitor** is a microcomputer and information management system. This equipment is placed with the network manager (the leader of a small group of people who supervise the offender and encourage him to succeed). It receives information from the offender and coordinates communications among the network members. Each local network can handle 15 to 25 people.<br><br>If required, a **central base station** can be added to provide increased security and back-up functions. |

*Source*: A. Schmidt (1986), "Electronic Monitors," *Federal Probation* 50(2):59.

at times when they are supposed to be at home. The offender must answer the phone, and place the transmitter in a special telephone connection, so that the transmitter sends a message to the computer. In the passive system, a transmitter attached to the offender emits a continuous signal. The transmitter must be kept within range of an amplifier/transmitter or the signal will not reach a monitoring computer. This continuously signaling system requires the offender to remain within 150–200 feet of the fixed amplifier, which is usually installed in the offender's home (Huskey, 1987:19–20). See Box 5. A more recent innovation is the use of the global positioning system (GPS) to maintain constant surveillance of the whereabouts of a person being electronically monitored (Padgett, Bales & Blomberg, 2006).

Electronic monitoring systems have tamper alarms that signal a warning to monitors if the devices are removed or altered. The random calling system allows for both voice identification and the transmission of a monitoring signal. As it operates over telephone lines, this system is unaffected by interruptions in transmission caused by walls, structural steel, or other radio transmissions. The active surveillance random calling system appears to have a lower false-alarm rate than the passive surveillance system. The passive surveillance continuous transmission system, while more prone to false alarms, provides a continuous monitoring of the offender's whereabouts.

Most jurisdictions have adopted one or the other form of monitoring technology, and a few have used both. The random calling system allows somewhat greater freedom. For example, the offender could be next door at a neighbor's house and still be called to the telephone. The use of both systems could provide a gradation in the severity of monitoring. Thus, a probationer who is given the random calling monitor and then misses a call could be "punished" by being issued a continuous transmission monitor. The possibility of varying the level of restriction within a category of penalty called "monitoring" adds to the attractiveness of this sanction.

Baumer, Maxfield, and Mendelsohn (1993) evaluated three electronically monitored home detention programs. They found that these programs differed in their effectiveness based upon the agency under which they were operated and the characteristics of the people placed on monitoring. Pretrial detainees were more likely to violate program conditions, but these offenders were more clearly diverted from jail. Further, there was some evidence to suggest that one effect of electronically monitored home confinement was to encourage offenders to seek employment. Finally, the assessment indicated that offenders on home confinement were not as securely incapacitated as are those incarcerated. Renzema and Mayo-Wilson (2005) reviewed scores of studies of electronic monitoring and concluded that the best evidence available suggests that the effect of electronic monitoring on reducing recidivism is limited. Padgett, Bales, and Blomberg (2006) compared GPS systems to radio frequency systems and found no differences between either of the electronic monitoring systems and offenders not being monitored in terms of recidivism.

In 1949, George Orwell's book *1984* was published. In that book, Orwell assessed the future of the human race under the conditions of the arms race. He suggested that society would become increasingly bureaucratized, and governments would become more totalitarian. The leader of one government, "Big Brother," would retain power through torture and brainwashing. The dominant aspect of life in this society would be that everyone was under surveillance by the government. It was in *1984* that Orwell coined the slogan, "Big Brother is watching." Because of the time period in which he wrote the book, much of what he described appeared to be science fiction. However, as evidenced by our current level of sophistication, it appears that George Orwell only missed by a few years when he titled his book *1984*. Lilly's (1992) assessment of the electronic monitoring movement on an international scale is reminiscent of Orwell.

The issues involved in electronic surveillance recall the questions raised about the development of probation and parole supervision. On the one hand are critics who suggest that monitoring is an insufficient penalty for many offenders. They contend that this leniency reduces the deterrent effect of the law. Other critics argue that the use of monitoring technology to allow the release from incarceration of "dangerous" offenders poses too great a risk to the community. On the other hand are those who criticize this technology as too oppressive, that is, it violates current standards of privacy and infringes on constitutional rights to protection against unreasonable searches and seizures. Finally, some critics fear that electronic monitoring, in practice, will be used to increase the severity of community supervision for those who would otherwise have been released to traditional probation or parole.

Proponents of surveillance argue that the technology enhances public safety by ensuring supervision of offenders in the community. Further, surveillance itself deters offenders from committing crimes. Similarly, the proponents suggest that the ability to monitor offenders results in a lessening of penalty severity. They argue that some offenders are sent to prison who do not actually need to be incarcerated. Continual supervision will allow judges and parole boards to leave these offenders in the community. While the current focus may be on the electronics of contemporary surveillance, at base, the questions and criticisms are the same ones that have always surrounded community supervision.

Despite the ongoing debate, electronic monitoring as a sanction, either alone or in combination with other forms of community supervision, appears to be here to stay. Harry Boone (1996) surveyed judges and policymakers about their perceptions of electronic monitoring. More than 90 percent of both groups said they felt electronic monitoring was here to stay, with almost two-thirds noting that they believed the use of electronic monitoring would grow in the future. Most observers believe that electronic monitoring is a cost-effective alternative to incarceration for many offenders (Evans, 1996). Camp and Camp (1996:160) reported that more than 90 percent of probation agencies responding to their survey indicated that they used electronic monitoring with a capacity of monitoring more than 12,000 offenders. The typical offender was monitored for a period of about three months.

Learning how well electronic monitoring can meet the other goals of community supervision (e.g., fairness; a reduction in future crime; etc.) must await further study (Cohn, Biondi & Flaim, 1996). Thus far, evaluations of electronic monitoring have not shown these programs to have an impact on future crime (Austin & Hardyman, 1991; Mackenzie, 1997).

## Day Reporting and Other Sanctions

Unlike many other intermediate sanction alternatives, **day reporting** is of relatively recent origin. While there was earlier use of day reporting in England, the first day reporting program in the United States was started in Massachusetts in 1986 (McDevitt, 1988). This program was designed as an early release alternative for prison and jail inmates near the date of their parole. Participants in the program were required to report to the center each day, prepare an itinerary for their next day's activities, and report by telephone to the center throughout the day (Larivee, 1990).

At midyear 2003, jails reported supervising almost 8,000 offenders in day reporting programs. Parent (1990) reported that day reporting programs were operational in six states by the late 1980s, and many more states were considering the option. These programs (and the clients they served) varied. McDevitt and Miliano (1992:153) observed that programs tend to have similar components, including frequent contact, formalized scheduling, and drug testing. In general, day reporting represents a significant increase in surveillance and contact over even intensive probation or parole supervision programs. By

## Box 6. Services Provided by Day-Reporting Centers

Total Number of Centers: 114

| Services: | At Center | Elsewhere | Both | Centers Providing |
|---|---|---|---|---|
| Job seeking skills | 79% | 13% | 8% | 98% |
| Drug abuse education | 69% | 17% | 14% | 96% |
| Group counseling | 80% | 12% | 18% | 96% |
| Job placement | 62% | 34% | 14% | 93% |
| Education | 55% | 31% | 14% | 93% |
| Drug treatment | 31% | 54% | 15% | 92% |
| Life skills training | 92% | 16% | 12% | 91% |
| Individual counseling | 72% | 17% | 11% | 89% |
| Transitional housing | 13% | 81% | 16% | 63% |
| Recreation & leisure | 74% | 16% | 10% | 60% |

*Source*: D. Parent, J. Byrne, V. Tsarfaty, L. Valade & J. Esselman (1995), Day *Reporting Centers, Volume 1* (Washington, DC: National Institute of Justice):13.

1992, there were six day reporting centers in operation in Massachusetts, with a total average daily population of several hundred offenders. By 1994, there were 114 day reporting centers operating in the United States (Parent et al., 1995). Box 6 offers a description of day reporting centers in the United States in 1994.

At midyear 2003, more than 12,500 jail inmates were supervised outside the jail facility through electronic monitoring (Harrison & Karberg, 2004). Day reporting clients typically make at least one in-person and several telephone contacts with center staff daily, yet they are allowed to remain in the community throughout much of the day. Most programs are limited to between two and four months in duration, followed by a period of probation or parole supervision. Often, day reporting clients work with program staff to develop and obtain substance abuse, psychological and employment treatment and services. These programs are still too new to have been adequately evaluated, but they promise to reduce prison crowding and costs, protect community safety, and provide needed services to offenders.

In Chapter 12 we discussed furlough programs. Work and study furloughs, as well as prerelease programs, have been developed to help inmates make the adjustment from incarceration to living in the community. Placements in residential community corrections facilities are also used to provide custodial supervision of offenders who are not seen as needing or deserving jail or prison incarceration (Holsinger et al., 1997). Other changes in probation and parole have similarly bridged the gap between traditional supervision and incarceration. There has been an increasing use of community service sentencing and the imposition of monetary penalties (such as fines and restitution to crime victims). All of these changes in traditional community supervision have worked to make probation and parole more severe as penalties, and to provide greater restrictions and controls over offenders in the community.

Shock probation and parole, split sentencing, and intensive supervision programs blur the distinction between incarceration and community supervision. The experience of being "on paper" becomes much more like that of being incarcerated. In these programs, the probationer or parolee faces additional deprivations of autonomy, liberty, and the like. It is difficult to determine whether the development of these programs has led to the increasing use of community supervision for felons and dangerous offenders. It is possible that these developments are in response to a changing population. Alternatively, these changes may have been successful in creating community-based sanctions that are seen as appropriate for prison and jail-bound offenders. In that case, the changing population of community corrections programs may be a response to changes in programs available.

## Issues in Community Supervision

As prison populations have increased since the 1970s, so have the numbers of people under community supervision. The change in types of offenders being placed on probation and parole supervision is an important factor in understanding changes in community supervision. The simple growth in the size of the population, regardless of its characteristics, also has led to changes. Three areas in which such changes can be seen are the financing, management, and technology of probation and parole. These changes merit attention, regardless of whether they involve special programs such as shock or intensive supervision.

### Financing

Several states implemented **community corrections legislation** that includes various funding formulas to support community supervision activities. These laws provide financial incentives to counties to reduce their prison commitments and to retain offenders in the community. The typical law either authorizes a subsidy for counties that reduce their commitment rates, or provides financial support for improved and increased community corrections programs. The state reduces the subsidy if the commitment rate is increased (Clear & Cole, 1986:399–400; National Advisory Commission, 1973:315). The Kansas Community Corrections Act, for example, "penalizes" counties for not reducing their commitments to state prisons (Jones, 1991).

California was the first state to employ an incentive program in order to encourage communities to keep offenders out of the prison system. In 1965, the California legislature passed the **Probation Subsidy Act**, which paid counties for each offender who was not sentenced to prison in each county. The state developed a formula that estimated the number of offenders expected to be sentenced to prison, and then paid $4,000 to the county for each offender less than that number who was not sentenced to prison. If a county was expected to commit 1,000 offenders to prison, but actually committed only 900, the county received a subsidy of $400,000 ($4,000 x 100). Subsidy funds were earmarked for the improvement of local correctional services. Other states subsequently developed similar models.

The California subsidy program faced several obstacles (Clear & Cole, 1986). There was no subsidy assistance to law enforcement, although the effect of the program was to keep offenders in the community. There was no inflation factor included, so that within 10 years, the purchasing power of the subsidy declined by more than one-third. There also was no adjustment for counties that historically had kept offenders in local correctional custody. For example, a county traditionally may have kept nonviolent offenders in the community on probation. Under the subsidy formula, that county had a lower estimate of commitments. Another county may have traditionally incarcerated nearly every felony offender. Under the subsidy program, the first county could only receive aid by keeping violent or more serious offenders in the community. The second county could begin to use probation for minor, nonviolent offenders, and could reap a large subsidy.

Later funding formulas for community corrections attempted to overcome some of the original difficulties in the California subsidy program. Minnesota, Oregon, and Colorado passed community corrections legislation that included more options for counties. These states also tried to adjust for crime and incarceration rates, and included inflation factors. Other states, such as Ohio, began subsidy programs for specific practices that counties could adopt to reduce prison commitments. In each of these cases, funding is tied to the development and expansion of community programs. The effects are to support probation and other community services and to assist the counties in handling their increasing caseloads.

Another more recent development is in the charging of **supervision fees**. Several state parole authorities and probation offices now require that the client make a monthly payment to the agency to offset the costs of supervision (Wheeler et al., 1989). This requirement further increases the cost advantage of probation and parole over incarceration. Similarly, it is common for a condition of supervision to be the payment of court costs. This requires that probation and parole officers serve (at least part time) as bill collectors for the courts.

A related financial alteration in the operation of probation and parole is the growing use of **restitution**. Offenders on probation and parole are increasingly being ordered to make restitution to the victims of their crimes. One-quarter of felony convicts in 2002 were assessed fines, and 12 percent were ordered to pay restitution (Durose & Langan, 2004). Probation and parole officers are then required to manage the payment process for restitution (Clear & Cole, 1986:110–111).

On the one hand, these developments assist community supervision by providing enhanced resources and by reducing costs of operation. On the other hand, these programs also add to the burden of probation and parole officers, who generally dislike working in the role of "bill collector." These practices reflect the tradition of experimentation with correctional practices in probation and parole. Box 7. shows financial conditions imposed on probationers in 1995, the most recent year for which data are available.

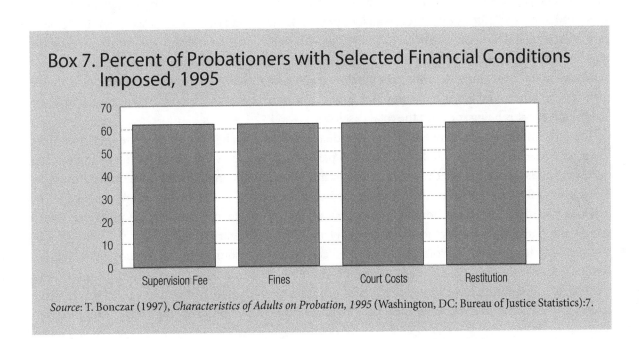

Box 7. Percent of Probationers with Selected Financial Conditions Imposed, 1995

*Source*: T. Bonczar (1997), *Characteristics of Adults on Probation, 1995* (Washington, DC: Bureau of Justice Statistics):7.

## Management

The traditional approach to probation and parole supervision consisted of the casework model. In casework, each officer was responsible for a caseload of offenders. The officer was a generalist expected to supervise a variety of persons having a variety of needs. The **casework model** expected the single officer to be capable of providing needed services to all of the offenders.

Beyond this, several other models of organization and caseload management have been proposed and adopted. Several jurisdictions now use teams of officers responsible for large groups of offenders. In **team supervision**, officers can take advantage of their varied strengths and skills. Thus, an officer who is particularly effective with offenders that require employment services can concentrate on that type of case for the entire team (Dell'Apa et al., 1976).

Another development involves the classification of offenders by objectives of supervision, rather than the general assignment of offenders to officers. This process clarifies the goals of supervision for the officer, and it allows officers to set priorities in responding to the needs of offenders (Clear & O'Leary, 1983). A related adaptation involves identifying the offenders who are least in need of supervision and service, and assigning them to a very low level of monitoring. This practice reduces the caseloads of officers who are providing service, and it maximizes (at least in theory) utilization of supervision resources (Vito & Marshall, 1983). As with objectives-based supervision classification, recent practice involves the identification of supervision levels on the basis of assessments of both the needs and risk of offenders.

The National Institute of Corrections has developed a **model case management system** (NIC, 1981). The system relies upon two case-assessment instruments: a risk assessment and a needs assessment. Each supervising officer completes these two questionnaires and then reviews them with the offender. Through discussion of the instruments, the officer and the offender develop a plan for dealing with needs. They develop case objectives from that plan. This system helps identify concrete actions that the officer should take, and it provides an ability to assess case progress.

As a management system, the model system involves three components: (1) classification, (2) case planning, and (3) the assignment of workload units. Classification is accomplished through the assessments mentioned above. Depending upon the levels of need or risk, or upon combinations of the two, the offender is placed in a supervision category that is somewhere between "high" (frequent officer attention) and "low" (little or no direct contact by officer). The second component, case planning, creates case objectives based upon a structured interview with the client. The officers' supervisors review the objectives and approve or modify them. Finally, cases are assigned varying "degrees of difficulty" or workload units. These units describe how much of an officer's time will be consumed by the case. In this manner, the officer and his or her supervisor know how much effort to expend on that case, and know how much effort is being spent on the total caseload.

From the information derived through individual case planning, it is possible for the agency or office to assess its needs, objectives, and progress. If 35 percent of the agency's caseload has high employment needs, administrators can see the utility in providing officers with employment development training. The agency might assign some officers as employment specialists. If a large enough percentage of the caseload has high-risk scores, administrators may want to create special surveillance units that would serve risk-control goals distinct from service delivery (Clear & O'Leary, 1983).

The National Institute of Corrections devoted considerable resources to the development and dissemination of this case management program. Training, technical assistance, and the provision of written documentation have spread the model program to probation and parole agencies across the country. With some adaptation for local considerations, the model program may have revolutionized the organization and administration of community supervision. Since then, other models of case classification and management have emerged and been adopted in a variety of institutional and community settings (Dowdy et al., 2002; Holsinger et al., 2003). These models sort offenders into distinct categories based on the expected risk of supervision or program failure, and identify treatment needs of offenders allowing correctional personnel to target treatments to the most important needs of offenders.

Not only has the spread of case assessment and classification technology changed the organization of service delivery and the assignment of cases to types of supervision, it has been linked to what some have called a "flight from discretion." Schneider, Ervin, and Snyder-Joy (1996) observed that even when case assessment and classification do not result in better case processing, community supervision staff support these practices. They suggest that the existence of classification and assignment procedures make case decisions more routine, and reduce the responsibility of supervising officers for what may turn out to be "wrong" case decisions. The increasing numbers of more serious offenders in community programs have raised the stakes and produced increased public scrutiny of supervision practices.

Management innovations in community supervision include the development and adoption of automated information systems to improve case supervision and monitoring. Edwin Zedlewski (1996) observed that existing software programs designed for salespeople are also well suited to probation and parole use. This software manages scheduling, keeps tracks of contacts, and otherwise performs the information storage and retrieval functions most useful to probation and parole officers. In recent years there has been increased emphasis in two important management areas. First, community supervision agencies are moving toward "evidence-based practice" (Latessa et al., 2002). Coupled with automated information systems, administrators seek to assess the effects of different practices on specific types of offenders or specific problems. Boone and Fulton (1996) reported the development of performance-based measures of community supervision effects. Increasingly, community supervision managers seek information about how to affect the behaviors of offenders. In 2001, the American Probation and Parole Association began revising accreditation standards for probation and parole agencies to include performance-based standards. As described by Taylor (2004:21), the new standards not only include compliance with policies and procedures but also include "measurement not only of what an agency does, but how well it does it."

## Technology

A final area of recent innovations in community supervision involves the application of communications and other technologies to supervision. These applications have taken a number of forms, such as the information technologies mentioned above. Developments in areas including word processing, telecommunications, and video recording have had some effects and can be expected to play a larger role in the future. We have already addressed some of the effects of improved information systems and classification and assessment procedures as a form of information technology.

**Drug testing** is currently a hot topic throughout all of our society. Repeated or continuing wars on drugs, increasingly tough drunk-driving laws, deaths of celebrities from drug-related causes, and notorious transportation accidents attributed to drug use all have focused attention on substance abuse. There are today a number of relatively simple technologies for the detection of alcohol and other drug consumption. They range from the Breathalyzer test to determine if a person has been driving under the influence of alcohol, to blood tests to determine alcohol or other drug content. Urine testing is becoming an increasingly common component of community supervision conditions.

Judges and parole boards seek to reduce the incidence of substance abuse among convicted offenders in the hopes of reducing future criminality. They traditionally have prohibited probationers and parolees from the consumption of excessive amounts of alcohol or the use of other recreational drugs. When this author worked for the Oregon Board of Parole, a standard condition of parole limited drinking for all parolees. Parolees were either not allowed to drink alcohol to excess, were not allowed to drink alcohol at all, or were required to take Antabuse. Antabuse is a drug that reacts with alcohol to produce very unpleasant symptoms in the drinker. These symptoms include nausea, shortness of breath, dizziness, and other sensations that are generally unpleasant enough to deter the drinker.

Regardless of the attempts to control substance abuse, probationers and parolees continue to acquire and use alcohol and other drugs. The development of easily administered detection tests has strengthened the ability of probation and parole officers to identify and control substance abuse among their clients. Many believe that merely testing for use will deter offenders. As Atmore and Bauchiero (1987) reported:

> We have noted significant behavioral improvements when we test regularly, because it serves as a deterrent. Therefore, we are returning less people to higher security for positive urines because they know they are taking a huge risk by substance use. In other words, test regularly! You need to have a consistent policy for testing and sanctions for positive results, or else word will get around quickly that one should not take this seriously.

> There are some easy to use and very reliable machines for urine testing now available … Any probation or parole officer could be trained to use basic urinalysis equipment in a short period of time …

In addition to the urine test described by Atmore and Bauchiero, probation and parole officers have a wide array of other testing technologies available to them. These include the Breathalyzer and blood tests, as well as some newer developments, such as a saliva test for alcohol use. With the saliva test, the subject's saliva is placed on a "blotter" that is actually a form of litmus paper. If the subject has recently used alcohol, the paper will change colors. Efforts are currently underway to develop similar saliva tests for other drug use.

Camp and Camp (1996:158–159) reported that all community supervision agencies responding to their survey used drug testing in 1995. These agencies reported a total of nearly 3.7 million drug tests. Most of these tests (98.7%) did not result in revocation of supervision for offenders. Often, even positive drug tests do not result in revocation. The development of drug courts, with their emphasis on drug treatment, for example, use tests as measures of case progress. A positive test result (showing the use of drugs) is likely to result in some change in status (assignment to a new treatment, increased contact, etc.), but is unlikely to result in revocation. Nonetheless, offenders seek ways to avoid detection, and officers must continually guard against altered urine samples (Elbert, 1997).

Substance abuse testing technologies enhance the ability of officers to control the risks of crime posed by their clients. These procedures also may change the nature of the job. The officers must now test their clients, serve as medical technicians, and otherwise assume the role of "cop" instead of "helper." Some believe that testing alters the nature of the officer's job and his or her relationship with offenders. In the Georgia Intensive Supervision program, special officers were designated as "surveillance officers" and charged with conducting urine tests and investigations. Using special officers protected the helping relationship between the probation or parole officer and the offender (Erwin & Clear, 1987).

Developments in geographic information systems have been applied to community supervision. Harries (2003) described a program in which the Maryland Division of Probation and Parole used geographic information to improve supervision. As described by Piquero (2003), Maryland used geographic analysis of crime to develop programs involving police, probation, community members, and other agencies to develop coordinated efforts to reduce and prevent crime. Geographic analysis can improve community supervision in a variety of ways ranging from describing "good" and "bad" environments in which to place offenders through minimizing supervision officer travel time by assigning caseloads based on geography. Related to this, as mentioned earlier, it is now possible to use the global positioning system (GPS) to track offenders. A popular service available on new motor vehicles (known as OnStar or by other titles) is now available for the tracking of offenders. With GPS monitors, it is possible to monitor the location of probationers and parolees at all times.

## Due Process, Crime Control, and Community Supervision

Many of the changes in community supervision were grafted onto existing practices of probation and parole supervision. Thus, restitution orders and supervision fees have been added as conditions of probation. Periods of confinement have been added to supervision conditions to enable courts to achieve split sentencing, or to create programs like shock incarceration. Supervision has been changed to create intensive monitoring programs for the more serious offenders now placed in probation and parole caseloads.

Some of the changes in community supervision represent the development of new programs that complement traditional probation and parole supervision. Day reporting centers, for example, are often operated as adjuncts of the jail or as institutional components of local community corrections agencies. The growth of residential community correctional facilities similarly has been outside of probation and parole agencies. Such facilities serve as a resource to those agencies.

Indeed, one of the problems inherent in estimating the numbers of persons participating in these various programs is that the participants may be reported as members of the probation and parole population. Thus, probation and parole supervision now includes thousands of cases in which offenders are under electronic monitoring, residing in halfway houses, attending day reporting centers, or receiving other forms of intermediate sanctions. As perceptions about the adequacy of sentences have changed, and as the number of offenders eligible for correctional supervision has increased, a large proportion of the burden of adapting to these changes has fallen on the community supervision agencies of the criminal justice system.

Traditionally, community supervision has taken the role of assistance to convicted offenders through the provision of services and a reduction in the severity of criminal sanctions. In this regard, throughout most of the twentieth century, probation and parole could be viewed as supporting the interests and needs of the individual, and thus having a due process orientation. In more recent years, however, the role of community supervision in crime control has come to dominate. Sluder, Sapp, and Langston (1994) have suggested that offender reform for the purposes of crime control is becoming the guiding philosophy of community supervision. In response, Jennifer Hartman (1997) has argued that current changes in community supervision represent extensions of state power and control over individuals. Garland (1990) and Simon (1993) take similar positions. Hartman (1997:193) concluded, "The definition, technology and expectations of community supervision today are such that control is the operating principle and dominates practice."

Joan Petersilia (1996) presented the argument that criminal justice policymakers must invest in community corrections if they hope to reduce crime in the future. Consistent with the position taken by Sluder, Sapp, and Langston, she contends that community supervision and alternative sanctions can support crime control efforts efficiently. The choice is not whether to mitigate the severity of criminal punishments, or whether it is better for offenders to be kept in the community. Rather, her position is that community supervision, including intermediate sanctions, is best designed to achieve reductions in future crime.

While crime control advocates might argue that sanctions short of incarceration inadequately protect the public and fail to deter offenders, due process advocates fear increasing the numbers of offenders who are subjected to criminal justice processing (i.e., net widening) or increasing the restrictiveness of interventions on the lives of offenders. In addition, due process proponents fear that the proliferation of intermediate sanctions has simply meant that offenders who would otherwise have received regular probation now are being subjected to such programs as electronic monitoring, intensive supervision, and day reporting (Harland, 1996). They believe that instead of providing true alternatives to incarceration, intermediate sanctions have brought more offenders under tighter control by the correctional system.

The growth of the community corrections population, especially if coupled with that of the prison and jail populations, suggests the due process proponents may be correct. By the end of 2003, more than 3 percent of the adult population of the United States was under correctional control. What remains unsettled is whether the offenders or society as a whole have benefited as a result of this increased correctional intervention. On one hand, more offenders than ever before are in the custody of corrections officials. On the other hand, intermediate sanctions may have saved tens of thousands of offenders from serving prison and jail terms, and may result in improved conditions for them in the future.

Community supervision represents a compromise between due process and crime control proponents. Offenders under community supervision are subjected to supervision, restrictions, and control. Still, these offenders are under less onerous control than those who are incarcerated. Community supervision often seeks to provide the "right" level of state control over the lives and behavior of convicted offenders. We will return to this issue in the final chapter, but growing interest in restorative justice seeks to balance the interests of the community, victim, and offender. In most restorative justice programs, community supervision plays a key role precisely because it is well suited to serve both due process and crime control ends.

## Discussion

National prison release trends are important to mention before we delve into the California experience. Nationally, of the 300,000 prison inmates released from custody in 1994, 68% were re-arrested within three years; 47% were convicted of a new crime, and 25% were re-committed to prison with a new sentence (CDCR).

# AB 109 and the California Experience

## Timeline:

- 2006: Governor Arnold Schwarzenegger transferred 8,000 prison inmates to out-of-state prisons due to overcrowding
- 2006: A class action suit is filed against the state for unconstitutional poor care for sick and mentally ill inmates
- 2009: The court rules that California state prisons are overcrowded and in violation of constitutional standards for medical and mental health services
- 2009: Governor Schwarzenegger signs into law SB 678 California Community Corrections Performance Act. Ten thousand state prisoners are transferred to prisons in Arizona, Mississippi, and Oklahoma
- May 2010: The United States Supreme Court rules that overcrowded conditions in the CA state prison system are so severe that they violate the Eighth Amendment on cruel and unusual punishment
- April 2011: Governor Jerry Brown signs into law AB 109, the Criminal Justice Realignment Plan

# Factors in Realignment

Realignment in California was the state strategy to reduce the prison population. The program was designed so certain convicted felons could be released back into the community. The idea was instead of placing these offenders on state parole, they were released into community supervision programs. The program was structured so that these felons would be supervised by county probation departments.

Under the old system, felons who were released on parole were supervised by the state for three years. Realignment changed that policy. Offenders released to community supervision had to remain on probation for six to twelve months. The length of probation time was left up to individual counties. In Los Angeles County, offenders are required to complete twelve months on probation.

In the first year of the program, 30,000 state inmates were released into community corrections programs. Over 12,000 felons were released back to Los Angeles County in that first year.

Another important factor in the realignment plan was the reclassification of certain types of felony convictions. Reclassification of these crimes allowed state prison inmates to be eligible to serve their sentences in the county jail instead of in a state prison. State officials believed that the realignment program would significantly reduce prison overcrowding and in turn the plan would meet the legal requirements rendered by the court decision.

Realignment focuses on criminal sentencing, punishment, and community corrections. To be eligible for the AB 109 program, prisoners had to be convicted of non-violent, non-serious, and non-sexual offenses. These offenders also had to be returned to the county were they were convicted (LA County Chiefs).

The problem with the plan lay in the fact that serious offenders were still released because their current offenses were considered non-serious. No one took into account the fact that many offenders were dangerous felons who had histories of committing acts of violence in pervious offenses (LA County Chiefs).

Under the authority of 1170 (h) of the penal code, 500 crimes have been reclassified so offenders can qualify for realignment release. That means there are only 70 crimes that have sentences for housing in the state prison (California Penal Code, 2013).

According to the California Department of Corrections and Rehabilitation, 1.2 billion dollars has been allocated to the 58 counties for realignment purposes. The State of California forecasts they will save two billion dollars by 2015. To reach this goal means that one-third of the current prison population will be transferred to community supervision.

## The Follow-Up Study

After realignment was implemented, a follow-up study revealed that the plan did not significantly impact recidivism rates. Sixty-two (62) percent of pre-alignment offenders were arrested again compared to a slight decrease of 58% of post-alignment offenders being re-arrested. Convictions for new offenses were not much different: 21.3% of pre-alignment offenders were convicted of new offenses while 22.5% post alignment offenders were convicted of new crimes (CDCR).

## Does Realignment Work in California?

Some experts report that keeping low-level offenders near home under the authority community supervision is more effective than confinement. The program also allows the offenders to work close to home and maintain family ties (Prizmich, 2013).

According to the California Department of Corrections and Rehabilitation, a new study showed post-prison arrests have declined and convictions are remaining at the same level under the alignment program. The program is promising to reduce prison expenditures by half a billion dollars (Prizmich, 2013).

In contrast, the program has its flaws. Realignment offenders are committing new crimes. Leaders in Bakersfield, CA, have reported a 16% spike in crime by low-level offenders being released to the community. They are considering hiring more police officers to deal with the program (ABC 23 News).

Bakersfield City Councilmember Russell Johnson stated: *This is not a city-created problem, this is a state problem. We have to keep our residents safe.* Later, he stated that adding police officers is an option but: *that is in jeopardy because we have all these predatory government agencies seeking to take local money.*

Flaws in the Los Angeles County program may have wider implications than just in communities. In a Press Telegram article, almost 2,000 offenders are out of compliance state wide. An investigation by Beatrice Valenzuela of the Press Telegram discovered that while 8,298 offenders were either in county jail or released on alternative sentencing programs, 1,844 were out of compliance and had disappeared. The Los Angeles County Probation Department has staff looking for the offenders; but they are still out there willing to commit new crimes (Valenzuela, 2013).

The Long Beach Police Department established a compliance team consisting of six officers and a sergeant. One of the team members is a Los Angeles County probation officer. This team has been much more successful than that of the County of Los Angeles. Long Beach has 537 offenders in the program or in jail. Only 11% are unaccounted for.

Chief James Hunt of the Monrovia, California, Police Department stated: *In [October] 2011, the State of California implemented AB 109. Approximately, 12,000 state prisoners were released into communities in Los Angeles County over the first twelve months of the program. The Los Angeles County Probation Department was unprepared to monitor this sudden influx of state parolees. Communities in the San Gabriel Valley, including, Monrovia began to experience a rise in property crimes, especially residential burglaries and auto burglaries. In 2012, Monrovia had a 5.1% increase in property crime and a 6.6% increase in violent crime. Through the first eight months of 2013, Monrovia has had a 30% increase in burglaries.*

Realistically not every low-level offender is a right fit for this program. In September 2013, Erick Balint engaged in a gun battle with Long Beach police officers and was killed by the officers in the city of Carson. The offender qualified for realignment release because his current conviction was for grand theft auto and evading police. The flaw in this entire program is that Balint's past convictions were not taken into account before his release. He had served time for being in possession of a firearm, domestic violence, and theft.

A number of San Gabriel Valley chiefs of police designed a strategy to combat the rise in property crimes and monitor these offenders. Realignment offenders are monitored under a new program called Post-Release Community Supervision; the offenders are called Post-Release Supervised Persons, or PSP's for short (Hunt, personal conversation, October 31, 2013). The chiefs created the West San Gabriel Valley Anti-Crime Task Force (WSGVACT) that includes officers from Monrovia, Pasadena, Arcadia, South Pasadena, Monterey Park, and El Monte.

Chief Hunt said: *I am short on police officers but I made a commitment to assign a detective to the task force to help reduce property crime in my city and also to monitor the PSP's in our region. Monrovia later received $90,000 a year out of the funds provided to local jurisdictions from the state to deal with crime issues created by realignment. These funds helped to pay for the detective's salary and benefits. His salary and benefits cost more than what Monrovia is receiving but the return is worth the cost. The team was the first such full time regional team created in Los Angeles County. We had the team before realignment and added compliance checks of the PSP population as part of their duties. One member of the team is a Los Angeles County probation officer and he has access to the PSP database. The team has been quite successful in dismantling burglary rings. In addition the team has also had success at arresting PSP's for various crimes.*

Chief Hunt closed by saying that Los Angeles County was not prepared for the number of PSP's released to the county (J. Hunt, personal communication, October 21, 2013).

For Monrovia, the chief stated that the department needs to change the way they police and to enhance technology in order to work more effectively with fewer officers. Monrovia has lost 20% of their sworn positions due to the down turn in the economy.

## Questions for Class Discussion

1. Discuss the pros and cons of community supervision programs
2. Evaluate whether or not new technologies are effective to balance efficient supervision of the offender and still keep them in the community.

3. Compare and contrast California's AB 109 program. How would you manage the program if you were the governor?

## Class Activities for the Professor

1. Assign the students the discussion questions in an on-line chat
2. In the classroom establish student panels to debate the AB 109 issue
3. Assign the students to research a trend or a technology in corrections and have them locate a journal article. The student should write a short paper and be prepared to discuss their findings in class.
4. Divide the students into pairs. Assign them to develop questions that they would ask a low-level offender to evaluate them for alternative sentencing.

## Works Cited

No author, (2013, May), CDCR Today. "New Study Shows Post Prison Arrests Are Down, Convictions Are Static Under Realignment." Retrieved from www.cdcr.gov/

Valenzuela, B. (2013, October 19), "Whereabouts of 2,000 Potentially High-Risk Probationers in LA County Unknown", Press Telegram. Retrieved from www.presstelegram.com

Prizmich, K. (2013), "AB 109". Retrieved from www.bi.com/industrynews/AB 109/

Los Angeles County Chief, Realignment Notes provided by Chief James Hunt, Monrovia Police Department.

# References

Anderson, J., L. Dyson & J. Burns (1999). *Boot Camp: An Intermediate Sanction.* Lanham, MD: University Press of America.

Atmore, T. & E. Bauchiero (1987). "Substance Abusers: Identification and Treatment." *Corrections Today* 49(7):22–24, et seq.

Auerhahn, K. (2007). "Do You Know Who Your Probationers Are: Using Simulation Modeling to Estimate the Composition of California's Felony Probation Population, 1980–2000." *Justice Quarterly* 24(1):28–47.

Austin, J. & P. Hardyman (1991). *The Use of Early Parole with Electronic Monitoring to Control Prison Crowding.* Washington, DC: National Institute of Justice.

Baumer, T., M. Maxfield & R. Mendelsohn (1993). "A Comparative Analysis of Three Electronically Monitored Home Detention Programs." *Justice Quarterly* 10(1):121–142.

Beck, A. & C. Mumola (1999). *Prisoners in 1998.* Washington, DC: Bureau of Justice Statistics.

Benda, B., N. Toombs & M. Peacock (2006). "Distinguishing Graduates From Dropouts and Dismissals: Who Fails Boot Camp?" *Journal of Criminal Justice* 34(1):27–38.

Bennett, L. (1991). "The Public Wants Accountability." *Corrections Today* 53(4):92–95.

Boone, H. (1996). "Electronic Home Confinement: Judicial and Legislative Perspectives." *APPA Perspectives* (Fall):18–25.

Boone, H. & B. Fulton (1996). *Implementing Performance-Based Measures in Community Corrections.* Washington, DC: National Institute of Corrections.

Byrne, J. (1986). "The Control Controversy: A Preliminary Examination of Intensive Probation Supervision Programs in the United States." *Federal Probation* 50(2):4–16.

Byrne, J. & A. Pattavina (1992). "The Effectiveness Issue: Assessing What Works in the Adult Community Corrections System." In J. Byrne, A. Lurigio & J. Petersilia (eds.), *Smart Sentencing: The Emergence of Intermediate Sanctions.* Beverly Hills, CA: Sage, 281–303.

Camp, C. & G. Camp (1996). *The Corrections Yearbook 1996.* South Salem, NY: Criminal Justice Institute.

Clear, T.R. & J. Byrne (1992). "The Future of Intermediate Sanctions: Questions to Consider." In J. Byrne, A. Lurigio & J. Petersilia (eds.), S*mart Sentencing: The Emergence of Intermediate Sanctions.* Beverly Hills, CA: Sage, 319–331.

Clear, T.R. & G.F. Cole (1986). *American Corrections.* Monterey, CA: Brooks/Cole.

Clear, T.R. & V. O'Leary (1983). *Controlling the Offender in the Community.* Lexington, MA: Lexington Books.

Clear, T.R. & C. Shapiro (1986). "Identifying High Risk Probationers for Supervision in the Community: The Oregon Model." *Federal Probation* 50(2):42–49.

Cohn, A., L. Biondi & L. Flaim (1996). "The Evaluation of Electronic Monitoring Programs." *APPA Perspectives* (Fall):28–37.

Corbett, R. & G. Marx (1991). "Critique: No Soul in the New Machine: Technofallacies in the Electronic Monitoring Movement." *Justice Quarterly* 8(3):399–414.

Cullen, F., J. Wright & B. Applegate (1996). "Control in the Community: The Limits of Reform." In A. Harland (ed.), *Choosing Correctional Options That Work.* Thousand Oaks, CA: Sage, 69–116.

Davies, G. & K. Dedel (2006). "Violence Risk Screening in Community Corrections." *Criminology & Public Policy* 5(4):743–770.

del Carmen, R. & J. Vaughn (1986). "Legal Issues in the Use of Electronic Surveillance in Probation." *Federal Probation* 50(2):60–69.

Dell'Apa, F., W.T. Adams, J.D. Jorgensen & H.R. Sigurdson (1976). "Advocacy, Brokerage, Community: The ABC's of Probation and Parole." *Federal Probation* 40(4):3–8.

Dowdy, E., M. Lacy & N. Unnithan (2002). "Correctional Prediction and the Level of Service Inventory." *Journal of Criminal Justice* 31(1):29–39.

Durose, M. & P. Langan (2004). *Felony Sentences in State Courts, 2002.* Washington, DC: Bureau of Justice Statistics.

Elbert, M. (1997). "The Use of Creatinine and Specific Gravity Measurement to Combat Drug Test Dilution." *Federal Probation* 61(4):10.

Erwin, B. (1986). "Turning Up the Heat on Probationers in Georgia." *Federal Probation* 50(2):17–24.

Erwin, B. & T.R. Clear (1987). "Rethinking Role Conflict in Community Supervision." *Perspectives* 11(2):21–24.

Evans, D. (1996). "Electronic Monitoring: Testimony to Ontario's Standing Committee on Administration of Justice." *APPA Perspectives* (Fall):8–10.

Flanagan, T. (1985). "Questioning the Other Parole: The Effectiveness of Community Supervision of Offenders." In L.F. Travis III (ed.), *Probation, Parole, and Community Corrections: A Reader.* Prospect Heights, IL: Waveland, 167–183.

Ford, D. & A. Schmidt (1985). "Electronically Monitored Home Confinement." *NCJRS Update* (November).

Fulton, B., E. Latessa, A. Stichman & L. Travis (1997). "Up to Speed: The State of ISP: Research and Policy Implications." *Federal Probation* 61(4):65–75.

Garland, D. (1990). *Punishment and Modern Society.* Chicago: University of Chicago Press.

Goldstein, H., W. Burrell & R. Talty (1985). "Probation: The RAND Report and Beyond." *Perspectives* 9(2):11–12, et seq.

Gottfredson, M., S. Mitchell-Herzfeld & T. Flanagan (1982). "Another Look at the Effectiveness of Parole Supervision." *Journal of Research in Crime & Delinquency* 18(2):277–298.

Gowdy, V. (1993). *Intermediate Sanctions*. Washington, DC: National Institute of Justice.

Guynes, R. (1988). *Difficult Clients, Large Caseloads Plague Probation, Parole Agencies*. Washington, DC: U.S. Department of Justice.

Harland, A. (ed.) (1996). *Choosing Correctional Options That Work*. Thousand Oaks, CA: Sage.

Harland, A. & C. Rosen (1987). "Sentencing Theory and Intensive Supervision Probation." *Federal Probation* 51(4):33–42.

Harries, K. (2003). "Using Geographic Analysis in Probation and Parole." *NIJ Journal* (July):32–33.

Harris, P., R. Petersen & S. Rapoza (2001). "Between Probation and Revocation: A Study of Intermediate Sanctions Decision-Making." *Journal of Criminal Justice* 29(4):307–318.

Harrison, P. & J. Karberg (2004). *Prison and Jail Inmates at Midyear 2003*. Washington, DC: Bureau of Justice Statistics.

Hartman, J. (1997). "Operating Principles in Community Supervision." In M. Schwartz & L. Travis (eds.), *Corrections: An Issues Approach*, 4th ed. Cincinnati: Anderson, 187–195.

Holsinger, A., C. Lowenkamp & E. Latessa (2006). "Exploring the Validity of the Level of Service Inventory-Revised with Native American Offenders." *Journal of Criminal Justice* 334(3):331–337.

Holsinger, A.., C. Lowenkamp & E. Latessa (2003). "Ethnicity, Gender, and the Level of Service Inventory-Revised." *Journal of Criminal Justice* 31(4):309–320.

Holsinger, A., E. Latessa, M. Turner & L. Travis (1997). "High Level Alternatives to Incarceration: Examining Community Based Correctional Facilities." Paper presented at the annual meeting of the Academy of Criminal Justice Science, Louisville, KY, March 1997.

Hughes, T., D. Wilson & A. Beck (2001). *Trends in State Parole, 1990–2000*. Washington, DC: Bureau of Justice Statistics.

Huskey, B. (1987). "Electronic Monitoring: An Evolving Alternative." *Perspectives* 11(3):19–23.

Ingraham, B. & G. Smith (1972). "Electronic Surveillance and Control of Behavior and its Possible Use in Rehabilitation and Parole." In *Issues in Criminology*, Vol. 7. Beverly Hills, CA, Sage, 35–52.

Jones, P. (1991). "The Risk of Recidivism: Evaluating the Public-Safety Implications of a Community Corrections Program." *Journal of Criminal Justice* 19(1):49–66.

Larivee, J. (1990). "Day Reporting Centers: Making Their Way from the U.K. to the U.S." *Corrections Today* 52(6):84.

Latessa, E.J., F.T. Cullen & P. Gendreau (2002). "Beyond Correctional Quackery: Professionalism and the Possibility of Effective Treatment." *Federal Probation* 66(2):43–49.

Latessa, E.J. (1980). "Intensive Diversion Unit: An Evaluation." In B. Price & P.J. Baunach (eds.), *Criminal Justice Research*. Beverly Hills, CA: Sage, 101–124.

Latessa, E. (1993). *An Evaluation of the Lucas County Adult Probation Department's IDU and High Risk Groups*. Cincinnati: University of Cincinnati.

Lilly, R. (1992). "Selling Justice: Electronic Monitoring and the Security Industry." *Justice Quarterly* 9(3):493–503.

Lutze, F. (2001). "The Influence of a Shock Incarceration Program on Inmate Adjustment and Attitudinal Change." *Justice Quarterly* 29(3):255–267.

Lutze, F. (1998). "Are Shock Incarceration Programs More Rehabilitative than Traditional Prisons? A Survey of Inmates." *Justice Quarterly* 15(3):547–563.

Mackenzie, D. (1997). "Criminal Justice and Crime Control." In L. Sherman, D. Gottfredson, D. MacKenzie, J. Eck, P. Reuter & S. Bushway (eds.), *Preventing Crime: What Works, What Doesn't, What's Promising?* Washington, DC: National Institute of Justice, 9.1–9.76.

Mackenzie, D. & D. Parent (1991). "Shock Incarceration and Prison Crowding in Louisiana." *Journal of Criminal Justice* 19(3):225–237.

Mackenzie, D. & J. Shaw (1990). "Inmate Adjustment and Change During Shock Incarceration: The Impact of Correctional Boot Camp Programs." *Justice Quarterly* 7(1):125–150.

McDevitt, J. (1988). *Evaluation of the Hampton County Day Reporting Center.* Boston: Crime and Justice Foundation.

McDevitt, J. & R. Miliano (1992). "Day Reporting Centers: An Innovative Concept in Intermediate Sanctions." In J. Byrne, A. Lurigio & J. Petersilia (eds.), *Smart Sentencing: The Emergence of Intermediate Sanctions.* Beverly Hills, CA: Sage, 152–165.

McGaha, J., M. Fichter & P. Hirschburg (1987). "Felony Probation: A Re-examination of Public Risk." *American Journal of Criminal Justice* 12(1):1–9.

Morris, N. & M. Tonry (1990). *Between Prison and Probation: Intermediate Punishments in a Rational Sentencing System.* Oxford: Oxford University Press.

National Advisory Commission on Criminal Justice Standards and Goals (1973). *Corrections.* Washington, DC: U.S. Government Printing Office.

National Institute of Corrections (1981). *Model Probation and Parole Management Project.* Wash-ington, DC: National Institute of Corrections.

National Institute of Justice (1999). *Keeping Track of Electronic Monitoring.* Washington, DC: National Law Enforcement and Corrections Technology Center Bulletin, October.

Note (1966). "Anthropotelemetry: Dr. Schwitzgebel's Machine." *Harvard Law Review* 80:403.

Padgett, K., W. Bales & T. Blomberg (2006). "Under Surveillance: An Empirical Test of the Effectiveness and Consequences of Electronic Monitoring." *Criminology & Public Policy* 5(1):61–92.

Parent, D. (1990). *Day Reporting Centers for Criminal Offenders: A Descriptive Analysis of Existing Programs.* Washington, DC: U.S. Department of Justice.

Parent, D., J. Byrne, V. Tsarfaty, L. Valade & J. Esselman (1995). *Day Reporting Centers, Volume 1: Issues and Practices.* Washington, DC: National Institute of Justice.

Parisi, N. (1980). "Combining Incarceration and Probation." *Federal Probation* 44(2):3–11.

Petersilia, J. (1985). *Probation and Felony Offenders.* Washington, DC: U.S. Department of Justice.

Petersilia, J. (1996). "A Crime Control Rationale for Reinvesting in Community Corrections." *APPA Perspectives* (Spring):21–29.

Petersilia, J. & S. Turner (1993). *Evaluating Intensive Supervision Probation/Parole: Results of a Nationwide Experiment.* Washington, DC: National Institute of Justice.

Petersilia, J., S. Turner & J. Peterson (1986). *Prison Versus Probation in California: Implications for Crime and Offender Recidivism.* Santa Monica, CA: RAND.

Piquero, N. (2003). "A Recidivism Analysis of Maryland's Community Probation Program." *Journal of Criminal Justice* 31(4):295–307.

Renzema, M. & E. Mayo-Wilson (2005). "Can Electronic Monitoring Reduce Crime for Moderate to High-Risk Offenders?" *Journal of Experimental Criminology* 1(2):215–237.

Renzema, M. (1992). "Home Confinement Programs: Development, Implementation, and Impact." In J. Byrne, A. Lurigio & J. Petersilia (eds.), *Smart Sentencing: The Emergence of Intermediate Sanctions.* Beverly Hills, CA: Sage, 41–53.

Rhine, E. (1997). "Probation and Parole Supervision: In Need of a New Narrative." *Corrections Management Quarterly* 1(2):71–75.

Schmidt, A. (1987). "Electronic Monitoring: Who Uses It? How Much Does it Cost? Does it Work?" *Corrections Today* 49(7):28–34.

Schmidt, A. (1989). "Electronic Monitoring of Offenders Increases." *NIJ Reports* (January/February:2–5).

Schneider, A., L. Ervin & Z. Snyder-Joy (1996). "Further Exploration of the Flight From Discretion: The Role of Risk/Need Instruments in Probation Supervision Decisions." *Journal of Criminal Justice* 24(2):109–121.

Schwitzgebel, R. (1969). "A Belt from Big Brother." *Psychology Today* 2(11):45–47, 65.

Simon, J. (1993). *Poor Discipline.* Chicago: University of Chicago Press.

Sluder, R., A. Sapp & D. Langston (1994). "Guiding Philosophies for Probation in the 21st Century." *Federal Probation* 58(2):3–10.

Sontheimer, H. & L. Goodstein (1993). "An Evaluation of Juvenile Intensive Aftercare Probation: Aftercare Versus System Response Effects." *Justice Quarterly* 10(2):197–227.

Szasz, T. (1975). "The Control of Conduct: Authority vs. Autonomy?" *Criminal Law Bulletin* 11.

Taylor, D. (2004). "Agency Accreditation: The Performance-Based Standards Experience." *Perspectives* 28(2):21–23.

Travis, L.F., III (1984). "Intensive Supervision in Probation and Parole." *Corrections Today* 46(4):34.

Vito, G.F. (1985). "Probation as Punishment: New Directions." In L.F. Travis III (ed.), *Probation, Parole and Community Corrections.* Prospect Heights, IL: Waveland, 73–80.

Vito, G.F. (1986). "Felony Probation and Recidivism: Replication and Response." *Federal Probation* 50(4):17–25.

Vito, G.F. & F.H. Marshall (1983). "The Administrative Caseload Project." *Federal Probation* 46(3):33–41.

von Hirsch, A. & K. Hanrahan (1978). *Abolish Parole?* Washington, DC: U.S. Department of Justice.

Wilson, J. (2005). "Bad Behavior or Bad Policy? An Examination of Tennessee Release Cohorts, 1993–2001." *Criminology & Public Policy* 4(3):485–518.

Wheeler, G.R., T.M. Macam, R.V. Hissong & M.P. Slusher (1989). "The Effects of Probation Service Fees on Case Management Strategy and Sanctions." *Journal of Criminal Justice* 17(1):15–24.

Worrall, J., P. Schram, E. Hays & M. Newman (2004). "An Analysis of the Relationship Between Probation Caseloads and Property Crime Rates in California Counties." *Journal of Criminal Justice* 32(3):231–241.

Zedlewski, E. (1996). "NIJ News: Gotta Get IT." *APPA Perspectives* (Fall):16–17.

# Unit 2

---

# External Impacts

Unit 2 examines external factors that have had significant impact on service delivery by law enforcement and corrections. The editor selected topics on the globalization of crime, terrorism, homeland security and national trends fleshed out by experts in the field.

Two decades of warring in Iraq and Afghanistan, the 9/11 attacks, and other mass-casualty events thrust our nation into a paradigm shift, asking; how safe are we? Emerging threats impacting law enforcement by violent fringe groups bent on killing Americans here and abroad fundamentally changed policing forever. Threats from domestic and international terrorists, Jihadists, rogue nuclear nations, drug cartels, and narco-terrorists dominate our collective identity as Americans.

## Objectives:

- From a management perspective, identify social and global contemporary issues in criminal justice
- Compare and contrast global, community, organizational and individual responses to contemporary issues in criminal justice
- Assess the intended and unintended consequences of criminal justice policies developed in response to contemporary issues in the field

# Chapter 6: Modern Slavers

## The Evil of Human Bondage

## Student Objectives

1. Compare and contrast debt bondage and illegal immigration
2. Evaluate the concepts of dignity and decency to the issue
3. Examine national responsibilities in a global setting

The practice of slavery has been part of the human condition since the dawn of humanity. Slavery is mentioned in the Bible when God commands Moses to tell the pharaoh to let the Jews return to the Promised Land (King James, 2010). Eighteen centuries later the United States would fight a bitter Civil War to bind the Union together and to abolish the slavery of African-Americans.

The article that the student is about to read is best summed up by the words of Harvard Professor Stanley Hoffman who wrote in *Duties Beyond Borders* (1981), "There is no way of isolating oneself from the effects of gross violations abroad: they breed refugees, exiles and dissidents" who come knocking at our doors. Human trafficking is an international problem that impacts nations and communities (Logan 2009).

# Trafficking and Human Dignity

### By Mark Lagon

Human trafficking is the slavery of our time. Exactly 200 years ago, Britain and the United States formally outlawed the transatlantic slave trade. A few decades later the practice of slavery was expunged from North America (with a heavy dose of justice enforced by the British Navy and of bloodshed in the American Civil War). While much has changed since the days of the transatlantic slave trade, the lie which fueled that horrific chapter in history is at the root of sex trafficking and slave labor today—a belief that some people are less than human.

Consider Carlo, a 27-year-old man from a rural area of the Philippines, recruited along with ten other men and women for a highly valued job in an American Midwestern hotel. The men were promised higher wages, reasonable hours, and benefits. Filipino recruiters charged each worker $1,200 as a "processing fee" for securing the jobs. Hotel managers added new non-negotiable charges for "rent." This debt was used to coerce Carlo and the others to work endless hours.

Carlo's passport was confiscated by the traffickers to keep him from fleeing, which also rendered him undocumented and subject to potential arrest and deportation if caught by immigration officials off hotel premises. Toiling for 16 to 18 hours a day, Carlo and the other Filipinos endured total control by hotel managers over every aspect of their lives—what they ate, where they lived, and the hours they worked.

# Debt Bondage

Carlo's story includes several threads which I increasingly see in my work at the State Department's Office to Monitor and Combat Trafficking in Persons. Carlo is a migrant. His nightmare began at the hands of a recruiter who used fraudulent offers of employment and extracted a large recruitment fee which Carlo could only pay by taking a loan. Carlo was uniquely vulnerable to exploitation once in the destination country, the U.S., due to the debt he carried as a direct result of recruitment. This home-country debt was exacerbated by fraudulent expenses, such as "rent," added by an exploitative U.S. employer.

Carlo's debt led to debt bondage. Lacking any form of power, not to mention identification, in a country not his own, Carlo was robbed of his dignity as a victim of forced labor.

Current trends fleshed out in the 2008 *Trafficking in Persons (TIP) Report* released by the Secretary of State in June, and produced by my office, paint a grim picture of the diffuse and diverse factors which contribute to the vulnerability of more than 175 million migrants in the world today—vulnerability not just to minor labor infractions but to gross exploitation.

Among these factors is the flagrant use of excessive debt as a tool of manipulation, the fraudulent practices of some middle-men brokering the movement of millions across international borders, weak laws—and weak enforcement of laws—governing labor exploitation, some aspects of sponsorship laws in Persian Gulf states, and a fundamental lack of understanding about human trafficking.

Debt bondage is a frequent form of forced labor. Too often, people are enticed into fraudulent offers of work abroad that require a steep payment up front for the services of a labor agency arranging the job or a payment that goes straight to the future employer. To pay such fees, workers in poorer countries either become indebted to the recruiter, or take out a formal or informal loan in their country of origin, with the expectation of payment based on future wages earned abroad. Often, worker expectations and repayment terms are based on exaggerated and false representations by recruiters regarding wages the workers can expect to earn in their new jobs. Once at an overseas worksite, such high levels of indebtedness can make workers vulnerable to exploitation by unscrupulous employers who subject workers to terms much less favorable than promised at the time of recruitment (such as much longer hours, less pay, and harsher conditions).

The very factors that push migrants to leave their home countries are often the factors which make them vulnerable to the exploitation of trafficking when they arrive in a new destination. For example, millions of Burmese, facing bleak economic conditions, brutal political repression, and the prospect of forced labor at home, have fled homes and villages, usually without legal documents. The International Labor Organization (ILO) considers Burma to harbor a significant share of the estimated 2.2, million victims of state-imposed forced labor globally.

Burma's repression bleeds out into the surrounding region. As Harvard University professor Stanley Hoffmann wrote in *Duties Beyond Borders* in 1981—and it is every bit as true today—"There is no way of isolating oneself from the effects of gross violations abroad: they breed refugees, exiles and dissidents."[1] The grim situation in Burma serves to drive desperate people from their homes, often in irregular, undocumented migration.

Shortly after I became U.S. ambassador to combat human trafficking, I met Aye Aye Win—a young Burmese woman in search of work beyond her own tortured country. A recruiter painted a promising picture of work in neighboring Thailand. Aye Aye Win assumed substantial debt to cover upfront costs required by the recruiter for this job placement. Together with some 800 Burmese migrants, many of them children, Aye Aye Win was "placed" in a shrimp farming and processing factory. But it wasn't a job. It was a prison camp. The isolated ten-acre factory was surrounded by steel walls, 15 feet tall with barbed wire fencing, located in the middle of a coconut plantation far from roads. Workers weren't allowed to leave and were forbidden phone contact with anyone outside. They lived in run-down wooden huts, with hardly enough to eat.

Aye Aye Win tried to escape with two other women. But factory guards caught them and dragged them back to the camp. They were punished as an example to others, tied to poles in the middle of the courtyard, and refused food or water. Aye Aye Win told me how her now beautiful hair was shaved off as another form of punishment to stigmatize her. And she described how she was beaten for trying to flee. In countries where desperation leads people to migrate, it is easy for human traffickers and recruiters to market a dream, or a lie, to vulnerable men, women, and children like Aye Aye Win.

## Dignity and Decency

It is important to clear up any misunderstanding about the difference between the issues of human trafficking and human smuggling or even illegal immigration—a charged topic in today's politics. Policies that conflate human trafficking and human smuggling or illegal immigration have the potential of punishing the very victims of trafficking whom we seek to protect. Human smuggling is the illicit transfer of someone across sovereign borders, often with the consent of the person being smuggled. Human trafficking involves a defining element of gross exploitation and control over an individual.

As recognized in both U.S. law and relevant international instruments, human trafficking victims either do not consent to their situations, or, if they initially consent, later become victims of force, fraud, or coercion—like Carlo. The ongoing exploitation of trafficking victims generates illicit profits. Yet the sooner we understand that migrants who are victims of human trafficking are just that—victims—the sooner we will have a proper perspective, which looks beyond simply law enforcement mechanisms, for grappling with how to confront this challenge.

Part of that perspective must be informed by a basic understanding of the human dignity which should be accorded to all people under natural law. By "natural law" I mean the broad category of universal principles of dignity and decency which, while not law in and of themselves, have historically informed our understanding of basic human rights from the Declaration of Independence to the United Nations Universal Declaration on Human Rights. President George W. Bush and Secretary of State Condoleezza Rice have called these principles "the non-negotiable demands of human dignity." Natural law has proved to be a powerful force—one which moves history. It triumphed over slavery before and it can triumph again.

For these principles to triumph, we must fashion instruments to overcome the rapacious and the sadistic. Presently there are national laws and policy, bilateral accords, and international instruments available which we can employ in the service of human dignity to eliminate the vulnerability of migrants to trafficking.

## International Trafficking

Among The Most compelling tools at our disposal is the *Protocol to Prevent, Suppress and Punish Trafficking in Persons, Especially Women and Children*, supplementing the *United Nations Convention against Transnational Organized Crime* (a mouthful, but a worthy one). This protocol requires parties to criminalize all trafficking in persons, including trafficking for purposes of forced labor or sex.

In some regions of the world, particularly Asia and the Middle East, a number of governments have entered into bilateral agreements or Memoranda of Understanding (MOUS) in order to encourage and formally manage the flow of migrant workers from one country to another. To date, however, very few contain provisions explicitly protecting workers from conditions of forced labor or other forms of trafficking in persons. Even a country such as Saudi Arabia, with an estimated 7 million migrant workers imported largely for "3D" work (dirty, dangerous, and difficult), does not have sufficient protection for migrant workers.

> *Natural law has proved to be a powerful force. It triumphed over slavery before and it can triumph again.*

We are encouraging labor-source and labor-destination governments in these regions to collaborate in confronting the problem of forced labor trafficking, including, when appropriate, through incorporation in bilateral agreements and Memoranda of Understanding specific measures to prevent trafficking in persons. Ironically, and tragically, some of those MOUS currently contain specific measures that promote trafficking, such as requiring the withholding of migrant workers' passports by employers in the destination country.

Labor-source governments should: 1) Prohibit and punish labor recruiters who participate in trafficking by securing workers through fraudulent offers or imposing fees meant to create situations of debt bondage; 2) Ensure that labor recruiters are properly vetted, licensed, and monitored; and 3) Increase efforts to raise awareness of the trafficking risk associated with labor recruitment and migration.

Labor-destination governments should consider steps to ensure that workers secured through third-party recruiters are not the victims of fraudulent work offers or conditions of debt bondage. The activities and practices of local labor brokers should be monitored, and such agencies, as well as employers, should be criminally accountable for acts of exploitation accomplished through force, fraud, or coercion against foreign workers.

All criminals responsible for human trafficking deserve potent penalties rather than suspended sentences or fines comparable to mere slaps on the wrist. Although there is still a massive lag in prosecution of forced labor trafficking versus sex trafficking cases, my office has noticed, in recent years, a rise in the number of reported cases of forced labor trafficking, some of which stem from otherwise legal transnational labor migration. But in many countries, there is official indifference in the face of labor trafficking, which is too often considered a civil, regulatory offense rather than a criminal act.

It is important that labor-destination governments encourage workers to report alleged cases of forced labor to law enforcement authorities and institute measures to ensure a worker can leave an abusive employer and seek legal redress without fear of automatic detention and deportation. Destination countries should take steps to make migrant workers aware of their rights. These efforts are invariably more effective where there are incentives for victims, such as provision of shelter, medical care, free legal aid with translation services, the ability to work while awaiting resolution of investigations, avenues for seeking restitution, and protection from possible retribution for having filed a complaint.

Finally, and perhaps most important, destination governments must ensure that exploitative employers and labor brokers are not allowed to abuse legal processes by having foreign workers who complain arrested, incarcerated, or deported. Workers who allege forced labor must have the opportunity to seek redress.

## Migrants

Human trafficking is also a phenomenon occurring within national borders. In Brazil, for example, forced labor has typically involved young men drawn from the impoverished Northeast states—Maranhao, Piaui, Tocantins, Para, Goias, and Ceara—to work in the northern and central western regions of the country. Although the law prohibits forced or compulsory labor, including by children, forced labor and trafficking of workers has occurred in many states, most commonly in activities such as forest clearing, logging, charcoal production, raising livestock, and agriculture, particularly harvesting sugarcane, coffee, and cotton. The ILO estimated that there were approximately 25,000 forced labor workers in Brazil during the year 2007.

Labor intermediaries trafficked most forced laborers to remote estates, where victims were forced to work in harsh conditions until they repaid inflated debts related to the costs of travel, tools, clothing, or food. Armed guards sometimes were used to retain laborers, but the remoteness of the location, confiscation of documents, and threats of legal action or physical harm usually were sufficient to prevent laborers from fleeing.

In Brazil, while the central government has announced a national plan to combat trafficking in persons, violators of forced labor laws enjoyed virtual impunity from criminal prosecution, and no landowner has ever been convicted and imprisoned for using slave labor. In a positive step forward, the Ministry of Labor and Employment did punish those who used slave labor by imposing fines, requiring that indemnities be paid to the workers and placing the names of violators on a "dirty list," which was published every six months on the Internet.

Given the nature of forced labor trafficking, it is necessary for our efforts to expand beyond government action. The ILO, for example, is reaching out to the private sector and has developed a list of ten promising practices to help employers prevent forced labor in their own enterprises and cooperate with broader efforts to combat forced labor and trafficking.[2] Goods enter the global marketplace while consumers have little or no knowledge of the supply chains and work conditions that resulted in their production. This is problematic for both the consumer and businesses which are increasingly faced with the challenge of ensuring that complex supply chains are untainted by forced labor.

Governments must protect victims of trafficking, including victims who are foreign migrants. For purposes of the annual U.S. *Trafficking in Persons Report,* one important component of victim protection considered is whether foreign victims of trafficking are provided with legal alternatives to deportation to countries where they face hardship or retribution. The *United Nations Protocol on Trafficking in Persons* also calls on state parties to consider offering victims of trafficking the ability to remain in their countries in appropriate cases.

North Koreans crossing the border with China are extremely vulnerable to trafficking given their illegal status in China and the harsh punishment they would face if they were to return home. Protection of victims should be the core principle of any effective anti-trafficking strategy. Greater government efforts need to be made to protect this highly vulnerable group.

At this time, China classifies North Korean refugees as "economic migrants" and forcibly returns some to the DPRK where, as noted, they may face severe punishment, including execution. The U.S. consistently urges China to treat North Korean asylum seekers in line with international agreements to which it is a signatory. The political sensitivity of this issue and a lack of transparency in China's law enforcement system have hampered our efforts to advocate effectively for change.

In many Persian Gulf states, which rely heavily on foreign migrant labor, individuals working as domestic servants, often migrant women, are particularly vulnerable to acute sexual and labor exploitation. They labor in low-paying, poorly regulated sectors. In many such countries, to be a woman or a migrant often means less than equal treatment under the law and in practice. But to be a woman migrant leaves you in a particularly precarious position. So-called sponsorship laws—prevalent throughout the Gulf—have in practice been abused in too many cases by unscrupulous employers who require the migrant worker to do whatever they demand or else run the risk of deportation due to alleged breach of contract.

## Less than Human

Nowhere is this more evident than in Saudi Arabia, where every month, hundreds of female migrants, recruited as domestic workers, flee Saudi households in which they face severe abuse including rape, physical beatings, confinement, and denial of wages. The perpetrators of these trafficking crimes are Saudi husbands and wives who, as part of the Gulf's "maid culture," see foreign servants as less than human and acceptable for exploitation. Unfortunately, Saudi Arabia's criminal justice system too often validates this culture of abuse by failing to hold traffickers accountable. Reflecting an abject lack of political will to address this crime, Saudi Arabia has been on the *TIP Report's* lowest ranking for four years in a row.

*Workers may escape abuse in private homes or work sites only to be denied an exit permit to leave the country.*

Take Nour Miyati, an Indonesian woman who sought a brighter future for her nine-year-old daughter. Nour worked as a domestic servant for four years in the Saudi Kingdom. She was treated fairly and was able to send money back home so that her daughter could stay in school. Then her fate took a turn under a new employer, who confined her to his house, denied her pay, and tortured her. Injuries she suffered to her hands and feet resulted in gangrene that required the amputation of her fingers and toes.

Tragically, Nour was twice victimized. Despite having escaped these horrific circumstances, she was arrested for "running away" under the country's sponsorship laws and was not accorded proper status as a victim of trafficking. Workers such as Nour may escape abuse in private homes or work sites only to be denied an exit permit to leave the country.

Labor-destination countries should have procedures in place to ensure that foreign workers are screened for evidence of trafficking prior to being removed for lack of legal immigration status. Training law enforcement officials and immigration officers on victim identification, or the deployment of trained victim identification specialists, are among the measures destination countries should consider in order to improve their ability to identify trafficking victims.

The exploitation of domestic workers is not unique to the Gulf. The 2008 *TIP Report* highlights the case of two women—Mala and Kamala—who came to the U.S. to work as domestic servants for an American family on Long Island, New York. They accepted an offer of work in a far-away country in hopes of improving the livelihood of their families back in rural Indonesia. Instead, what they encountered in an affluent community of suburban New York City was a form of modern-day slavery. The two domestic workers were subjected to beatings, threats, and confinement until, after years, they sought help. Their exploiters were tried and convicted on multiple criminal charges, including forced labor and "document servitude" (withholding a person's travel documents as a means to induce them into labor or service).

Trafficking of migrant women is particularly relevant in the realm of commercial sexual exploitation. As migration becomes increasingly feminized, more migrant women are at risk of being trafficked into prostitution. Lila, a 19-year-old Romanian girl, who had already endured physical and sexual abuse from her alcoholic father, was introduced by an "acquaintance" to a man who offered her a job as a housekeeper or salesperson in the UK. When she arrived in the UK, the man sold her to a pimp, and Lila was pushed into prostitution. She was threatened that she would be sent home in pieces if she didn't follow every order. After an attempted escape, her papers were confiscated and the beatings became more frequent and brutal. Months later, after being re-trafficked several times, Lila was freed in a police raid. She was eventually repatriated back to Romania, where after two months she fled from a shelter where she had been staying. Her whereabouts are unknown.

Migrants are abused nearby, not just in far-off lands. Molina, a 30-year-old Mexican, was held against her will and forced to work in a factory in Southern California making dresses from 5:30 in the morning until II at night, seven days a week. She was not allowed to take a shower or leave the factory; at night she shared a small bed with another woman. She received one meal of beans and rice a day. If she didn't sew fast enough, her boss would pull her hair, pinch and slap her. The factory doors were locked during the day and at night a watchman prevented her from leaving. "If we wouldn't do what she [her boss] said, she told us somebody who we love would pay the consequences," says Molina.

## Relief

To elicit cooperation from other nations in eradicating human trafficking, the U.S. needs to be seen as acknowledging that it confronts trafficking as well, as Molina's story illustrates, and that we are willing to share lessons learned as well as talk about areas where there is room for improvement. I work closely with domestic agencies to show other nations we are not just delivering diplomatic demands to others to change but are deeply committed to change ourselves. The U.S. government identifies our own areas for improvement in an annual self-assessment produced by the Department of Justice.[3]

Within the United States, the Trafficking Victims Protection Act of 2000 (TVPA), which created the office I direct, also created the "T" Visa which allows trafficking victims to remain in the United States to assist federal authorities in the investigation and prosecution of human trafficking cases, and to give them a place of refuge in the aftermath of severe exploitation. This status applies even to individuals who may have come here originally without proper documentation, if it is clear that they were victims of human trafficking.

From 2001 through January 2008, the U.S. Department of Homeland Security granted approximately 2,000 "T" visas to trafficking victims and their families, allowing them to remain in the United States. Human trafficking survivors from as many as 77 countries have been certified to receive certain U.S. federally-funded or administered benefits. Fortunately, Molina from the story above qualified for a "T" Visa under U.S. law and she now works as a security guard in Los Angeles; she's completed English classes and is working toward her GED.

While this victim-centered approach is laudable and something that we encourage foreign governments to consider, there is still room to improve at home. Many trafficking victims do not know that this form of relief exists. Greater government efforts need to be made to educate a highly vulnerable group of victims regarding what protections are available. Otherwise, as in so many countries, victims hidden in the shadows of complex, insidious manipulation—what sociologist Kevin Bales calls "disposable people"[4]—are afraid to come forward and seek help, afraid to be treated as criminals and illegal aliens.

The plight of exploited migrants, some of whom are susceptible to human trafficking, should not become enmeshed in our domestic immigration debate. We should be able to agree that those who arrive on our shores only to experience victimization in the form of human trafficking deserve proper care. As a global leader, we encourage the same response abroad.

## What To Do

In order to improve our awareness of forced labor abroad, and to discourage labor exploitation, the U.S. Department of Labor is currently developing a list of goods that the department has reason to believe are produced through forced labor or child labor in violation of international standards. The list, due in 2009, will serve as an awareness-raising tool for U.S. enforcement agencies, for the public, for governments, for NGOS, and ultimately for the business community. It is also consistent with U.S. government efforts to deny specific items produced, in part or wholly, by forced labor access to the U.S. market.

Amid the tremendous benefits that international migration brings, we cannot be blind to the dark side of the global economy—for it is in these shadows that trade in human beings is permitted to flourish. Whether it is an Indonesian migrant worker trapped in a factory in the Middle East, or an Eastern European girl prostituted and held captive in a brothel in Western Europe, or a young North Korean bride forcibly married to a Chinese man—these are the faces of modern-day slavery. They have become ensnared in human trafficking and forced labor and they demand our attention as they yearn for dignity.

Governments, both at the domestic level and through international cooperation, must work to improve protection for those migrants who are victims of trafficking while respecting their human rights—ensuring they are not treated as nonpeople. Most of these arrangements need not take the form of new treaties and multilateral institutions. As Anne-Marie Slaughter pointed out in *The Real New World Order,* "In this context, a world order based on government networks, working alongside and even in place of more traditional international institutions, holds great potential."[5]

To end the enslavement of some of the world's migrants, we need to focus on legal tools as well as other arrangements that further the fundamental principle of human dignity. This principle inspired Myres McDougal and Harold Lasswell, of the so-called New Haven school of legal thought, who wrote in 1959, "Our overriding aim is to clarify and aid in the implementation of a universal order of human dignity." To decrease migrants' vulnerabilities to human trafficking, we indeed need to focus on tools in public law (and also in less formal arrangements) which take into account the underlying concern of the New Haven school in advancing human dignity.

International cooperation can be achieved as well through the most prominent international instrument in this area, the *UN Trafficking in Persons Protocol,* a state-of-the-art UN instrument adopted in 2000, the same year that the U.S. Trafficking Victims Protection Act passed. The UN Protocol should be a touchstone, alongside ILO conventions and migration agreements, for confronting the special calamitous horror of human trafficking. More important than ratifying the protocol is implementing it. As important as enacting laws consonant with the protocol is vigorously enforcing them. Promoting human dignity is the common denominator in these arrangements, formal and informal, among or within nations designed to fulfill the natural law principle that fellow humans not be treated as less than human—as slaves. All governments, ours included, must embrace this obligation.

## Discussion

In 2010, the United Nations Office of Drugs and Crime [UNODC] generated a report entitled: "The Globalization of Crime—A Transnational Organized Crime Threat Assessment." The issue of human trafficking made the top of the list as a global concern. The trends identified in the report were alarming. In 2010, the UNODC identified victims from 127 countries. In addition, 137 countries identified trafficking victims within their borders [UNODC], 2010, p. 3).

Two-thirds of trafficking victims are women and 79% of victims are trafficked for sexual exploitation. After the collapse of the Soviet Union, Europe became a mecca for Eastern European women migrating mainly from Eastern Europe to the West. The end of the Soviet domination in the Balkans, and the former Soviet Union produced a shift in labor trends. From 2005 to 2006, fifty-one percent of these women came from the aforementioned countries and worked as prostitutes (UNODC. 2010). In the UNODC 2010 report, a new trend identified that most of women trafficked for the sex industry were from non-European countries. Once rescued, these laborers and sex workers find themselves classified as both victims and suspects. They are victims because of their detainment and exploitation by their captors, and suspects because in most cases they volunteered to violate the immigration laws of their host countries.

The UN identified smuggling of migrants (illegal immigration) as a major concern for the United States. The average worker in Latin American earns the equivalent of two U.S. dollars per day. These migrants are streaming across the Mexico–U.S. border. In 2008, 792,000 migrants entered the United States illegally.

Eighty-eight percent of the migrants were from Mexico and ninety percent of these migrants utilized professional smugglers (UNODC, 2010, p. 4). After paying a portion of their smuggling fee, the migrants began their hazardous journey from the border into the United States. They ended their travels in U.S. safe houses and were held as virtual hostages until their relatives paid the remainder of their smuggling fee. Eventually many of these illegal migrants are discovered by law enforcement and deported to their country of origin or are prosecuted by the federal authorities.

Why is this topic relevant to the criminal justice student or practitioner? The exploitation of humans for material gain is evil. It is the duty of practitioners to protect everyone regardless of their status as victim or suspect. We are bound by our professional ethos to do so.

As Americans survivors of the post 9/11 attacks, and citizens, we must remain vigilant to terrorist-related activities in our neighborhoods. As global citizens, we must apply that same level of vigilance to detecting cases of human slavery. After all, those victims are hidden in stash houses in our cities, towns, and neighborhoods awaiting rescue. They deserve our help.

## Questions for Class Discussion

1. Discuss debt bondage. Why is his practice so popular with workers? What risks do the workers take and why?
2. Compare and contrast the concepts of dignity, decency, and less-than human teatment.
3. Examine the relief efforts taken by the United States and other countries to curb human trafficking.

## Class Activities for the Professor

1. Utilize the questions for on-line discussions
2. In the classroom, divide the class into two panels and have them compare and contrast factors about international human trafficking.
3. Assign the students to find another journal article on human trafficking and have them write a research paper on past and current trends.
4. Assign the students to find another journal article or other reading on the topic. Assign the students to write a one-page summary and present those findings to the class.

## Works Cited

United Nations Office on Drugs and Crime, (2010), The "Globalization of Crime—A Transnational Organized Crime Threat Analysis", Vienna: United Nations.

"The King James Holy Bible". Hendrickson Bibles: (1873).

# Notes

1. Stanley Hoffmann, *Duties Beyond Borders: On the Limits and Possibilities of Ethical International Politics* (Syracuse University Press, 1981), III.

2. International Labour Organization. Special Action Program to Combat Forced Labour (SAP-FL). http://www.ilo.org/sapfl/Events/ILOevents/lang–en/WCMS_092176/index.htm.

3. *Attorney General's Annual Report to Congress and Assessment of the U.S. Government Activities to Combat Trafficking in Persons Fiscal Year 2007* (May 2008). http://www.usdoj.gov/ag/annualreports/tr2007/agreporthumantrafficing2007.pdf.

4. Kevin Bales, *Disposable People: New Slavery in the Global Economy* (University of California Press, 2000).

5. Anne-Marie Slaughter, *The Real New World Order* (Princeton University Press, 2005).

# Chapter 7: Boot Prints in the Sand

## The Global War on Afghan Heroin

> *Opium is a poison undermining our good customs and morality*
> Qing Empire, China, 1810

## Student Objectives

1. Compare and contrast Afghan culture and its relationship to opium production
2. Evaluate the link between the Taliban and transnational organized crime groups in Afghanistan
3. Analyze factors in opium cultivation before and after the U.S. invasion
4. Examine heroin trafficking trends and the impact on the world
5. Analyze the impact of Afghan heroin in the United States

My family was down range. My son Glenn, his wife Brialynn, my son-in-law Jason, my nephew Scott, and Glenn's uncle Ernest all left their boot prints in the sands of Afghanistan, Iraq, or in Jason's case, both countries. The invasion of Kuwait and the terrorist attacks on September 11, 2001, brought American troops and dozens of other coalition forces to the desert to fight terrorism and state-sponsored aggression.

As of this writing (2013) American troops and other coalition countries are still bringing the fight to the Taliban and other enemy fighters. The Afghanistan operation is called "Operation Enduring Freedom." According to the National Post (2013), 2,261 Americans have been killed in action and 19, 080 have been wounded fighting in Afghanistan. Most of the military troops killed are from the U.S. Army. The second highest casualty rate has been suffered by the marines. The deadliest years have been 2005–2008.

| | |
|---|---|
| **2008** | **1019 Killed in Action (KIA)** |
| **2007** | **918 KIA** |
| **2006** | **942 KIA** |
| **2005** | **900 KIA** |

This article and analysis that follows examines the global impact of Afghan opium cultivation and the power brokers who control the Central Asian heroin trade. These transnational crime groups are also directly involved in the chemical transformation of opium into morphine and heroin. The student will learn the methodologies used by transnational organized crime figures, "warlords" who traffic heroin throughout the world, and the unintended consequences of Afghan heroin use emerging in American communities.

## Understanding the Cultural Landscape

*Where is Afghanistan and how does its location contribute to regional conflicts?*

Afghanistan is located in Central Asia, bordering Turkmenistan, Uzbekistan, and Tajikistan to the north; China and India on the east; Iran on the west; and Biauchistan and Pakistan on the southeast (Rubin, 2007). Afghanistan's 1,270 mile border with its northern neighbors was a significant factor in the Soviet war in Afghanistan and contributes to the current drug trade (Rubin, 2007). The country is very poor and landlocked (CIA, 2014).

*Who are the Afghans and how do they live?*

With a population exceeding 31 million, Afghanistan is ethnically diverse. In the tribal areas more emphasis is placed on tribe, clan, and family, and less on government structure (Rubin, 2007).

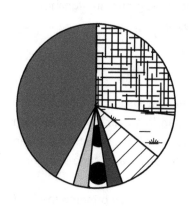

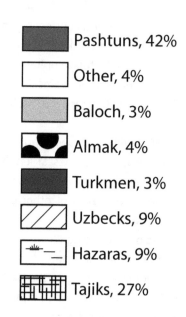

Pashtuns, 42%

Other, 4%

Baloch, 3%

Almak, 4%

Turkmen, 3%

Uzbecks, 9%

Hazaras, 9%

Tajiks, 27%

The economy has greatly improved due to international aid (Rubin, 2007). The majority of Afghans (78%) practice farming and sheep herding. The number one crop is opium followed by wheat, fruit, nuts, wool, and mutton. The standard of living is one of the lowest in the world and the unemployment rate is 35%. Young people comprise the largest group by age. The median age for males and females is equal at 17.9 years of age (CIA, 2014).

Health standards are extremely low. Medical care, especially in the tribal areas, is nearly nonexistent. Safe drinking water is a major problem and contributes to the water borne disease problem. Afghanistan has 0.21% physicians per 1,000 people. Infant mortality rate is number one in the world. Major infections include bacterial diarrhea, hepatitis A, typhoid fever, malaria, and rabies. "I was more afraid of rabies than of the enemy. It was common on patrol to have dogs charge soldiers near the farms and villages" (G. Lacher, personal communication, October 20, 2013).

## Describe what a Village Looks Like

Sergeant Glenn Lacher said: The people look as if they are in Biblical times. *The people are poor. The houses are made out of mud. There are no toilets. People will step out of their house and relieve themselves right next to the house. There were camel herders in the area. They were nomads who would migrate yearly from Pakistan. They would set up their tents by the side of the roads and in the fields,* (G. Lacher, personal communication, October 20, 2013).

### What are the Important Factors in Afghan Religion?

The majority of Afghans are Sunni Muslim (80%), while Shia Muslims account for only 19% of the population. Only one percent of the population practice religions other than Islam. Animosity between the Sunni and Shia Muslims is prevalent in the Muslim world. Globally, there are 100 million Shia while Sunnis number 1.7 billion. Sectarian violence is common place (Abdo, 2013).

Sergeant Glenn Lacher was embedded with Afghan troops. The American soldiers were trained to respect Islam. *Muslims are required to pray five times a day. When it was time to pray, our Afghan interpreter would inform us it was prayer time. So, even if we were in the middle of a combat patrol, the American soldiers would set up security. The Afghans would unroll their prayer rugs, and take off their shoes. They would wash their hands and feet with water from their canteens and pray. Once they were finished we continued our mission until the next prayer cycle* (G. Lacher, personal communication, October 20, 2013).

**Figure 1** Afghan women and children at stream (Source: Glenn Lacher)

## HEROIN

The next step in the trail of Afghan opium is the chemical conversion into morphine. Morphine was distilled in 1804. It appears in either liquid or powder form and was first widely used in the American Civil War. In 1857, the hypodermic needle and syringe were invented. These two close inventions led to the ability to inject morphine directly into the bloodstream. Indiscriminate morphine use on wounded Civil War soldiers caused widespread addiction problems (Narconon, 2013).

In 1874, a German chemist discovered heroin as a cure for morphine and opium addiction. The discovery of heroin led to the introduction of a powerful addictive substance. Heroin was marketed as a cure for morphine addiction.

Heroin (diacetylmorphine), is the potent derivative of morphine and is highly addictive (DEA, 1983, p. 170). Legally heroin is classified as a narcotic. Pharmacologically, heroin, morphine, and other opiates are called narcotic analgesics because they relieve pain and produce sleep.

I have debriefed hundreds of heroin users in my career. Heroin users describe that injecting or smoking heroin produces a "rush" or a warm feeling followed by euphoria, a feeling of well-being. Users report a reduction in fear and anxiety. The muscles in the neck relax to the point that users go into a state called being "on the nod." This state is characterized by the user resting their chin on their chest. They appear be in a state of drowsiness or lethargy (DEA, 1983, p. 170). The user is slow to react to verbal stimuli but is completely aware of their surroundings.

## SIGNS OF INFLUENCE

All the narcotic drugs will constrict the pupils except Demerol. Demerol is mainly abused by those in the medical field; due to its availability and the presence of normal size pupils mask influence or detection by other medical personnel. Raspy voice, drowsiness, on the nod, slow deliberate movements, slow speech, dry mouth, droopy eyelids, itching of the face, and the presence of recent

## What are the Roles of Afghan Women?

My son-in-law, Sergeant Jason Lilley served tours in Iraq and Afghanistan with the United States Marine Corps. He participated in helicopter operations in Iraq during the 2003 invasion and served in Afghanistan from 2009 to 2010.

In *the rural areas, women have no voice in Afghan culture. Long clothes and veils hide their features. Their primary function is child bearing and child care. You would see the women walking in the villages but they did not participate in conversations with outsiders. When we would talk to village elders, women were noticeably absent. Women and girls were not allowed to attend school or did not have schools to attend. Women are now attending the university in Kabul so things were changing in the cities but not in the tribal zones.*

*The Marine Corps sent female marines alongside female Afghan interpreters to talk to women in the tribal areas. The goal of the program was to establish trust, collect intelligence, and help rural women*

injection sites indicate being under the influence. Injection sites may not be present if the user ingests opiates orally, nasally, or smokes the drug.

## DEFINITIONS

**Figure 2.** Heroin

### Addiction

The user cannot abruptly stop using heroin without physically and psychologically desiring the drug.

### Withdrawal

If the user stops taking the drug they become sick. Symptoms include nausea, vomiting, severe tremors, muscle spasms, slow shallow breathing, clammy skin, convulsions, coma, and death.

### Cross-Tolerance

All opiate drugs, with enough strength or volume, will stop withdrawal symptoms.

### Overdose

Overdose is a medical condition where the ingestion of a substance causes the need for medical attention or death, due to the purity or volume of the drugs or combination of drugs

*understand what was happening outside of their villages. This idea was radical for the culture* (J. Lilley, personal communication, October 19, 2013).

Glenn Lacher agreed with Jason Lilley. *When we searched a village for weapons, the women would run into a room. We had American female soldiers with us on patrol with female Afghan interpreters. Our female soldiers would search the Afghans and ask them questions about the Taliban. As men we never talked to women. To do so would anger the Afghan men to the point of violence.*

## What are Some of the Cultural Norms?

Glenn Lacher gave his observations on the Afghan culture. *Showing respect to men and especially the village elder is central to Afghan culture. You shook hands with your right hand. You right hand also was for eating while your left was reserved for wiping your butt. Also if you were sitting down, you never showed the bottoms of your boots to an Afghan. Doing so was disrespectful.*

# The Rise of the Taliban

A short history lesson on Afghanistan and the rise of the Taliban will help connect the dots for this chapter on the Afghan heroin trade. Afghanistan is landlocked in the middle of Central Asia. The country is surrounded by Pakistan, Iran, China, Turkmenistan, Uzbekistan, and Tajikistan. The Stan countries were occupied by Russia for seventy years. Islam was crushed by the Soviets so the religion is not widely practiced in the Stans and northern Afghanistan. In contrast, in the remainder of Afghanistan, faith is a central part of life.

In 1978, the Saur Revolution overthrew the government in a bloody coup. After several political assassinations, a Marxist-Leninist government was formed. Islamic tribes waged war on the pro-Russian government.

In 1979, Russian Spetsnaz (1), disguised as travelers arrived in Afghanistan to support the Communist government. Over the next ten years, more than 500,000 Russian troops would fight the Mujahideen (2). The Mujahideen were Afghan tribal groups who followed the teachings of the Qur'an (3). During the Soviet occupation, more than 50,000 Russians were killed and over a million Afghans lost their lives.

Secretly, the United States, India, China, and the Saudis supported the Mujahideen by supplying weapons and Stinger missiles. One of the prominent Mujahideen leaders was Osama bin Laden. In 1989, the defeated Russian military left Afghanistan. After the Soviets retreated, the Hazara, Tajik, Uzbek and Pashtun tribes, who fought the Russians, waged a civil war against each other. In the ensuing conflict thousands of men, women, and children were raped, tortured, and murdered.

By 1994, the civil war had destroyed the government infrastructure creating chaos. Tribal areas were controlled by warlords. Bandits roamed the country killing and robbing at will. The people turned to Mullah Mohammed Omar (4) who was a Pashtun and an Islamist (5). Omar hated the warlords of the Hazaras, Tajiks, and Uzbeks whom he considered infidels (6).

Omar grew a 25,000-man Taliban army (7) from Islamic schools in Pakistan called Madrassas. Dating back to the middle ages, the schools taught the fundamental teachings of the Prophet Mohammad. Omar's goal was to create a 14th-century Islamic society in Afghanistan by Jihad (8). The Taliban effectively put an end to large scale opium cultivation.

By 1996, the Taliban controlled Kabul and banned music, photography, movies, television and perfume. People suffered greatly under Taliban rule. Women were forced to wear burkas (9). Offenders were beaten with rubber hoses. Women were banned from schools and medical care. One out of three women died in childbirth, and the literacy rate dropped to five percent. Public executions became the entertainment before soccer matches. Women were shot for various Islamic crimes. Persons suspected of theft had their hands cut off. Their severed hands were displayed on poles.

The Taliban fought the Mujahideen tribes called the Northern Alliance. On September 11, 2001, agents of Osama bin Laden flew planes into the Twin Towers in New York and the Pentagon in Washington D.C. Over three thousand Americans were killed in the attacks, including Muslim-Americans.

In November 2001, CIA para-military officers secretly entered Afghanistan and convinced the Northern Alliance to help America fight their mutual enemies; the Taliban. A team of U.S. Army

Special Forces (Green Berets) joined the CIA and fought the Taliban with the Northern Alliance. As of the writing of this book, the war continues against the Taliban. In addition to Pakistani and Afghan troops, Muslims from the Arab states, Chechnya, China and the United States, called "enemy fighters," have joined the fight against American and coalition forces. Currently, many of the aforementioned tribes figure prominently in the Afghan opium and heroin trade.

## Footnotes

1. "Spetsnaz", Russian for "special purpose forces"; they were established after World War II and were trained to fight U.S. soldiers in Europe. Spetsnaz troops are highly trained forces attached to the army and the navy. They conducted counter guerrilla warfare against the Mujahideen and have fought in Chechnya. Spetsnaz troops are part of the current coalition forces; U.S. forces train with the group. In 1993, I lectured to Spetsnaz-trained Lithuanian Special Forces called "Black Wolves." I was invited by Lithuania to teach western policing methods and met the Black Wolves commander. The colonel was former Spetsnaz and I happened to have brought a U.S. Green Beret lid with me to trade. The colonel was delighted when I gave him the beret as a gift. A few days later he presented me with a Russian general's winter dress cap. He later visited me at the Monrovia Police Department and we taught him how to shoot an MP-5 sub-machinegun.
2. "Mujahideen" translates to "strugglers or people doing jihad."
3. "Qur'an" or "Koran" is the holy book and teachings of the Prophet Mohammad in the religion of Islam.
4. "Mullah" refers to a Muslim who is educated in Islamic theology and sacred law.
5. Islamists support and advocate Islamic fundamentalism
6. "Infidel" means " without faith." To Muslims, the term refers to a person who rejects the belief in Allah as the True God.
7. "Taliban" means "seekers of knowledge."
8. "Jihad" means "holy war" or "struggle in the way of Allah;" the Islamic God. There are two types of Jihad mentioned in the Koran. The non-violent definition refers to the fulfillment of religious duties. It also means an armed struggle against persecution and oppression.
9. A burka or burqa is a full body garment worn by women when in pubic in the Islamic tradition.

## Works Cited:

Stanton, D. (2009). Horse *Soldiers: The extraordinary Story of a Band of U.S. Soldiers Who Rode to Victory in Afghanistan.* New York: Scribner

Moore, R. (2003). *The Hunt for Bin Laden.* New York: Random House

**Figure 3.** Afghan riding in horse chart. Afghan man riding in horse drawn cart next to US military vehicle. Photo by Glenn Lacher. (Source: Glenn Lacher)

*When we entered a village, the elder would greet us. We would sit down with him and he would make us an offering. The elder would offer us either a green tea or a milk tea. He would also give us flat bread and meat; usually goat. We would eat while the team leader, through our interpreter, would ask the elder about Taliban activity.*

## Do the Afghan People Want Americas in their Country?

Barnett Rubin, a U.S. diplomat who served in Afghanistan states that the feelings among Afghans are mixed. Certainly, the Taliban does not want Americans in the country. An elder who complained about government corruption told Rubin: *We have been with the Taliban and have seen their cruelty. People don't want them back.* A fruit trader from Kandahar commented: *The Taliban beat us and ask for food, and then the government beats us for helping the Taliban.*

Jason Lilley, USMC, observed just how important the American presence is to some Afghans: *I was admitted to a military hospital with a severe elbow infection. The doctors were talking about amputation. I was awaiting word if I would be transferred to the hospital in Germany. In a bed next to me was an Afghan interpreter. He had been shot in the back or the side by an enemy sniper. Interpreters are targeted first by the Taliban. Even with his wounds, he was talking of his appreciation of the marines for giving him food, clothes, money and status. He was worried what would happen to him when the Americans left the country. This was a common feeling amongst local Afghans*

*Another patient was brought into our room. An air Force para-rescue crew evacuated a six-year-old Afghan boy who had suffered shrapnel wounds over his entire body. The interpreter spoke to the boy's grandfather. The grandfather stated that even if his grandson's injury was from U.Sf fire he was glad we were in the country protecting them from the Taliban.*

*The child's injuries were inflicted by insurgents. The grandfather understood that his grandson received the wounds because of the American military presence but accepted it. He appreciated what the Americans were doing to defeat the Taliban and other enemy fighters. Once a local Afghan is discharged from the International Security Assistance Force Hospital, the Afghan is given food, money, clothes, and transport back to their village* (J. Lilley, personal communication, October 20, 2013).

## What do the Afghans Think of Drug use?

Sergeant Glenn Lacher stated: *I was not deployed in an area where they grew opium. Opium, marijuana, and hashish use among the Afghans is common-place. The local people chewed Neswa. The substance looked like brown balls. It could contain anything tobacco, marijuana, hashish, and sometimes opium. It was common for our Afghan army troop or border police to be on patrols with us and be high on opium, hashish, and they always chewed Neswa.*

**Figure 4.** Typical Afghan village. Photo by Glenn Lacher. (Source: Glenn Lacher)

**Figure 5.** Afghan compound owned by wealthy land owner. Notice rock used instead of mud typical of poor villages. The field is wheat. Photo by Glenn Lacher. (Source: Glenn Lacher)

## Chasing the Afghan Dragon

The expression "chasing the dragon" is a Chinese saying referring to smoking opium. In this chapter, we begin our analysis of the Afghan heroin trends utilizing the concept of interdisciplinary study. The chapter is about heroin but the reading is from the Journal of International Affairs. CJM students and police managers must have a firm grounding in foreign affairs, terrorism and homeland studies, and international relations to effectively evaluate contemporary issues.

Law enforcement must blend other academic disciplines with their experiences in criminal justice to effectively manage contemporary and future policing issues. Gaining interdisciplinary skill sets and applying new knowledge about organized transnational criminals is the only way to protect our nation and American interests abroad.

After reading the article, you will understand the pharmacology of opium, heroin and other drugs that mimic opiates. You will also have a firm grasp on the role that the Afghan drug trade plays on the international stage.

# Gaming the System: How Afghan Opium Underpins Local Power

By Justin Mankin

Afghanistan's non-democratic local powers grow stronger while international efforts to ballast Kabul's government falter, so robust central governance continues to remain elusive to Afghanistan's leaders. Despite the influx of foreign aid, development agendas, democratic processes and urbanization at the center, localities at the state's periphery—predominantly in the south—are heavily reliant on self-administration and service provision. Entrenched local administrative procedures, based on authority from tribalism or local power brokers' influence, continue to be resilient, while faith in the state is decreasing. Central incompetence, reinforced by endemic corruption and entrenched tribal mores, have fomented a growing sense of confusion and impotence within the country's institutions. This deterioration represents a failure of governance for the Afghan state: the inability to deliver services to the populace. 70 percent of the Afghan population still resides outside of the centrally administered areas in historically fragmented communities, creating political bulwarks that the Afghan government must breach to attain domestic legitimacy and build strong national institutions. Yet some successes are rightly highlighted. In the wake of the 2001 Bonn Agreement, ripples of change advanced: the foundation of the bicameral legislature was poured, de jure human and equal rights were established and the ground for democratic growth was tilled. These successes, however, should be noted with caution for one needs only to look to the fraudulent elections of 2009 to see that these young democratic fields are salted with many of the despotic power structures that have characterized their landscape for centuries.

Some of the very global economic forces that should, theoretically, overthrow the local political status quo are actually playing an important role in sustaining it. Afghanistan's local power brokers are using new opportunities arising from global integration within existing traditional power structures to augment and entrench their power in ways previously unachievable. The term "traditional," however, has two principal limitations. First, there is a question of how much today's tribal structures resemble those of the past; the structures are not static. Second, today's power brokers are revising and overturning "traditional" structure hierarchies, albeit governing in a similar fashion. As Barnett Rubin notes astutely, "Tribalism in the modern world is more often a strategy of state control or social resistance than the culture of an autarchic, kinship-based world that no longer exists, if it ever did."[1] Nonetheless, structures akin to those that have long prevailed still remain to the detriment of the state.

Among the most important forces that sustain these structures—and the focus of this essay—is economic integration. Specifically, it looks to the recent evolution of the Afghan opium trade as a case study. The opium trade includes all opiate-related activities bringing revenues to Afghanistan, from water rights and land tenure for poppies to heroin processing and trans-shipment.

Some observers paint a unidirectional relationship between the evolution of the opium trade and the Taliban insurgency, with the rise of a well-funded insurgency driving increases in cultivation in areas under their control. The impulse to view the opium trade as an indicator of instability is informed by at least two notions.[2] First, civil conflicts rage where they are financially viable—a function of natural resources ripe for exploitation—and eventually devolve into a conflict about the economics of war itself. This was convincingly articulated in Paul Collier's influential work on greed and grievance.[3] Second, the American experience in Colombia can be projected onto Afghanistan. There is considerable pressure to see the Taliban as analogous to the FARC and the drug-terror nexus as symbiotic and linear. It is natural for policymakers to view similar problems as analogues of one another, though it can come at the sacrifice of lasting policy solutions. The view of the Taliban as being similar to FARC may largely be shaped by the U.S. Drug Enforcement Administration's prominent role in both Colombia and Afghanistan.[4] Regardless of the logic to which they subscribe, the account is reductionist; it misses the richness of understanding and implications for policy that comes from viewing the opiate economy as a function of local power dynamics rather than simply insurgency or criminality.

Observers of Afghanistan rightly argue that the drug economy is evolving; modes of opiate production are consolidating in the southern provinces as poppy cultivation declines in the northern provinces. Some argue that the opium economy is reflective of successful counternarcotics (CN) campaigns in the north and the insurgency-fomented instability in the south, and further, that the southern consolidation is illustrative of progress in the fight against the drug trade. Touting the northern poppy cultivation decline as a success, Antonio Maria Costa, director of the United Nations Office on Drugs and Crime (UNODC), claimed in September 2009 that, "The bottom is starting to fall out of the Afghan opium market … the regional divide of opium cultivation between the south and rest of the country [mirrors] the security situation between the lawless south and relatively stable north of the country."[5]

I argue that the opiate economy's evolution is both a consequence of Afghanistan's local power structures and a cause of their further entrenchment. Local actors have developed innovative ways to participate in the drug economy consistent with their power typologies. It is this dynamic—not simply counternarcotics and insurgency—that has shaped the opium economy. Furthermore, despite regionalization, the trade is more nationally integrated than at any previous time. Progress in the drug war or

**Figure 6.** Enemy fighter detained by Afghan border police. Armed with a pistol and Russian hand grenades, this youth shot at US soldiers after he crossed into Afghanistan from Pakistan. Photo by Glenn Lacher. (Source: Glenn Lacher)

insurgency should therefore not be measured linearly, and attempts to categorize successes and failur such miss important considerations. Viewed through the lens of local power, the opium trade's southern consolidation is not a progression, as UNODC would claim, but rather a regression. It portends significant implications for the future of the democracy-building and development projects in Afghanistan.

In making my case, I will show that Afghanistan's local power structures principally have two typologies: those powers formed by the Afghan state, and those powers formed by Afghan society. The terms "state" and "society" are problematic when applied to Afghanistan as they do not accurately reflect what they purport to describe. "State" is here meant to capture the various attempts by domestic and foreign powers to politically consolidate the territory of Afghanistan. "Society," in contrast, describes the myriad societies and functions associated with tribal and traditional forms of governance. I use this paradigm to counter arguments about the causes and implications of change in the opiate economy. From a strategic perspective, my account aims to contribute to the larger discourse on local power in an era of globalization.

## Mapping Local Power in Afghanistan

In exploring the continued importance of Afghanistan's local power structures, it is useful to map two local power typologies: those powers that form out of the state and those borne of society. The projection of this simple map is informed by two prevailing theories of the genesis of local power. The first argues that local despotic power structures are the form, function and manifestation of the state, even a democratic one. The second claims that the source of local power lies with society.[6] Using both of these theoretical approaches, a simple geographic model can be generated: local power structures in the north of Afghanistan are generally more a product of the state, while those power structures in the south are more reflective of society. In very general terms, good proxies for evaluating the state and society model are ethnicity, which is distinctly geographical in Afghanistan, and proximity to the governmental center, Kabul, as will be explored below. Tajiks and Uzbeks largely control authority and local power in the north with their power stemming more from the state; in the south, local power is generally controlled by Pashtuns and the Baluch and is borne more of society. This paradigm is too simplistic to capture or account for the myriad exceptions to it, but it is useful in examining the evolution of the drug trade from the perspective of local power.

Many of the modern forms of local power in northern Afghanistan are products of militarism, an outcome of the country's long history of failed attempts at national consolidation, from Ahmad Shah Durrani to the current Karzai regime. Northern local power elites were generally created by the state as well as by world powers. Colonization strategy generated and exploited power asymmetries; the Soviets co-opted the ethnic Tajiks and Uzbeks in the north rather than the southern Pashtuns, more due to geography than innate ethnic characteristics. Tajikistan and Uzbekistan were Soviet republics and comprised of the very ethnic groups that make up northern Afghanistan. Further, much of the "economic and security infrastructure of the Afghan regime was located in [the north], which was increasingly integrated [ … into] the Central Asian Republics."[7]

The new Afghan elites and rulers are a product of an education system created by foreign powers and designed to overthrow social mores of familial and tribal identity, creating a new intelligentsia.[8] This education, coupled with billions of dollars in military aid to these elites, gave them the means and, once the aid dried up, the incentive to raise militias.[9] Northern power broker and Junbish-e-Milli leader Abdul Rashid Dostum, for example, was a product of Soviet training, despite eventually turning on his patrons.[10] Although leaders in the north, such as Dostum, do claim kinship identities, their form of

.itarism. In contrast to the Pashtuns and Baluch of the south, tribal codes and
.nwali do not characterize Tajik and Uzbek pedigrees.[11]

.re the focus of much discussion about traditional and tribal governance in
, the successful maintenance of local power is contingent first and foremost on
This may be, in part, reflective of the general political disenfranchisement many
to Kabul, which begets further reliance on tribal structures. Pashtun tribal dynam-
.. There have been cases where, like northerners, Pashtun warlords have risen to
prom... .bb and flow of tribal dynamics among Pashtuns, however, has meant that the political
space at the .. . level for a modern conception of the state is fleeting, if it even exists at all. Insofar
as state-legitimized power has existed among Pashtuns, tribal legitimization has also been necessary.
Muhammad Nasim Akhundzada, for example, was legitimized as a powerful Helmandi warlord by both
military prowess and his tribal lineage.[13]

## The Opium Economy and Local Power

The opiate trade plays a convoluted role within the larger political economy of governance and violence
in Afghanistan. It would be reductionist to suggest that the drug trade foments instability or, further,
that the drug economy *is* the war economy. Unfortunately, as others have noted, it is challenging to
separate the role of resource exploitation in the origins of conflict from its influence on the conflict's
longevity and form.[14] Fundamentally, the Afghan opiate economy does play a part in sustaining the
Taliban insurgency; it is a symptom of and fuel for the larger political economy of war.[15] Were the drug
trade removed from Afghanistan, however, the Taliban would still be a powerful insurgent force seeking
to overthrow the Karzai regime. The Taliban-led insurgency is by no means the drug trade's *raison d'être*,
nor does it follow that the insurgency is a product of the drug trade.[16] Clearly there are overlaps between
Taliban elements and opium–the two influence one another and are being driven closer together–but it
remains the case that the two are discrete entities and will be treated as such for this analysis.

Far more important for the purposes of this essay is the opium trade's role in underpinning and
perpetuating local power. Integral to the increasing strength of local power structures in southern
Afghanistan has been the recent consolidation of the opiate economy, the evolution of which is a by-
product of globalization. The trade is undergoing an evolution from a decentralized and diffuse economy
to one governed by a pattern of geographic hierarchy. It is further characterized by vertical and national
integration of the opiate business and prosperous local governance.[17] Savvy tribal leaders and warlords
in the south are slowly building a model of accumulating social and political capital via the provision
of political protection from the north. Primitive accumulation from the evolving drug economy has
been pivotal to the development of this model of governance, which is one that reaffirms local power
structures in both the north and south.

## The Evolution of the Opiate Economy and Local Power in the North

Poppy cultivation in eastern and northern provinces, particularly in major production hubs such as
Badakhshan and Nangarhar, dropped precipitously in 2008 compared to years past.[18] Northern power
brokers are, however, no less complicit in the new opium economy. The UN is quick to cite the northern
cultivation decline as a success, resultant from "the extensive eradication of opium poppy crops …

conducted by Governors," particularly in 2007.[19] Low cultivation levels in the north have held for 2009 as well. This account sees declining cultivation as sufficient for success, whereas I do not. The drop in cultivation may in part be spurred by lower farm gate prices of opium, as some argue, but can alternatively be viewed as a product of the prevailing local power structures in the north. Much of the drug trade in the north and east of Afghanistan was once controlled by many of the warlords and power brokers who have since reached accommodation with the state.[20] This is reflective of the fact that many of the power structures in the north and east are endowed more with authority from the state than from traditional Afghan society. Those power brokers who were drug producers (many of whom serve as Kabul's security officials) were subject to political pressure to stop illicit activities. Given that many local power brokers in the north garner legitimacy from the state, however, it is likely that they stand to profit whether or not poppy is planted in northern ground. This is the case for three reasons. First, they maintain their official positions and by extension their local power. Second, local power brokers stand to gain considerable rewards and political currency with good performance on poppy cultivation. Finally, local profits from the opiate economy do not end with poppy production. Local power brokers in the north stand to gain from eradication, the emerging "criminal protection industry," and the processing and trans-shipment markets.[21]

For northern strongmen, by virtue of their intimate relationship with the state, control of their local bailiwicks is in part dependent on their continued legitimacy vis-à-vis the state. Thus, they cannot participate in the drug trade in a way that exposes them to anything beyond rumor of involvement. Some officials have been rotated out of official positions (to the detriment of their local power structures and influence) because of their direct involvement in the trade. In many cases, though, demotion was more likely a product of political targeting than effective counternarcotics. These cases of political rotation have nonetheless helped drive the northern evolution, a reduction in direct production involvement with the opium trade and a consolidation of ancillary functions associated with the opium economy. Northern power brokers help engender the political climate that allows for tremendous cultivation in the south.

The cases of Mohammed Atta and Haji Zahir illustrate the new realities of how those local power brokers that are connected with the state participate in the drug trade.[22] Haji Zahir, unlike many northern officials, is Pashtun, and provides an example of how proximity to the political center, Kabul, can be a proxy for the typology of local power. His case illustrates how, for northern powers, direct involvement in the drug trade comes at the detriment of their position with the state, and by extension, their local power. Zahir was a well-connected border commander in Nangarhar Province who, despite his pedigree, was not immune to the state's ability to disrupt local power structures.[23] Zahir was rotated out of his palatial Jalalabad home and sent to a new post far to the north in Takhar province, a major trans-shipment point for opium. His corruption, however, was viewed as egregious, and Zahir was stripped of his position.[24] Zahir's example demonstrated to other northern officials that there were limits to how one could participate in the drug economy, reinforcing a southern consolidation of the means of opiate production.

The Zahir case highlights that northern officials are vulnerable to scrutiny by the state. Practically, this means that northern power brokers cannot be as close to the drug trade as southern power brokers. This may be a product of the fact that Karzai does not rely on the northern power brokers for political support and power projection as he does the southern ones. It remains, however, that northern strongmen no longer have legitimacy by virtue of their military might alone; support from the state is necessary as is reflected in the evolution of the opium economy into a mostly southern phenomenon.

**Figure 7.** Typical mud huts inside Afghan village with local residents. Photo by Glenn Lacher. (Source: Glenn Lacher)

---

The case of Mohammad Atta shows how indirect involvement is more politically viable for a local power broker who fits the northern typology. Mohammad Atta, governor of one-time opiate hub Balkh province, and a former opium profiteer, successfully enforced a cultivation ban in 2006, "consolidat[ing] his power while also building his legitimacy and bargaining position vis-à-vis central government and international players."[25] Despite a lack of cultivation there, Mazar-e Sharif (Balkh's capital), is still a destination of a significant number of drug-related money transactions from southern cities.[26]

Northern local strongmen like Atta stand to gain from counternarcotics campaigns. "Good performers" receive political currency and development aid for enforcing Kabul's counterdrug edicts. Further, other drug crops that garner less scrutiny, such as cannabis, are profitable, viable and are likely funding northern power. Many power brokers use drug proceeds to invest in and develop the local community as a mechanism for ensuring their longevity. It is likely arbitrary for a northern power broker if this development comes from aid or from drugs—now it comes from both. Local officials can then claim credit for helping to establish hubs of prosperity and maintaining an obliged populace of satisfied locals.

The Atta case shows that northern local power brokers stand to profit through both the corruption surrounding eradication and the state incentives to enforce alternative livelihoods. The bargaining around planting and eradication is subject to corrupt dealings and profits, particularly when pursued by local power brokers.[27] Further, those officials who have opium stockpiles benefit from the increase in opium prices caused by the decrease in northern production. Poppy eradication can raise profits for local power brokers, for it "raises the price of opium [and further ... it] does not provide for a sustainable reduction in the drug economy, nor does sustainable reduction of the drug economy start with eradication."[28]

Another feature of the evolution of the drug trade in the north is the possible trend toward regional specialization of the opium trade's ancillary functions. As recourse for profiting while maintaining plausible deniability, northern officials have specialized in protection rackets, or what some call the "criminal protection industry." An anonymous Afghan official said of criminal protection, "This is [not] illegal business in Afghanistan … this is business."[29] And business is good. Thus, as in many other developing countries, clientelism abounds; the process of appointments generates big profits. Officials along smuggling routes in the north of Afghanistan, major trading arteries to consumer markets in Russia and the Commonwealth of Independent States (CIS), are in the business of securing bribes for the appointment of sympathetic, corrupt or weak officials.[30] Once a corrupt official is in place, s/he becomes part of the reinforced web of protection and patronage.

Profits stem from more than protection rackets, appointment bribes and international aid packages to good performers. Despite a decrease in cultivation in the north, Afghan poppy crops still total well over 100,000 hectares—more than double the average cultivation between 1994–2001.[31] Opiates still traverse the Afghan landscape prolifically, which means profits from smuggling. "One border police commander in eastern Afghanistan was estimated by counternarcotic officials to take home $400,000 a month from heroin smuggling."[32] Though speculative, this commander is likely Haji Zahir who, during his time in Nangarhar Province, oversaw the important trade route through the Khyber Pass into Pakistan.

Northern local power brokers have monopolized the profits from the ancillary aspects and support activities of the opium economy—those sectors of the trade outside of traditional opiate operations. Thus, for northern power brokers who also serve as Kabul's local administrators, the anti-poppy

**Figure 8.** Afghan 9 year old boy shooting an AK-47 (Source: Glenn Lacher)

campaign has become as much a function of their local power structure as the cultivation once was; the evolution of the drug trade is both a cause and consequence of their local power. The trend points to the evolution of the opium trade as a product of their power: the functionalism of corruption and the decline in cultivation are both shaping and sustaining the structure of local power.[33]

## The Evolution of the Opiate Economy and Local Power in the South

The north's new supporting role has allowed the south to consolidate the sectors of production. Increased risks have led to rewards associated with the opium economy. Due to the pyramids of protection and patronage, now, "only larger traders can afford the increased bribes and protection from political authorities."[34]

A consolidation of the means of opiate production in the south of Afghanistan is consistent with and reflective of the forms of local power there. In the north, the local power stems largely from militarism; the legitimacy associated with governance may prove elusive to these power brokers, which is why so many northern powers rely on state-endowed legitimacy. In contrast, in the southern Pashtun belt, charismatic leadership and authority within tribal structures are generally the primary sources of power. Southern power brokers, therefore, have to maintain an obliged populace that is integral to sustaining their position. Authority within the tribe is a project of constant maintenance; southern power brokers

**Figure 9.** A local reporter interviewing an Afghan poppy farmer in his field. (Source: http://commons.wikimedia. org/wiki/File:Afghan_poppies.jpg. Copyright in the Public Domain.)

"must procure and redistribute resources from [without; … their] followers expect material or symbolic advantages from them."[35]

Self-administration and local governance is key, as local *khans* amass political capital through the provision of political and economic goods in the absence of the state. Vertical integration on the part of southern power brokers has meant an increase in their share of the value chain of opium production. The technical capacity and expertise required for opium refinement formerly resided outside of Afghanistan in Turkish and Kurdish laboratories.[36] Refining opium into morphine base and refining morphine into heroin are arduous processes with both potential missteps and profits increasing dramatically along the value chain. Southern Afghanistan has increasingly developed the capacity to perform these refinements, thus capturing more of the added value. Some 90 percent of the opium is now processed in Afghanistan. With this vertical integration comes a windfall of profits: The potential value of the 2008 opium harvest for the Afghan economy was about US $3.4 billion.[37]

Competition within the trade has consolidated modes of production into the hands of a few. The barriers to entering the opiate trade have increased due to the requirements of technical savvy, international connections, manpower and wealth, all of which are needed to run a more vertically integrated opium smuggling business. By some estimates, there are about twenty high-level traffickers, many of whom wield tribal authority and provide de facto governance structures.[38] As local power brokers in the south assert more control over the value chain, accumulation of capital occurs. Some of the accumulation is reinvested in the local tribe as smugglers make the import-export contacts to bring in cellular phones, vehicles and other goods in a local area. This use of opiate revenues to enrich not just the trafficking organization, but also an obliged populace of tribal followers is important in the south. Though the rules governing tribal hierarchies have been distorted in response to huge drug revenues, the forms of local power remain resilient.

The simplistic view that drugs equal instability and insurgency does not capture this complexity: the drug trade can alternatively be viewed as a metric for local development. The trade resides in border communities, prompting exchanges in goods and the creation of infrastructure for service provision. This in turn leads to the establishment of legitimate businesses that fortify illegitimate ones—tea houses, fuel depots and schools, vehicle, cell phone and durable good imports—all of which give power brokers stature and play a role in their opiate operations while providing political and economic goods for locals. The drug trade "also funds the real estate speculation behind the construction boom and rise of business," many of which would not be built were it not for the drug trade.[39] Again, the assumption that the correlation between drugs and instability is linear does not hold. The stability and opportunities the trade provides, though strategically pernicious, are important to the local level and thus are important to understand.

Tribal largesse is part of the equation as well. Trafficking lieutenants with tribal authority use capital from drug revenues for the important performances associated with the maintenance of tribal power such as weddings, burials and pilgrimages.[40] Particularly in the wealthy areas, drugs provide locals with land, credit, water and employment.[41] There is an impulse to reduce the role of these networks to simple criminality—to make them indivisible from the insurgency—but these power brokers play an important political and developmental role for their obliged populaces. Moreover, this dynamic is entirely consistent with traditional forms of southern power.

Take, for example, the case of Haji Juma Khan, a Baluch trafficker recently extradited to the United States.[42] Khan long ran a tribally based smuggling empire on the Afghanistan-Pakistan frontier, from Nimroz province to Quetta.[43] His nephews and his Mohammadhasni clan continue to operate a significant network.[44] Khan, despite having wielded tremendous tribal authority, is discussed more in terms of his relationship with the Taliban, having in the past provided drug revenues and safe haven for their attacks on coalition forces.[45] This association is what prompted the eventually successful, though decade-long, targeting by international law enforcement and intelligence.

If instead of simply viewing Khan as a drug trafficker, however, one examines him as a local power broker, his relationship with the Taliban appears more nuanced. As a powerful Baluch tribal leader, he was responsible for a significant number of people in a predominantly Pashtun region, where there is considerable tension between the two ethnicities. Khan more likely paid the Taliban (a Pashtun-dominated movement) out of political expediency to maintain stability in both his business and in his tribal populace than out of sympathy for the Taliban ideology. Further, Khan sought to ensure his power through the use of the criminal protection industry of the north; he pursued amnesty in return for investing his drug revenues into rebuilding the country.[46] Khan's strategy was to use his drug proceeds to develop, govern and provide security for his followers in the absence of the state.

More notable than the difficulty of targeting Khan, this case highlights the role of maintaining an environment conducive to opium production and local power. An environment suspended between strategic instability and tactical stability is ideal for the cultivation of poppies and the processing of opium. Thus, many of the overtures that local power brokers make to the Taliban are likely efforts to strike this balance between tactical stability and strategic instability, rather than out of ideological alignment. Khan, for example, likely paid the Taliban to ensure that his operations moved along unabated at a tactical level, while fomenting the instability and power vacuum through tacit support of the insurgency at a strategic level. This highlights the danger with policymakers' tendency to paint drug networks and the Taliban with the same broad brush: while defining and targeting them the same way drives them closer together, there exists a means to cleave the two apart.

Another mistaken analysis is to confuse a correlation between insecurity and poppy cultivation with causality. Stability at the local level is necessary not only for poppy cultivation—crops are static, labor-intensive and require security—but also for maintaining allegiance from tribal followers. The opiate economy not only provides the economic opportunities at the local level, it also provides the incentives and revenues for stability. Local and tribal elites provide political goods to build their power, but by extension also build local stability, prosperity and its maintenance therein.

The case of Musa Qala in Helmand province during the 2006 cultivation season provides an instructive example. Helmand is the most prolific opium source in Afghanistan, and Musa Qala is one of the province's most prolific cultivation districts and fiercely contested by the Taliban.[47] Thus, for the local power structure invested in the opiate trade, stability comes at a high cost: negotiating a ceasefire with the Taliban. The *shura*, or tribal council, negotiated a settlement with the Taliban after the insurgent force overran the town center in October of 2006.[48] Notably, this ceasefire was negotiated in the weeks just prior to the closing of the poppy-planting window in the district, the month of November. Once the crop was in the ground, the incentives for the local Alizai tribe to ensure the stability to harvest would have been significant. The heavy fighting in the district center and fields might have meant farmers could not plant the crop without risk to their lives. If the fields were too insecure to harvest, my simple calculations indicate a potential profit loss of nearly US $46 million to Musa Qala's populace.[49] This would be a huge loss for any developing local economy to sustain, let alone a small district in southern Afghanistan. A huge source of labor, tribal largesse and prosperity would have disappeared if the *shura* had not pursued ceasefires concurrent with the lead-up to poppy planting or the harvest.

In this case, the local power brokers, consistent with their power typology, that of society, sought to provide the stability needed to maintain their authority in their bailiwick, even though that meant dealing directly with the Taliban. The revenues from the drug trade provide not just the hard currency for prosperity in a local area, but also the political currency needed to hold authority over their people. In the absence of a strong state, local power brokers are able to use the exploding opium economy to entrench themselves within their community as de facto administrators, indispensable to both locals and the central administration of the government.

## Conclusion

I have argued that a major linchpin for the trend toward further entrenchment of non-democratic governance structures has been the opiate economy, as both a cause and consequence of local power. This paper highlights that attempts to paint the evolution of the opiate economy as a sign of counternarcotics' success need to be carefully considered. Success may actually be failure in this instance, as the powers that participate in the trade find innovative ways to entrench themselves, the trade and their ability to generate profits and to govern at the sacrifice of the state. Though self-administration by local power brokers with nominal allegiance to the state is strategically beneficial to Kabul in the short-term, this reliance on rural self-administration will inhibit the unification and democratization of the Afghan state in the long-term. Like the difficulty in addressing late development in the contemporary world, Afghan democratization within the context of globalization presents numerous obstacles that must first be acknowledged so that they might be overcome.

**Figure 10.** Nomadic Kuchi People. (Source: http://commons.wikimedia.org/wiki/File:Nomadic_Kuchi_people. jpg. Copyright in the Public Domain.)

# Discussion

## Walking the Opium Trail

The opium poppy looks like any of the other over 200 types of poppy found in the world. Our culprit is the only poppy plant that produces opium. Opium is produced by *Papaver somniferum L.* Opium is a naturally occurring alkaloid found in this poppy (Drug Enforcement Administration [DEA], 1983, p. 169).

The most important chemicals found in opium include morphine, codeine and thebaine. Thebaine is paramophine. It is poisonous and used to produce two strong synthetic opiates called oxymorphone and oxycodone (DEA, 1983).

Opium will grow in all temperate climates. Afghan opium poppies produce a higher potency of opium than the Southeast Asian countries of Laos and Myanmar. Afghanistan now produces 90% of the opium on the planet (UN, 2010).

The majority of Afghan opium is grown in a few provinces that ironically are controlled by the Taliban. Afghan law enforcement experts fear that when the United States military withdraws from Afghanistan, the nation will become a true narco-state (UN-Afghan Assessment, 2013).

For years the United States and Afghan Ministry of the Interior have conducted poppy eradication efforts in the country, including aerial chemical dusting. The efforts have eradicated hundreds of acres of opium but the unintended consequence is that these antidrug efforts allowed the Taliban to win the loyalty of the opium farmers (Rubin, 2007, p. 63).

For centuries, opium cultivation has used hand methods to extract the opium liquid. That certainly is the case in Afghanistan. After the leaves fall from the flower, the exposed bulb is sliced with a knife and the latex substance oozes out and quickly dries. After the bulbs are dried, the substance is collected into bags for transport to heroin labs (DEA, 1983).

In the past, morphine and heroin were not chemically converted from opium inside Afghanistan. Raw opium was transported by truck and converted into heroin in Pakistan. A new trend has developed. Afghan transnational groups have established large conversion labs in the tribal belt along the Pakistani border (UNODC, 2013).

This area is controlled by the Taliban. Protection money from drug profits placed in the pockets of the Taliban fuel the insurgency against the coalition. Experts believe if the U.S. military and the Afghan National Army swept through and conquered these few provinces, the heroin market would fall (UNODC, 2010).

# Heroin Consumption and Trafficking Trends

Since 2010, 450 tons of heroin have hit the global market. It is estimated that 50 tons of the drug are exported by Myanmar and Laos. In contrast, Afghanistan exports 380 tons of heroin/morphine annually (UNODC, 2010). The Taliban has taken advantage of antidrug policies established by the United States to protect and win the loyalty of the opium farmers. This practice funnels money back to the Taliban to fight the U.S. military and coalition forces (Rubin, 2007, p. 63).

Five major drug trafficking groups on the Afghan side of the border and one insurgent group (Hizb-I-Islami) control the distribution operations. The Traffickers have established a sophisticated truck transport system to reach foreign markets. Tapping into ties in the region with their ethnic brethren, the Tajiks, heroin crosses out of Afghanistan and into border countries to reach the international markets. Assisting the Afghan traffickers are corrupt officials, warlords, and smaller tribal clans, and family groups (UNODC, 2010).

Experts estimate out of the 380 tons of heroin processed in Afghanistan, 105 tons travels through Pakistan and 95 tons snakes through Tajikistan, Uzbekistan, and Turkmenistan to reach markets in Europe, Russia, and Asia (UNODC, 2010).

The profits are staggering, 20 billion dollars earned from Western European markets, while the sales in Russia hit 13 billion U.S. dollars. Profit information was not available for Afghan heroin reaching Southeast Asia, China, India, Iran and Australia. There is evidence to suggest that Afghan heroin has reached Latin America and Mexico. Experts believe that a significant amount of Afghan heroin may have entered the United States (UNODC, 2013).

Who is consuming this much heroin? With a user population of 1.5 million addicts, the Russian Federation consumes most of the world's heroin. Iran and Europe are tied for second place. China follows third. The U.S. and Canada combined are tied for fourth place. The continent of Africa takes fifth place.

## Connecting the Dots

What impact will Afghan heroin have on the United States? Heroin is a significant problem in the nation. According to the National Institute on Drug Abuse, it is estimated that there are 4.2 million Americans, 12 years and older who have tried heroin once. There are approximately 1.2 million occasional heroin users in the U.S. of which, 200,000 are classified as addicts. The Centers for Disease Control and Prevention [CDC] reported that heroin users account for 201,000 ER visits annually. A new trend has been identified. Due to stricter controls on prescription opioids, users are turning to heroin because it is easier to obtain. Based on this trend, the United States is likely to see a significant increase in Oxytocin and Vicodin users switching to heroin to prevent withdrawals.

Every street cop will tell you that heroin users commit crimes to support their habit. The most common crimes are thefts and prostitution. Many addicts commit more serious crime such as robberies and residential burglaries.

Mexico grows opium and produces Black Tar heroin. The country is the source for the smuggling of heroin and cocaine into the United States. Black Tar is a very potent type of heroin. Afghan heroin has the highest purity level and is cheap to buy. I wonder what future trends will be identified as Afghan heroin becomes widely available on the streets.

I think the most significant impact that Afghan heroin will pose in America will be the response by Mexican drug cartels. Will the cartels partner with the Afghani groups or will warfare erupt between the groups for control of the heroin trade in the United States. The federal government has not effectively sealed our border from the Mexican drug cartels so any scenario is plausible.

Will the cartels employ new terror techniques that they learn from Afghani terrorists against U.S. interests? Another impact to consider is the 2014 troop reduction in Afghanistan. Will this move plunge Afghanistan into civil war?

One only needs to study history. After World War II and the Korean and Vietnam conflicts many indigenous people were granted asylum in the United States. If civil war erupts, Afghans will migrate to American in droves. Such an influx of Afghans into the U.S. will give transnational heroin groups and terrorists the means to hide within Afghan communities.

If Afghan transnational organized crime groups establish working relationships with the Mexican drug cartels, the move will pose a significant risk to our homeland security efforts. In addition, this trend will have a profound impact on law enforcement and corrections.

## Questions for Class Discussion

1. What have been the results of U.S. anti-poppy policies in Afghanistan?
2. What measures by the U.S. and the Afghan governments might curb opium poppy cultivation?
3. What steps can be taken to curb the market appeal of heroin?

## Class Activities for the Professor

1. Assign the students to write a research paper comparing and contrasting Afghan heroin traffickers with Latin American cocaine traffickers.
2. Assign the students to find a journal article on any factors related to heroin. The students should write a reflection paper and present their findings in class.
3. Utilize the discussion questions for on-line chats.

## Works Cited

Abdo, G., (2013, October). "Why Sunni-Shia Conflict is Worsening", Retrieved from www.cnn.com/opinion.

Centesr for Disease Control, (2010. July), "Unintentional Drug Poisoning in the United States", Retrieved from www.cdc.gov.

Central Intelligence Agency, (2014), "CIA World Fact Book", *New York,* Skyhorse Publishing.

Drug Enforcement Administration, (1983), "Narcotic Investigators Manual", Washington DC.

Rubin, Barnett, (2007), "Saving Afghanistan", Foreign Affairs, Volume 86, No 1.

United Nations Office on Drugs and Crime, Islamic Republic of Afghanistan, Ministry of Counter Narcotics, (2013), Afghanistan-Opium Risk Assessment, Vienna.

United Nations Office on Drugs and Crime (2010), The Globalization of Crime—A Transnational Organized Crime Threat Assessment, Vienna

# Notes

\* Afghanistan was the author's professional focus for several years while he worked as a U.S. intelligence officer.

1. Barnett Rubin, *The Fragmentation of Afghanistan: State Formation and Collapse in the International System* (New Haven: Yale University Press, 1995), 5.

2. For many people examining the Taliban insurgency, "opium has become an index of insecurity," but this is too simplistic, as there "is no universal, one-directional relationship between drugs, corruption and conflict." Jonathan Goodhand, "Poppy, Politics and Statebuilding," in *Afghanistan: Transition Under Threat,* ed. Geoffrey Hayes and Mark Sedra (Waterloo, Ont.: Wilfrid Laurier University Press & CIGI, 2008), 51–89.

3. See Paul Collier, "Economic Causes of Civil Conflict and their Implications for Policy," in *Leashing the Dogs of War: Conflict Management in a Divided World,* ed. Chester Crocker, Fen Osier Hampson, and Pamela Aall (Washington, D.C.: USIP Press Books, 2007), 197–218; Paul Collier and Anke Hoeffler, "Greed and Grievance in Civil War," World Bank Policy Research Paper 2355 (Washington, DC: World Bank, 2000).

4. See in particular the summary of remarks of U.S. Drug Enforcement Administration (DEA) assistant administrator Michael Braun to the special policy forum at the Washington Institute in July 2008: "[t]he DEA [ … ] estimates that the Taliban is currently at the organizational level of operations at which the FARC operated ten years ago."; cf. Gretchen Peters, "Take the War to the Drug Lords" *New York Times,* 18 May 2009; idem, "Taliban Drug Trade: Echoes of Colombia" *Christian Science Monitor,* 21 November 2006; idem, *Seeds of Terror: How Heroin Is Bankrolling the Taliban and al Qaeda* (New York: St. Martins Press, 2009).

5. United Nations Office of Drugs and Crime (UNODC), *Afghanistan Opium Survey 2009, Summary Findings* (Vienna: UNODC, 2009).

6. See Joel S. Migdal, *Strong Societies and Weak States: State-Society Relations and State Capabilities in the Third World* (Princeton, N.J.: Princeton University Press, 1988); Joel S. Migdal, Atul Kohli, and Vivienne Shue, eds., *State Power and Social Forces: Domination and Transformation in the Third World* (New York: Cambridge University Press, 1994); and Michael E. Meeker, *A Nation of Empire: the Ottoman Legacy of Turkish Modernity* (Berkeley: University of California Press, 2002).

7. Rubin, *Fragmentation,* 144.

8. Ibid., 20.

9. "From 1955 to 1978 the Soviet Union provided Afghanistan with $1.72 billion in economic aid and roughly $1.25 billion in military aid, while the United States furnished $533 million in economic aid." (Ibid.)

10. Jane's Information Group, "Political Leadership: Afghanistan," *Jane's Sentinel Security Assessment,* online edition, www.janes.com (accessed August 2008); "Profile: General Abdul Rashid Dostum," *BBC News,* 21 September 2001.

11. Rubin, *Fragmentation,* 30.

12. Antonio Giustozzi and Noor Ullah, "Tribes' and Warlords in Southern Afghanistan, 1980–2005," Working Paper No. 7, Crisis States Development Research Centre (London: London School of Economics, 2006).

13. Ibid., 9.

14. Chris Cramer, "Homo Economicus Goes to War: Methodological Individualism, Rational Choice and the Political Economy of War," *World Development* 30, 1849.

15. Goodhand, "Poppy, Politics."

16. See, for example, General McChrystal's recent remarks on Taliban funding, "[e]liminating insurgent access to narco-profits … would not destroy [Taliban] ability to operate," Eric Schmitt, "Many Sources Feed Taliban's War Chest," *New York Times,* 18 October 2009.

17. See, for example, UNODC, *Opium Survey 2009*; and Doris Buddenberg and William A. Byrd, eds., *Afghanistan's Drug Industry: Structure, Functioning, Dynamics, and Implications for Counter-Narcotics Policy,* (Kabul: UNODC & World Bank, 2006).

18. UNODC, *Afghanistan Opium Winter Rapid Assessment Survey* (Vienna: UNODC, January 2009), 42.

19. UNODC, *Afghanistan Opium Winter Rapid Assessment Survey* (Vienna: UNODC, February 2008), 2.

20. Goodhand, "Poppy, Politics," 59.

21. Buddenberg and Byrd, eds., *Afghanistan's Drug Industry,* 195.

22. Mohammed Atta is also known as Ustad Atta Mohammed Noor.

23. See Farah Stockman, "Karzai's pardons nullify drug court gains," *Boston Globe,* 3 July 2009; and Jason Burke, "A Year of Living on the Edge," *Guardian,* 6 October 2002.

24. See Stockman, "Karzai's pardons."

25. Goodhand, "Poppy, Politics," 68.

26. Buddenberg and Byrd, eds., *Afghanistan's Drug Industry,* 178.

27. Thomas Schweich, "Is Afghanistan A Narco-State?" *New York Times Magazine,* 27 July 2008; The Senlis Council, "Hearts and Minds in Afghanistan–Zroona Aw Zehnoona" (London: The Senlis Council, 2006).

28. Barnett Rubin and Jake Sherman, *Counter-Narcotics to Stabilize Afghanistan: The False Promise of Crop Eradication* (New York: New York University Press, 2008), 11.

29. Kim Barker, "If heroin rules, kingpins walk free," *Chicago Tribune,* 26 July 2008.

30. See Sarah Lister and Andrew Wilder, "Strengthening Subnational Administration in Afghanistan: Technical Reform or State-Building?" *Public Administration and Development* 25, no. 1 (2005), 42, 39–48; Anthony Loyd, "Corruption, bribes and trafficking: a cancer that is engulfing Afghanistan," *Times,* 24 November 2007.

31. UNODC, *Opium Survey,* 2009.

32. Loyd, "Corruption, bribes."

33. See structural-functionalism theorist Alfred Radcliffe-Brown.

34. Mark Shaw, "Drug Trafficking and the Development of Organized Crime in Post-Taliban Afghanistan" in Buddenberg and Byrd, eds., *Afghanistan's Drug Industry,* 199; Rubin and Sherman, "Counter-Narcotics."

35. Giustozzi and Ullah, "Tribes," 3.

36. Jason Burke, "Afghan Drug Lords Set Up Heroin Labs," *Observer,* 11 August 2002.

37. UNODC, *Opium Survey,* 2008.

38. Duncan Walsh, "Flower Power," *Guardian,* 16 August 2008; Buddenberg and Byrd, eds., *Afghanistan's Drug Industry;* Rubin and Sherman, "Counter-Narcotics."

39. Barnett Rubin, Road to Ruin: Afghanistan's Booming Opium Industry (New York: CIC NYU, 2004), 6–7.

40. UNODC, Afghanistan Opium Survey 2007 (Vienna: UNODC, 2007), v.

41. Rubin and Sherman, "Counter-Narcotics," 17.

42. Peters, "Take the War to the Drug Lords."

43. See Walsh, "Flower Power;" Peters, "Take the War to the Drug Lords;" idem., *Seeds of Terror.*

44. Peters, *Seeds of Terror,* 158.

45. See, for example, Peters, "Take the War to the Drug Lords;" idem, *Seeds of Terror;* Greg Zoroya Donna Leinwand, "Rise of drug trade threat to Afghanistan's security," *USA Today,* 26 October 2005; Tim Mcgirk, "Terrorism's Harvest," *Time,* 2 August 2004.

46. Walsh, "Flower Power."

47. UNODC, *Opium Survey,* 2007; idem, *Opium Survey,* 2008; Jane's Information Group, "The Battle for Musa Qala," *Jane's Terrorism and Security Monitor,* 4 April 2008.

48. Ibid.

49. The average farm gate price of dry opium, P, in 2007 was US $122/kg. The average opium yield per hectare, Yh, for 2007 was 42.5 kg. The area under cultivation in Musa Qala, A, for 2007 was 8,852 ha. Based on averages, the farm gate price potential of Musa Qala district, X, in 2007 is X = [P * Y] *A = [122 * 42.5] * 8,852 = US $45,897,620. This is significantly higher than any alternative development aid that might have reached the district.

# Chapter 8: Attacks on American Kids

## School Threats and the Active Shooter

*Children are the hands by which we take hold of Heaven*
Henry Ward Beecher

## Student Objectives

1. Compare and contrast causal factors in school shootings
2. Examine actual school shooting events and analyze causal factors identified in the chapter
3. Explore the changes that law enforcement and school administrators have had to enact to respond to the threat of active shooter attacks

Why are people murdering our kids at school? Sometimes I am afraid to watch the news anymore because these senseless killings just continue. Research shows including the October 2013, Sparks, Nevada school shooting that left a teacher dead. There have been 17 shootings at American schools since the Sandy Hook attack in December 2012 (Aborn, 2013). What can we do to protect our children at school from random or planned acts of violence? I selected the article you are about to read because it is written from a school security management perspective. As students or members of law enforcement, the courts or corrections, we need to broaden our perspectives in an interdisciplinary fashion.

# School Security: Best Practices

By Kent C. Jurney and Steve Cader

In the wake of the heartbreaking shooting at Sandy Hook Elementary, parents, school administrators, teachers and communities everywhere are left wondering how to keep our children safe when they are at school, and how to prevent future tragedies.

What are the answers to safer schools? Government and community leaders are looking at options that include armed guards and teachers, stronger gun control, regulation of the video game industry and identifying better mental health initiatives, among others.

In January, President Obama took action and put gun control on the national agenda when he issued his Gun Violence Reduction Executive Actions. Unfortunately, even with this increased spotlight and presidential executive orders, there is no simple or foolproof way to protect schools from violence.

While there's no way to predict or prevent school massacres, experts do agree there are best practices that schools can adopt to be more aware and prepared when these incidents occur. These protective measures can include procedures, personnel and equipment designed to mitigate the effects of an attack.

Fortunately for cash- and resource-strapped schools, the issuance of the president's Jan. 16 Gun Violence Executive Actions will help facilitate and fund security programs for schools nationwide. For the full list of President Obama's executive orders, go to www.whitehouse.gov/sites/default/files/docs/wh_now_is_the_time_full.pdf.

Here's an outline of best practices to mitigate shootings and other violent events on school grounds:

## Planning and Training

School shootings are unpredictable and evolve quickly. Preparedness is critical in any school incident, whether an active shooter, a bomb threat or other terrorist activity. Typically, it takes 10 to 15 minutes before law enforcement arrives on scene to stop the shooter and mitigate harm to victims. This means everyone on campus must be prepared mentally and physically to deal with such situations.

*Preparation:* While 84 percent of schools had a written response plan for a shooting in 2010, only 52 percent had drilled their students in the past year, according to the White House. This spring, a set of model plans will be made available, and $30 million in grants is proposed to help districts develop their own plans.

Here are some ways schools and students can be more prepared:

- **Develop model emergency response plans**—this is one of President Obama's Gun Violence Reduction Executive Actions required for schools, houses of worship and institutions of higher education.
- **Hire a security director** or appoint an employee who will be responsible for creating and implementing these emergency response plans, and coordinating all security activities for the school.
- **Establish a command and control center** to mobilize, deploy and report information regularly to local law enforcement and emergency responders.
- **Designate individuals familiar with the campus to serve as liaisons** with responding emergency personnel.

- **Provide floor plans and schematics to emergency personnel** beforehand, or have them available digitally for quick access when an emergency occurs.
- **Post evacuation routes in conspicuous locations** throughout a facility and ensure the facility has at least two main evacuation routes.
- **Create and assemble crisis kits** containing radios, floor plans, keys, staff roster and staff emergency contact numbers, first aid kits and flashlights. Distribute them to appropriate staff and employees.
- **Place removable floor plans** near entrances and exits for emergency responders.
- **Conduct security audits** on a regular and continuing basis.

*Training:* There is no better way to prepare for emergencies than training and education. Knowing what to do can save lives and reduce injury of staff and students. One of President Obama's recent executive orders was to "provide law enforcement, first responders and school officials with proper training for active shooter situations." This should help raise awareness and funding for school emergency training and response programs. Education training practices that should be followed include:

- Train staff to know and follow standardized procedures in an emergency and incorporate security into employee training programs.
- Provide security information and training to all students.
- Conduct regular exercises for active shooters. For years children have been exposed to fire, earthquake, and even bomb drills. The most effective way to train your staff to respond to an active shooter situation is to conduct mock active shooter training.
- Include local law enforcement and first responders during your training exercises and encourage law enforcement and emergency responders to train for an active shooter scenario at your location.

## Hire Right

Large concentrations of students gathering inside and around school buildings on a regular schedule make schools vulnerable to child predators, as well as shooters and terrorists. So it is critical for schools today to conduct diligent and thorough background checks and fingerprinting of all school personnel.

Vendors and service providers that have access to school grounds, such as janitors, landscapers and other maintenance workers, should have the same stringent background checks and fingerprinting as every teacher and administrator.

Cross-train every person who is employed on the campus—including vendors and contractors—to develop safety and security awareness protocols that provide support to and enhance existing security programs.

Look for vendors with "safe campus" programs. These vendors consult with administration and other school vendors to create a culture of safety awareness that includes every person on campus, and becomes part of the security/safety solution by increasing the number of people continually surveying the campus for potential suspicious activities and expanding the eyes and ears of campus security staff.

## Improve School Facilities

Because schools are relatively open access, it can be difficult to control access to schools without new technology and improved facilities maintenance. While these protective measures can be expensive, President Obama has earmarked $150 million for Comprehensive School Safety grants that will provide schools with funding for buying safety equipment, conducting threat assessments, and training crisis-intervention teams.

Best practices for maintaining access control to better protect students while on school grounds include:

- Define the facility perimeter and areas within the facility that require access control. Maintain building access points to the minimum needed.
- Photo IDs for all employees and students.
- Provide visitors with school-issued identification badges when on school grounds and require visitor check-in with the front office upon arrival and departure.
- Control vehicle access to school parking lots.
- Design a video monitoring, surveillance, and inspection program.
- Continuously monitor people entering and leaving the facility and establish protocols identifying suspicious behavior.
- Deploy personnel assigned to security duty to regularly inspect sensitive or critical areas.
- Vary security rounds and schedules to avoid predictability.
- Improve lighting across the campus and maintain the grounds.
- Make sure the school has enough utility service capacity to meet normal and emergency needs and provide adequate physical security.
- Make sure employees are familiar with how to shut off utility services, etc.

## Increase Communication

Good communication is critical in emergency situations to increase response times and reduce confusion, panic, misinformation, and possible injuries. All schools should have a communication plan in place. Schools should establish a liaison and regular communication with local law enforcement and community leaders. They should install systems that provide communication with all people at the school including employees, students, visitors, and emergency response teams; and establish protocol and systems—such as email and text messaging—that provide alerts and to communicate with parents in emergency situations.

Good communication strategies also include procedures for communicating with the public and the media regarding security issues, breaches and threats.

## Resource and Security Officers

Whether the threat is vandalism, student violence, terrorist threats or an active shooter, having a law enforcement officer or trained/armed security guard on campus can be a strong potential deterrent. Schools can work with local police to establish a school resource officer program. Or, schools can turn to private security companies to provide a trained and armed security guard to fulfill the role of school resource officer.

A school resource officer (SRO) is a law enforcement officer assigned to a school. Their main goal is to prevent juvenile delinquency by promoting positive relations between youth and law enforcement. SROs are not just "cops on campus"—they become part of the staff.

They educate students by teaching law-related classes, and counsel students and parents as well. The SRO becomes involved in the students' lives as a trusted figure and positive role model. The intent is that the officer becomes part of the school community, making the students feel safer, and provide another trained set of eyes and ears among students to help identify potential issues and vulnerabilities, and reduce juvenile crime.

SRO programs are not new—many schools have used them successfully in the past; however, the economic downturn slashed school budgets and stretched law enforcement resources extremely thin. With not enough officers to spare and schools not being able to afford them, most SRO programs have been cut. President Obama's new executive orders have provided incentives for schools to hire school resource officers once again.

An economical and effective alternative to an SRO is a fully trained, armed security officer. Many security officers are former law enforcement officers who can be employed through a security company for almost half the cost of the sworn officer.

*Kent C. Jurney, CPP, is Vice President of Client Services at ABM Security Services. He has been developing and delivering security protocol and training to schools and private industry for more than 40 years and developed the security curriculum for community colleges which is still part of the academic program in many colleges in Florida. For more information about ABM, visit www.abm.com.*

*Chief Steve Cader is branch manager for ABM Security Services in Northern Calif. He is in his 40th year as a California Peace Officer and is a retired Chief of Police for the town of Atherton, Calif. In addition to his responsibilities with ABM, he also works part time as a police officer, as well as an advisor to a homeland security contractor in bioterrorism and emergency notifications.*

## Discussion

The Bureau of Justice Statistics (BJS) provided some interesting statistics to consider about school shootings. There are 130,000 schools in the United States populated by 50 million, K through 12th grade students. From 1992 to 2011, 23 school-aged children were murdered at elementary schools, high schools or on their way to school events. This statistic rises to 45 violent deaths annually when you factor in teachers and staff who were also killed. The 45 deaths included murders and suicides.

The BJS reports that from July 1, 2010 through June 30, 2011, 31 students, staff, and non-students were killed at school. Of those numbers 25 were murdered and 6 committed suicide. When you look at school aged children ranging from 5 to 18 years, 11 were murdered and 3 committed suicide. These deaths occurred on school property (Bobers, 2013).

A murder committed on school property is a rare occurrence. During the 2009–2010 school year, 1,396 school age children; ages five to eighteen were murdered; 19 murders occurred at school. Causal factors including gang attacks and murders by non-gang members were cited in the article. Other causal factors to consider are mental health issue and that firearms are readily available. The debate continues about whether violent video games and other media cause actual violence. Bullying by other students is of grave concern to school officials. Do you think bullying is a leading factor in students who kill their peers and teachers?

The Bureau of Justice Statistics stated that bullying by other students is a factor in school violence. In 2011, 28 percent of all students reported being bullied at school. In the same year, 9 percent of all students reported being cyber bullied by fellow students.

Schools are reacting to the issue of violence on their property. Comparing statistics from the 2007–2008 school year to 2009–2010, there was a 63 percent increase in the installation of school-wide emergency systems and a 36 percent increase in structured, anonymous, threat-reporting systems.

Since the 1999 Columbine High School massacre where 15 students were killed, law enforcement has made some fundamental changes in response to active shooter events. Pre-Columbine, the standard tactic employed at schools, was to wait for SWAT before entering the school or other structures. Columbine changed that model of tactical thinking.

The new thinking developed by tactical experts was to train all officers to employ military urban tactics, to hunt down and neutralize the threat. Officers were taught team movement tactics and room-clearing techniques. They were taught not to stop and render medical aid but to step over the dead and wounded, until the shooter was located and engaged.

I was a SWAT lieutenant when the Columbine attacks happened. Our team, called the Tactical Response Team trained on a regular basis with the Los Angeles Police Department SWAT D-Platoon.

I remember a rainy day in November, learning new active-shooter tactics from the LAPD. The Los Angeles Police Department was far ahead of current practice in the field. When our team went to the LAPD training, LAPD was training every officer in their department on active shooter-techniques.

After completing the training we trained every Monrovia police officer in the active-shooter tactics we had learned. We actually conducted the training in schools that were closed for winter or spring breaks. We invited the fire department to train alongside us and practice victim rescue. We also used our police explorers who were students at the high school to be actors. I do believe to this day that the active-shooter training prepared our next generation of police officers to respond tactically in the event of an attack. Unfortunately, over the years, law enforcement officers across America have been forced to engage active shooters who have come to the campus to kill.

## Discussion Questions

1. What are the prevalent factors in school shootings?
2. What nationwide steps would you enact if you had the power to reduce school shootings?
3. What would have a greater impact on school shootings: stricter gun control or mental health improvements?
4. Do you think violent video games contribute to school shootings or bullying?

## Class Activities for the Professor

1. Discuss the questions in an on-line chat or in the classroom.
2. Divide the class into panels and debate gun control or mental health issues.
3. Assign the students to conduct a case study on a school shooting
   a) Assign the students to write a paper.
   b) Assign the students to prepare a Power Point presentation and present their findings.
4. Assign the students to prepare a press release on a real school shooting including an overview of the event, a time-line, background of the shooter(s), causal factors in the attack, and report on the results of the first responder units

## Works Cited

Aborn, R. (2013, October 31), Sparks Nevada Shooting. *Christian Science Monitor*. Retrieved from www.csmonitor. copyUSA

Robers, S., Kemp, J., and Truman, J. (2013), *Indicators of School Crime and Safety: 2012* (NCES 2013-036/NCJ 241446), National Center for Education Statistics, U.S. Department of Education, Bureau of Justice Statistics, Office of Justice Program, Department of Justice, Washington, D.C.

# Chapter 9: The Impact of Cannabis Legalization on Human Resource Management

By Donald C. Lacher, MS-Captain-Retired

*Sometimes I am asked by kids why I condemn marijuana when I haven't tried it.*
*The greatest obstetricians in the world have never been pregnant*
Art Linkletter

## Student Objectives

1. Compare and compare marijuana impairment with other drugs
2. Explore the role marijuana plays in poly-drug use
3. Examine issues in the marijuana legalization debate
4. Examine human resource ramifications in marijuana legalization

## The Marijuana Debate

I selected this topic for this textbook for two broad reasons. First, marijuana use is looked at so casually by society today. Marijuana use does pose significant problems for society, especially when users operate motor vehicles. If marijuana were legalized in California, use by law enforcement and correctional officers, fire-fighters, and other first responders would cause great concern for public sector management and human resource personnel.

I have studied marijuana all my professional life; no not by experimenting, but by research. Drug abuse, use, and sales are one of my areas of expertise. Police officers by the nature of their job are the great researchers of their time. They learn about drug abuse in their lab, the streets. They talk to junkies and other dopers all day long and they learn. That is why cops make good undercover officers because they learn from the best; those who belong the drug culture.

I learned that way too. As a patrol officer I searched out drug users and arrested them for drug influence, possession, and possession for sales. I always treated people with dignity and respect. I would talk to them off the record so I could learn about the drug subculture. I learned that taking a few minutes plus giving the users a smoke, soda, or candy bar leveled the playing field and averted the attention from their arrest. Many of my drug suspects were grateful to be in jail because jail was the only drug rehabilitation center available to them; a chance to "kick the habit." The techniques of the drug trade I learned from junkies helped me to be successful while purchasing illicit drugs in an undercover capacity.

## My Expertise and Experience

I believe that I have the expertise and experience as both a police officer and a law enforcement manager to write on this topic. I bring 31 years of experience, with 17, of those years at the rank of sergeant or above. From the time I was promoted to sergeant until my retirement at the rank of captain, human resource issues impacted me every working day. My responsibilities to the department did not finish at the end of my workday. My responsibility as a HR manager was a 24 hour job. No complaints from me; "just the facts" as Sergeant Joe Friday said on *Dragnet*.

While assigned as a detective, I worked narcotics and vice crimes for eight years. I completed the Drug Investigators course with the Drug Enforcement Administration. I attended many schools and eventually taught narcotics investigation to academy recruits and to advanced officers. I was selected by the California Department of Justice, Peace Officers Standards and Training (P.O.S.T.) to help design their forty hour narcotics investigation course.

I immersed myself in the drug subculture. Working undercover I purchased marijuana, heroin, cocaine, meth, LSD, PCP, and magic mushrooms many times. I served search warrants and seized all the aforementioned drugs. I arrested suspects for cultivation of opium poppies and marijuana.

For two summers I was assigned to the California State Department of Justice Campaign Against Marijuana Planting (C.A.M.P.) program. I worked on a task force with the California Bureau of Narcotics Enforcement (BNE), the Drug Enforcement Administration (DEA), Bureau of Land Management (BLM), United States Department of Forestry, CA Department of Forestry, Tribal Police, and the Humboldt County Sheriff's Department. In this program, law enforcement officers from around the state interdicted the flow of high-grade marijuana from Northern California destined for the south. We raided marijuana grow operations on private and public lands, national forest, and on Native American reservations.

**Figure 1.** Marijuana leaf on tree stump

I testified hundreds of time in municipal, superior, and federal courts as an expert. I qualified as an expert in the topics of drug influence, possession for sale, distribution networks, organized crime, gangs, and automatic firearms.

Many years later, while assigned as a traffic lieutenant I became a certified Drug Recognition Expert through a program with the Los Angeles Police Department and the National Highway Traffic Safety Administration. This training taught me to detect the poly drug user. My team and I targeted those persons driving under the influence of alcohol and drug combinations. Eventually, Monrovia became a training ground to certify DRE's from around the nation and abroad. We trained officers from Norway, Australia, Germany, and England. Again, I found myself testifying in DUI cases and again becoming an expert in this very interesting topic.

So we will explore the ramifications of marijuana use by public sector employees. We will also examine the impact the topic has on human resource management. I am writing this chapter at the student level for those not employed in the criminal justice system. I hope the information is also worthwhile to law enforcement and correctional officers, supervisors, and managers. This topic will certainly make you think about the significant factors about marijuana legalization and the impact on human resource management.

Consider that all criminal justice supervisors, managers, and executives are first and foremost human resource managers. The fundamental duty of a supervisor, manager, and executive is to balance the needs of their department with the needs of their employees. Effectively managing the humans in your organization creates harmony in the workplace, improves employee morale, increases performance and productivity; and in turn provides a higher level of service to your customers: the public.

## History

Marijuana was first written about in a Chinese manuscript in 2700 B.C. In 1545, it was discovered in the New World. In 1607, marijuana was grown for both its hemp for making rope and being smoked as a recreational drug. In 1617, marijuana was introduced in England as a cure for headache, menstrual cramps and toothaches.

In 1950s America, the drug was associated with jazz musicians who claimed their creativity increased when smoking marijuana. The drug is most widely associated with 1960s rebellion in the United States. In the present day, marijuana continues to create controversy especially in the continuing debate over decriminalization and legalization.

**Figure 2.** Flowering marijuana plant

## Identification and Pharmacology

*Cannabis sativa L* from the genus cannabis and the family Cannabiaceae is the botanical name for marijuana. Botanists describe marijuana as a tall, woody, annual shrub (DEA, 1983, p. 201). The leaf structure of the plant is very unique. Marijuana can vary in color from medium and deep green to as exotic as a light green with shades of red or orange.

The active alkaloid in cannabis that causes euphoria is called THC (delta-9-tetrahydrocannabinol). Cannabis comes in three forms: marijuana, hashish called concentrated cannabis, and oil.

Marijuana leaves and flowering tops (buds) are crushed and smoked in pipes; those rolled in paper as cigarettes are called "joints" (DEA, 1983). *Sinsemilla* (Spanish for "without seed") has been a very popular type of marijuana since the late 1970s. The goal of the cultivator is to produce a marijuana plant without seeds to boost its THC level. Male and female marijuana plants look different. The males tend to droop and are thinner than the females. The female plants are more upright as they reach toward the sun. The planters immediately destroy the male plants. The females are annual plants so to reproduce, they must drop seeds. To attract the male pollen, which is no longer in the immediate vicinity, the female plant produces increased levels of THC. The higher THC level produces marijuana that is much more potent than the plant would produce if allowed to grow naturally.

This high-grade marijuana is called bud. When I worked in the C.A.M.P. task force, *Sinsemilla* was the only marijuana plants we seized and this variety of marijuana was cultivated for the lucrative markets in Southern California. A couple years later, we were seizing *Sinsemilla* plants in Monrovia and all over Southern California.

Hashish or "hash" consists of THC rich resin. Hashish is Arabic for "assassin." The substance got its name from the Arabian Peninsula. In the ancient Arab world, assassins were paid in hashish; hence its name. The sticky resin is collected from the flowering tops of the marijuana plant, dried, and compressed into a cake form. Hashish is smoked or eaten (Lyman, 2011).

I attended the Narcotics Investigators course with the DEA. Our marijuana instructor was a DEA agent who just returned from narcotics interdiction duties in Pakistan.

He told us two unique methods for collecting the resin to make hashish. In India, men sat in steam baths to make them sweat profusely. The naked men would run through the marijuana fields and the sticky resin would cling to their bodies. Workers used flat wooden tools to scrape the pure hashish resin from the sweaty runners.

In Pakistan and Afghanistan, and in other parts of Central Asia, camels are utilized as living hash labs. The camels are starved and set loose in the marijuana field. After eating the marijuana nature takes its course. After the camels defecate, the substance is picked clean of undigested plant material. The camel hash is compressed in wooden blocks to form kilo bricks and the hashish is ready for market. Most hashish is produced in the Middle East, North Africa, Pakistan, and Afghanistan (Lyman, 2011

Hash oil is different from hashish. Solvents are used to extract the resin in the form of a sticky, oily substance. The oil, called "honey," is a more potent form of THC. THC levels can be as high as 15% whereas most marijuana contains 5% THC. The oil is placed on marijuana joints or tobacco cigarettes and smoked (Lyman, 2011).

Flash fire and explosions while extracting the oil are common when concentrated solvent fumes reach an ignition source. These extractions are conducted indoors making, explosions common place. I investigated a few extraction lab explosions in my career. On two occasions cooks died or were horrifically burned.

In Central Asia and India the resin is extracted from the flowering tops of the marijuana plant. The substance is kneaded into sticks and sometimes mixed with spices. It is called Charos or Dawamesk and either smoked or eaten. Bhang is smoked in North Africa. The leaves of the marijuana plant are powdered and mixed with spices, and honey or water, and then smoked or eaten. In North Africa the dried crushed tops are mixed with tobacco and smoked in pipes.

Chira is a form of hashish and is very popular in the Eastern Mediterranean and in the Arabian Gulf. Chira is made by reducing the raw resin to powder for smoking or kneaded into sticks for eating. Another hashish concoction from the same region is made by soaking the flowering tops in butter and water. The substance is laced with honey and almonds, and then eaten in the forms of cakes (DEA, 1983). In the United States and Canada, cannabis is commonly called marijuana, smoke, grass, pot, herb, weed, and chronic. Marijuana cigarettes are often called joints or blunts. Marijuana can also be smoked in water pipes called bongs.

## Cannabis Influence

Ingesting marijuana, hashish, or hash oil produces a reddening of the conjunctiva in the eye. Users will exhibit very red or bloodshot eyes. They usually have an odor of burnt marijuana about them and might have green material on their tongues. It is common to see users exhibit both eyelid and body tremors.

High-grade marijuana will cause the pupils of the eye to dilate to the point you will see very little of the color of their eyes. Certified drug recognition experts will examine eyes in a darkroom. Marijuana causes rebound dilation that can be detected in the darkroom. The evaluator will shine a penlight in the user's pupils. The pupil response is constriction. However, the pupils will slowly dilate and pulsate at the same time.

Levels of intoxication will vary from one individual to another. Intoxication levels can vary depending on the level of THC in their bloodstream or on the amount of time that has passed since they last

**Figure 3.** Marijuana plant

smoked cannabis. Users will experience relaxed inhibitions, disorientation, increased appetite, and in high doses paranoia (Lyman, 2011).

## Cannabis and the Poly Drug User

In 1979, the Los Angeles Police Department developed and tested a series of clinical and psychophysical tests that a trained officer could use to identify and differentiate between types of drug impairment (Lacher, 1993). The LAPD utilized these techniques to improve the enforcement of the drug-impaired driver and to reduce death and injuries in traffic collisions. These trained officers are called Drug Recognition Experts and quickly demonstrated that they could effectively recognize the drug-impaired driver (Lacher, 1993).

In 1984, the National Highway Traffic Safety Administration (NHTSA) and the National Institute on Drug Abuse (NIDA) sponsored a controlled laboratory evaluation of the drug-recognition procedures. Researchers at Johns Hopkins University conducted the evaluation and deemed that DRE-trained officers were effective in identifying the categories of drugs present in a subject. In 1985, a field validation study was conducted in the City of Los Angeles and proved that the Drug Recognition Expert program was an effective method to identify the drug-impaired driver.

In 1990, the Monrovia Police Department formed a partnership with the Los Angeles Police Department to train thirteen officers as Drug Recognition Experts. I was a lieutenant when I was certified as a Drug Recognition Expert.

The seven drug categories include depressants (alcohol and prescription meds), central nervous system stimulants (cocaine and methamphetamine), hallucinogens (LSD, peyote, mescaline, ecstasy, psilocybin), phencyclidine (PCP), narcotic analgesics (heroin, morphine, opiates), inhalants (glue, paint, gases), and cannabis.

Poly-drug users are those persons who have more than one of the seven drug categories in their system. More than one category of drugs in a human's system can mask the signs and confuse a non DRE-trained officer. The officer knows they are impaired but cannot determine what drug is affecting the suspect. The role of the highly trained drug recognition expert is to determine what drugs are impairing the suspect. This process is very important in the investigation of DUI-related deaths or injuries caused by the poly drug driver.

Part of my thesis was to collect data on subjects arrested for drug influence or driving under the influence. Our DRE-trained personnel collected blood or urine samples that were tested by the crime lab for the presence of all seven drug categories.

**Figure 4.** hash

In the study, we discovered some interesting trends about our poly-drug user population. Alcohol combined with any drug occurred most in our findings. The most prevalent combination was alcohol and cannabis, followed by cannabis and cocaine. Statistically, our findings showed that 20% of our suspects arrested for drug influence or driving while impaired were poly drug users (Lacher, 1993).

According to the 2009 study, "Drug-Related Hospital Emergency Room Visits" by the National institutes of Health, of the 2.1 million drug related emergency room visits, 14.3 percent involved alcohol in combination with other drugs. These visits included reports of drug abuse, adverse reactions to drugs, and other drug-related consequences (NIDA, 2011, 1).

Long-term cannabis abuse suppresses the immune system and causes lung and reproductive system damage. Long-term, frequent cannabis use causes *amotivational syndrome.* This conditional causes apathy and impairment of judgment, memory, and concentration; and a loss of interest in personal appearance and pursuit of goals (Lyman, 2011, p. 117).

Marijuana use is on the rise among teenagers. According to the "2011 Teenage Marijuana Use Is on the Rise", published by the National Institutes of Health, marijuana use among 8th-, 10th- and 12th-graders rose 10 percent (NIDA, 2011). In conclusion, cannabis is widely abused with other licit and illicit drugs. I have not been able to find a current validation study to see how the trends might have changed.

## Cannabis as a Gateway Drug

Globally, cannabis is the most frequently abused drug. The 2003 "Monitoring the Future" study concluded that in the United States 57 percent of adults aged 19 to 28 reported using marijuana in their lifetime. Among youth, 17.5 percent of eighth graders and 46.1 percent of twelfth graders had used cannabis in their lifetimes (Lyman, 2011).

Cops are the great sociologists of our time. They have the opportunity on a daily basis to conduct research about drug and crime trends. They do not sit in an office poring over journals, essays, and books. Cops collect their information directly from the source: the drug abuser.

For this piece of the chapter, I interviewed retired Officer William Couch from the Monrovia Police Department. Officer Couch worked in law enforcement for 37 years; 15 of those years he was assigned as a Youth Services Officer. His duties included teaching D.A.R.E., and juvenile delinquency intervention and enforcement. During his 17 years assigned to youth services, he personally taught D.A.R.E. to over 15,000 students. Over his career he estimates he has counseled hundreds of kids and their parents (Couch, W., personal communication, October 31, 2013). Officer Couch provided unique insight about marijuana use among youth. Remember, these youngsters grow up and enter the workforce.

Officer Couch said: *I would begin my interview with kids who are using marijuana and ask "why?" The number one answer was peer pressure. Kids want to impress their friends and that holds true with marijuana. The second most common response was that they used drugs to change how they felt about themselves because they suffered from low self-esteem.*

**Figure 5.** An illegal marijuana grow site with very tall plants. For scale, note the person in the background.

*All the years I was a cop, I wondered "does delinquency cause crime or does crime cause delinquency?" I believe that the answer is that delinquency causes crime, including marijuana use. In my experience kids do not just start smoking marijuana. First they experiment with tobacco and alcoholic beverages because both are easily available.*

*Status offenses are offenses that are not illegal for those over 18 and 21 years of age. Kids follow a pattern of committing violations of the law and status offenses. The term is "juvenile delinquency." They commit minor violations of the law such as smoking tobacco and drinking alcohol. They commit status offenses such as curfew violations and truancy. If they were a good student, their grades drop and they refuse to follow the directions of their parents.*

*The next step is experimenting with marijuana. I estimate that 96 percent of the youth I counseled were using some form of cannabis either marijuana or hashish. As these youth became more involved in the marijuana culture, they would look for a new drug to get high. Many went on to abuse cocaine, heroin, methamphetamine, LSD, magic mushrooms, inhalants, ecstasy or PCP.*

*To say cannabis is not a gateway drug would be ludicrous. Juveniles would decide to abuse these drugs for the same peer pressure and low self-esteem they suffered with while using marijuana. Juveniles who had a drug dealer selling them marijuana had the connections to hook them up with harder drugs. Of course the dealers were in the business to make money off their customers. When I was conducting my research for the Monrovia truancy ordinance, I discovered that the vast majority of those adults serving time in prison had marijuana backgrounds. Another factor in delinquency and marijuana abuse is single-parent homes. I would estimate that 65 percent of the youth I counseled for delinquent behavior were living in homes with one parent.*

## Is Marijuana Dangerous to Humans?

The evidence suggests that marijuana is dangerous. Dr. Robert Heath of Tulane Medical School concluded from his study on monkeys, that marijuana damages the part of the brain that controls motivation. In the book, "Marijuana: An Annotated Bibliography" published by the University of Mississippi, and containing 8,000 scientific research studies concluded that marijuana causes harm to the mind and body (Lyman, 2013).

Marijuana also contains known toxic and cancer causing chemicals. Marijuana causes the same respiratory issues associated with tobacco use including, bronchitis, emphysema and bronchial asthma (Lyman, 2013).

High concentration of cannabis in the bloodstream can cause serious situations that might need emergency care. Marijuana in high doses can cause hallucinations, fantasies and paranoia. According to the NIDA, in of the 4.2 million drug-related emergency room visits in 2009, marijuana was involved in 376,462 of them.

**Figure 6.** Detail view of an outdoor marijuana plant.

## Marijuana and Drugged Driving

The FBI reported that in 2010, 1,412,333 Americans were arrested for impaired driving. The statistic includes driving under the influence of all drugs including alcohol. It is interesting to note that France is very progressive on curtailing driving under the influence of alcohol. In 2012, all vehicle owners were required to install a breath testing device in their vehicles (Mosher, 2014).

Drugged driving is a concern because while under the influence of any drug that affects the brain, motor skills, reaction time, and judgment are impaired to the point, that the drivers are a danger to themselves, passengers and other motorists on the road way (NIDA, 2102).

All states have enacted laws regulating blood alcohol concentration (BAC) levels. If a person is driving under the influence of alcohol, the BAC is .08 and is presumptive in a court of law. It is not so simple for drug impairment while driving. Only 16 states have passed laws establishing impairment for drugs other than alcohol. Only Arizona, Delaware, Georgia, Indiana, Illinois, Iowa, Michigan, Minnesota, Nevada, North Carolina, Pennsylvania, Rhode Island, South Dakota, Utah, Virginia, and Wisconsin have passed laws that state that driving a motor vehicle with any detectable amount of drugs is presumptive.

So, in those aforementioned states, if you operate a motor vehicle and chemical tests shows any amount of cannabis in your system you are presumed to be under the influence of that drug. I find it interesting that California, Florida, Ohio and New York are not on the list. Below are some study highlights:

- 2004 Maryland study of crash victims to a trauma center 34 percent tested positive for drugs only (other than alcohol), whereas 16 percent tested positive for alcohol only
- 2004 study in several locations showed 4 to 14 percent of injured or dead drivers tested positive for THC
- 2007 results from NIDA's Monitoring the Future survey revealed 12 percent of high school seniors admitted driving under the influence of marijuana within the two weeks prior the survey

Cannabis impairs motor coordination thus impairing one's ability to drive a motor vehicle safely. The drug causes distortion of time and space; this distortion contributes to motor vehicle, occupational, and home accidents (Lyman, 2011). Cannabis also has lingering effects so one could still be too impaired to drive for several days after the last ingestion of the drug.

Further studies have shown that in 60 cannabis experiments, including laboratory, driving simulators, and on-road experiments, behavioral and cognitive skills related to driving performance were impaired and the subjects became increasingly impaired as THC levels rose in the body.

Evidence from on-road and simulator studies has revealed that cannabis negatively impacts a driver's attentiveness, and perception of time and speed. Research has also shown that impairment increases significantly for drivers who test positive for both alcohol and THC. The conclusion is that alcohol and cannabis use are linked behaviors. This trend bears out in my 1993 study of the DRE program.

## Human Resource Management Ramifications

So, readers, what impacts would marijuana legalization have on HR practices? Colorado legalized marijuana and they are in the thick of how this issue will impact employees and organizational drug policies. How will the private, public, and non-profit industries maintain drug-free workplaces?

So first we will examine the Colorado experience as a platform for states that might be forced by voters to legalize marijuana. As of this writing, 18 states including California have approved medical marijuana programs. In November 2013, Colorado and Washington legalized marijuana.

Under federal law cannabis is illegal and has been deemed as having no medical value. Caught in the middle between legalization in the states and federal law, companies are wondering how this issue will impact their workplace drug policies and drug testing. If marijuana is legal, will they be able to test for the drug and deny employment if the test is positive for marijuana? Well, they are not sure but they are sure that new laws will be created. Private and public sector managers are asking if federal laws will protect their current drug policies regarding marijuana. No one will have the answer until the issues reach the courts (Mont, 2013, 1).

Business owners with federal government contracts are wondering how the state law will impact their ability to do business. Emily Hobbs-Wright, a practicing attorney, in Colorado, said that Colorado has "lawful off-duty activity statutes that prohibits employers from disciplining or terminating workers for using any legal substance off-duty and off the premises." The law was enacted to protect tobacco users from losing their jobs when new public bans were enacted (Mont, 2013, 1). So can Colorado cops and other first responders smoke cannabis? Officials in Colorado and Washington are not sure either.

A pending law suit in Colorado might make new laws on this issue. DISH Network fired an employee who was a quadriplegic and medical marijuana patient. He was fired from his position as an operator when he tested positive for marijuana. DISH contends that they had the right to terminate the employee under federal law so to maintain the company's drug-free workplace designation.

The company argued that alcohol intoxication is easier to determine than marijuana influence. Marijuana can linger in the system for up to three weeks. DISH said they have an obligation to protect other employees and cannot take the risk that the marijuana user might injure themselves or other workers. The liability they say is just too great (Mont, 2013, 1).

Colorado companies are also worried how varying laws from state to state will impact their locations in multiple states. Michael Rush from a Delaware law firm said that: "their state's experience with marijuana laws added a new twist to counter federal laws. In 2011, the state passed a medical marijuana law and then gave registered marijuana users affirmative action protection so organizations they worked for could not terminate them under the authority of federal marijuana laws" (Mont, 2011, 2).

One thing is certain: legalization of marijuana by states will create new court decisions regarding drug-testing for applicants, random drug-testing of current employees, random drug-testing policies, and post-accident testing. So readers what impact will this topic have on law enforcement officers, fire fighters and other first responders? Do you want these first responders smoking marijuana?

## The Debate over Medical Marijuana Dispensaries

California police chiefs and sheriffs are very concerned what impact the legalization of marijuana would have on their industry. In 1996, California was the first state to allow medical marijuana to be dispensed. The Drug Enforcement Administration (DEA) went on a pot war with municipalities that gave permits to marijuana dispensaries.

The City of Los Angeles has been at the center of the marijuana debate. The city allowed medical pot shops to open in defiance of federal law. At one point the city did not even know how many pot shops were operating in the city. The DEA intervened and the entire mess became political. The Los Angeles Police Department reported that while most areas in Los Angeles saw a decrease of Part I crimes. The FBI classifies aggravated assaults, forcible rape, murder, robbery, arson, burglary, larceny and motor vehicle theft as Part I crimes. Areas close to pot shops experienced a 200 percent increases in robberies, a 52 percent in burglaries, and a 57 percent increase in aggravated assaults (Kanable, 2009).

This is an interesting trend to evaluate. Imagine that fact the robbers would target marijuana dispensaries for cash and product. The assault statistic might answer the question does "marijuana cause crime?" It is even more interesting to consider the 52 percent jump in burglaries. Is the burglary spike directly related to marijuana use? Or is the trend driven by an influx of criminals frequenting the area where pot shops operate?

According to Rebecca Kanable, the author of "Turning Over a New Leaf: California Chiefs and Others Aim to Keep the Country from Going to Pot", chiefs and sheriffs are going to fight any attempt in the state to legalize marijuana. The fight may be with the politicians who are going to bend to the pro-legalization camp. Politicians need to realize that the weak pot they smoked in high school or college is not the marijuana encountered today.

In May 2009, the Office of National Drug Control Policy released a THC study conducted by University of Mississippi. The study revealed that current marijuana has the highest THC levels since their testing program began. Marijuana seized by law enforcement was tested by the university's laboratory. The average THC level in 1983 was less than 4 percent. In 2008, the average THC level was 10.1 percent. The highest concentration found in current samples reached 27.3 percent.

This trend may account for the large number of marijuana emergency room visits mentioned earlier in this chapter. The article goes on to say that the NIDA reported that 6 to 11 percent of fatal collision victims test positive for cannabis. An interesting side note to consider is that on June 19, 2009 cannabis smoke was listed as a known cause of cancer under California's Proposition 65 (Kanable, 2009).

I decided to discuss this topic with an expert in the field of human resources. Danielle Tellez is a risk manager for a municipality in California. Danielle remarked: *If marijuana is legalized in California, it will significantly impact the ability of local governments to maintain a drug-free workplace. This possibly creates serious concerns for HR. Can you imagine police officers and fire fighters using marijuana off duty? The city would incur liability for marijuana-using employees who drive our vehicles or operate certain types of equipment.*

*This situation would impact our ability to discipline employees. New laws would be created by civil suits filed against cities by employees. In California, marijuana legalization would impact the Peace Officer Bill of Rights, labor law, and ADA, just to mention a few.*

*Marijuana legalization for the public sector would be in direct conflict with drug free workplace policies. We have a duty to protect the community and our employees. We need to consider our employees who do not use marijuana. How will their safety be jeopardized by fellow workers who smoke marijuana?*

*Under current California, law we can deny employment applicants who use tobacco because of the risk of cancer. The California Labor Code grants us that authority. I wonder if the labor code will be impacted if marijuana is legalized in California. Will be able to deny employment or discipline city workers who smoke marijuana?* (Tellez, D. personal communication, October 29, 2013).

The prospect of marijuana legalization for any state has serious and complex implications for private, public, and non-profit sectors to maintain a drug free work environment. The issue extends to the ability of employers to control the off-duty conduct of their workers and to shield them from civil suits filed by their employees. Certainly, the legalization of marijuana in California would have severe consequences on human resource management. There is no doubt in my mind that the lawyers will make money off this new legal opportunity if marijuana is legalized in any state where it is currently illegal.

# Case Study

I close this chapter with an HR scenario for you to consider and discuss in your college classroom. In this scenario you are the chief of police, sheriff or corrections chief. You are a retired captain from another jurisdiction. You have been a chief of police at your new department for three months.

Your state has just legalized cannabis in any form. It can be smoked in public or in private. The decision is immediate and new laws have not been developed to control marijuana use among employees.

"Officer Joint has been on a hash oil binge over his three days off. At 5:00 am he took one last hit before getting ready for work. At 7:00 am, Joint arrived at the police station. He dressed in his uniform and reported to briefing. After briefing he ate fast food for breakfast and began his patrol duties. He felt tired and drowsy from the effects of the hash. Later, he admitted the hash use to investigators and said he had difficulty with his driving skill."

"A few minutes before 8:00 am, he is dispatched to a domestic violence call. The path to the call took him on to a residential street and skid-mark analysis indicated he was driving seven miles over the speed limit. Joint was not using his lights or siren."

"Turning a corner too fast, the patrol car struck a mother pushing a baby carriage in a crosswalk. The crosswalk was adjacent to an elementary school. The mother, the baby in the carriage and a six-year-old child holding her mother's hand are all killed."

Officer Joint's supervisor and watch commander arrived and began their investigation. Believing that Officer Joint might be impaired, the criminal aspect of the case is referred to the highway patrol. Two highway patrol officers arrived at the scene to investigate the traffic deaths. One of them was a certified drug recognition expert. He determined that Officer Joint was mildly impaired. Officer Joint was arrested for driving under the influence and vehicular homicide. A urine sample concluded that Joint had trace amounts of THC in his system but not enough to justify a DUI charge.

Officer Joint is ultimately charged with three counts of misdemeanor manslaughter. The district attorney decided to file misdemeanor charges due to the lack of evidence of impaired driving.

After reading all the documentation on this case, you decided to make an example of Officer Joint, so this tragedy does not happen again. You terminated Officer Joint for conduct unbecoming an officer for his admitted hashish use. A factor in the termination was Joint's ultimate conviction on three misdemeanor manslaughter counts. Since Joint does not have a criminal record the court sentenced him to 90 days in county jail. The jail time was suspended. He was placed on probation for twelve months and ordered to complete drug rehabilitation counseling.

The husband of the decedents filed a multi-million dollar law suit again you the chief, and the city. The former officer Joint also filed a civil suit against you and the city for wrongful termination. Since he was not convicted of a felony, his civil suit maintains that he still can work as a law enforcement officer. Joint has also filed for a stress-induced medical retirement claim for psychological damage he suffered from the deaths and how your internal affairs personnel behaved toward him.

He alleged in his civil suit that the chief of police is discriminating against him for two reasons. First, since he is a former drug user he falls under the protection of the Americans with Disabilities Act (ADA). Secondly, the former chief disciplined an officer for a similar case. Three years before this incident, Officer Beere was convicted of misdemeanor manslaughter when he crashed his car and killed another driver. In that case the officer was off-duty and had a .07 blood alcohol concentration level. After serving a sixty-day suspension Officer Beere, was allowed to return to work and is still employed at the agency. In fact Beere was Joint's field training officer. How are you going to manage this situation?

## Case Study Questions

1. Compare and contrast the significant human resource factors in the case study.
2. Analyzes possible legal defenses for your actions in terminating Officer Joint.
3. Evaluate the administrative factors in the termination.

## Discussion Questions

1. What is your position on marijuana legalization? Defend your position.
2. If marijuana is legal in your state or were to become legal, should law enforcement, fire, and other ESM personnel be forbidden to use the drug off duty? Defend your position.
3. What impact would marijuana legalization have on the drug-free workplace?

## Professor Activities

1. Assign the Joint Case Study for discussion or a written assignment
2. Conduct student panels to debate the legalization of marijuana and human resource impacts in the drug free workplace.
3. Assign the students a marijuana project; ideas include but are not limited to:
    a)  Write a human resource (HR) policy for marijuana use by law enforcement, corrections, fire, or other public workers.
    b)  Write a drug-free workplace policy that includes marijuana for either the public, private, or non-profit sector.
    c)  Write a drug-testing policy for the public, private, or non-profit sector.

## Works Cited

DEA, (1983). "Narcotic Investigator's Manual", Washington D.C. U.S. Printing Office

Kanable, Rebecca (2009). "Turning Over a New Leaf: California Chiefs, Others Aim to Keep from Going to Pot" Law Enforcement Technology, 10. Retrieved from: http://www.galegroup/ps/i.do?id=GALE%.

Lacher, D (1993). "Program Evaluation: The Drug Recognition Expert Program".

Master's Thesis, University of La Verne, La Verne.

Lyman, M (2011). "Drugs in Society: Causes, Concepts and Control", New York, Anderson Publishing.

Mont, Joe, (2013). "Marijuana Laws Spark Employment Policy Review: Haze of Confusion Descends on Companies", Compliance Week, 16. Retrieved from: http//www.go.galegroup.com/ps/i.do?id=GALE%.

Mosher, C., and S. Akins. (2014). "Drugs and Drug Policy", Thousand Oaks, Sage Publishing.

National Institute on Drug Abuse. (2010), "Drug Facts: Drugged Drivers". Retrieved from: http://www.drugabuse.gov/publications/drugfacts/drugged-driving.

National Institute on Drug Abuse. (2011), "Teenage Marijuana Use Is on the Rise", Retrieved from: http//www.drugabuse/news-events/nida/2011/03/teeage-marijuan-use-rise.

National Institute on Drug Abuse (2011). "Drug Facts: Drug-Related Hospital Emergency Room Visits". Retrieved from: http://drgabuse.gov/publications/drugfacts/drug-related-hospital-emergency-room.

# Chapter 10: Looking Toward the Future

*For time and the world do not stand still. Change is the law of life. And those who look only to the past or present are certain to miss the future*

John F. Kennedy

## Student Objectives

1. Compare and contrast significant factors impacting the criminal justice field in the 21st century
2. Evaluate the impact of the 9/11 attacks on the nation and how those events changed policing
3. Analyze the significant factors in the USA PATRIOT Act
4. Examine the change roles of law enforcement, the courts, and corrections in the community

I selected this article for the last chapter in the book because it points us toward the future. The article examines trends likely to impact crime and restorative justice. Primarily, the chapter explores the significant factors in our nation's response to terrorism. I believe after you examine your perceptions about the global impact of terror in concert with the information you are about to read, you will become firmly anchored to make a difference in the world community.

# Looking Toward the Future: Criminal Justice in the 21st Century

By Joycelyn Pollock

## Chapter Outline

1. Two Directions
2. The Role of the Community in Crime
3. Restorative Justice Programs
4. Terrorism and Our Response
5. Conclusion

## What You Need to Know

- Crime has declined but is starting to inch upward again.
- The community has always been identified as a factor in criminal choice.
- Social disorganization theory is not unlike the Chicago or ecological school idea that crime was localized in distressed neighborhoods.
- Restorative justice changes the major focus of the justice system from punishment to restoring the victim to a state of wholeness.
- Restorative justice programs include victim-offender mediation, community reparation boards, family conferences, and circle sentencing.
- September 11, 2001, dramatically changed the governmental focus, agency structure, and laws regarding counterintelligence and protection of the public against the threat of terrorist acts.
- A controversial element of the USA PATRIOT Act is extending the right to use roving wiretap warrants, which apply to any telephone the suspect calls.
- The Department of Homeland Security has a budget of more than $30 billion. It includes all or part of the FBI, Customs, Border Patrol, and 19 other agencies.

What is the future of criminal justice in our country? Of course it is impossible to accurately predict what may occur in the future, but it is important to ponder the possibilities and prepare for them. In this last chapter, we will take the time to look forward. It should be clear that the criminal justice system is a massive, multifaceted, non-organization of police, courts, and corrections across 50 states and the federal government. It affects literally millions of individuals in this country. Change is unlikely to be systemic or coordinated. On the other hand, we can identify trends and the possible directions that might be taken by the many different agencies that make up the system of criminal justice.

Crime has dramatically decreased since the early 1990s—so much so that homicide rates are at 30-year lows, and all forms of personal and property crimes have decreased to levels not seen since the 1970s. Even so, it seems to be the case that citizens are not aware of this good news because media outlets tend to emphasize violent crimes disproportionately to their prevalence. Television reality "cop shows," court shows, and prime-time dramas focus on violent crimes and obscure the reality that crime may not be the major problem that people think it is.

In the last few reporting periods, we have seen a slight rise in crime, certainly in some reporting jurisdictions. This may be a troubling harbinger of things to come. One of the clear issues of the day is what to do about the 600,000 individuals released from prison each year, many of whom have been in prison since the early and mid-1980s. These individuals have served long periods of time, decades even, without any meaningful programs to help them conquer addictions and adapt to their freedom on the street. Are these individuals beginning to affect the crime rate? Perhaps a slowing economy might be why crime is now beginning a slight upward trend. Or the numbers may be simply artifacts of reporting changes. We will need to watch carefully to track whether crime rates will continue to rise.

We have, throughout this book, concentrated primarily on domestic crime and state and local responses to it. One thing that cannot be ignored since 9/11 is that the United States must prepare for future terrorist attacks. We briefly mentioned the Department of Homeland Security in an earlier chapter, but the response to terrorism must be a shared effort among all levels of law enforcement and public safety. Therefore, we come to an interesting observation.

## 1. Two Directions

In thinking about the future of the criminal justice system, or, more accurately, the various components of the *non-system* of criminal justice, it seems that an interesting juxtaposition of future trends must be considered. The first is that the system has been, for the last couple decades, moving toward, in fits and starts, a more community-oriented view of the causes of crime, prevention, and enforcement. Such things as community policing, community courts, re-entry programs, and restorative justice all have the basic theme that crime is a community problem and any solution to it must be found in the community.

Another factor, however, that has dramatically changed the criminal justice system is the threat of terrorism, and the legislative changes and executive response to it. This threat has led to a greater centralization of law enforcement, and greater federal powers to investigate and prosecute. Thus, we have two almost countervailing tendencies that will influence the future; the first would lead to decentralized, community responses to crime, and the second to increasing federalization and expanded powers of investigation.

The most monumental event of the decade was, of course, September 11, 2001, which will take its place in United States history beside such tragedies as the bombing of Pearl Harbor. The effects of this tragedy cannot be underestimated. In addition to the loss of lives, we must also consider the psychological effects of fear, the crippling costs of military efforts in Afghanistan and Iraq, and the continuing costs of protection here at home, including costs associated with TSA and the Department of Homeland Security.

The governmental response to the threat of terrorism within the boundaries of the country has dramatically reshaped the organization and mission of federal law enforcement. It has also created new questions for the courts to resolve and pitted federal courts against the executive branch in arguments regarding torture, renditions, executive privilege, civil liberties, and the security classification of government documents. Fear of crime has now been eclipsed by fear of terrorism, and new legal and ethical questions regarding the appropriate response to this threat have taken center stage in national debates.

So that brings us to an interesting paradox. We have, on the one hand, seen a renewed interest in community responses to crime, as evidenced by the popularity of restorative justice programs and a federally supported initiative to respond to the problems of re-entry of prisoners. These are examples of trends that tend to energize individual communities to deal with the issues of crime and juvenile delinquency by placing resources and the responsibility of crime prevention at the community level. Community responses are often less punitive, and require more comprehensive social responses to the problems of crime in the community.

On the other hand, we have also witnessed a series of federal responses to terrorism that centralizes resources, and promotes greater powers for the federal branch of government. Even conservative pundits are beginning to express concern at the cost of the "war on terror," as well as the expansion of federal crimes and the role of federal investigation and law enforcement in domestic crime fighting. Some argue, in fact, that the responses that have occurred after 9/11 are threatening the bedrock of state "police power" (the power of states to define and enforce most criminal laws), and even the very civil liberties that define our country.

So, in this last chapter, we will explore these disparate directions, looking at the policies and underlying philosophies and rationales of each. They seem to represent two different directions that the country can take. Some might argue they must be different because they respond to different threats.

## 2. The Role of the Community in Crime

There is a long history in criminology of looking at the community as criminogenic. Recall from an earlier chapter that the ecological or Chicago school of crime theory discovered that high crime rates existed in mixed zones, which are areas of the city where the functions of retail, residential, and commerce were mixed. These researchers further discovered that the **mixed zones** also were likely to display high levels of other social ills, such as alcoholism and mental illness in addition to crime. Further, indicators such as graffiti, abandoned houses, vandalism, and low home ownership characterized the zone.[1] The Chicago school approach led to 60 years of attempting to more closely describe in what way the community and/or the residents within the community influenced the individual to commit crime.

**Social disorganization theory** today continues this theoretical thread, and theorists such as Robert Sampson postulate that indicators of social disorganization, i.e., lack of social "capital," are also indicators of high crime.[2] A strong community can prevent criminal behavior. The following quote describes this idea:

> When multiple members of a community act for each other's benefit, an overarching sense of good will and community spirit develops. When there are patterns of such reciprocity, a sense of community capital emerges, and this capital can reap strong returns in reducing crime and establishing standards of conduct among its members. … even in impoverished, inner city neighborhoods, social capital can suppress criminal activity. [3]

Others, such as Robert Bursik and Harold Grasmick, also examine the informal controls on an individual that come from family, school, church, and neighborhood. They argue that formal controls, such as police, tend to undercut these more personal controls.[4]

The importance of the community on crime is recognized by such efforts as community policing. The idea behind this innovation was that the community itself needed to be involved and police officers could strengthen community resolve to conquer crime by acting as facilitators and resource mediators. Even community policing efforts become complicated, however, when attempts are made to draw the boundaries of good and bad, offender and victim, too simplistically. Some researchers note that community residents express mixed feelings toward the gang members whom the criminal justice system targets as offenders. In one sense, these youths are the problem because they create crime and scare away business development. In another sense, however, they are the community, because they are the sons and brothers of residents.[5]

Criminogenic communities have more comprehensive and pervasive social problems. Typically, the communities that offenders come from and go home to are characterized by long-standing poverty from lack of jobs and business development. Schools are sub-performing and drop-out rates are high. The residents are heavy users of government services. In fact, in a justice mapping research project in New Orleans (before Hurricane Katrina) it was found that there existed "million dollar blocks." These were areas of the city where more than a million dollars was spent incarcerating, returning, and revoking offenders from that street. Further, there is a substantial overlap between neighborhoods that are recipients of TANF (Temporary Assistance to Needy Families) and those who receive a disproportionate share of offenders (released on parole or probation).[6] Obviously, the best approach to the "crime problem" is to deal with the community's needs as a whole. For instance, all residents could benefit from revitalization efforts, and these efforts would also provide alternatives to criminal opportunities.

More generally, research is beginning to show that the huge increase in incarceration that occurred since the 1980s has not necessarily been helpful to the communities hardest hit by crime. Todd Clear and his associates found that a "**tipping effect**" occurred at high rates of imprisonment where imprisonment seemed to result in more crime in certain communities. Positive effects of incarceration included removal of problem family members and reducing the number of dangerous individuals in the community, but negative effects also occurred. In fact, there was an apparent increase of crime in the neighborhoods that experienced high incarceration rates.[7]

Further study with focus groups indicated that community members saw incarceration as both a positive and negative force in the community. Negative elements included the stigma attached to returning offenders for the offender and his or her family, the financial impact of imprisonment for both the offender and his or her family, and the difficulty of maintaining interpersonal relationships through a prison sentence. High levels of incarceration reduce the number of potentially positive role models for children, result in transient populations, and affect the ability of the community to control its members through informal and affective ties.[8]

It should be noted that one can argue that there may be a *correlation* between crime and high levels of imprisonment but it is difficult to show causation. Also, the correlation between high levels of imprisonment and low respect for formal social control agencies is also silent on directionality and so it could just as easily be that these factors lead to high imprisonment, not the other way around. In reviewing all the evidence, however, it seems that incarceration has mixed effects. It reduces crime by the removal of criminal offenders; on the other hand, if a community experiences high levels of incarceration, it increases social mobility and social disorganization, and weakens the ability of the community to utilize parochial methods of control.[9] The best policy recommendations based on the above research include limited incarceration and enriched services to the communities that experience moderate to high rates of incarceration. The community should be helped to reach a point where it can control its members through informal private means of control.

It cannot be ignored that prisoners almost always eventually get out and return to the community. Recently, there has been attention to the issue of the 600,000 prisoners who are released to the community each year. Community efforts are seen as essential in responding to the problem of huge numbers of prisoners being released. Because they will be returning to communities, these communities must be involved in efforts to help ex-offenders adapt and become productive citizens. Re-entry efforts have

## BOX 1

*Restorative Justice*

- The process of justice employs local leadership, is informal, and invites participation from community members.
- The goal is to repair the harm done to a community member by another community member in a way that will restore the health of the community relationship.
- The authority of the justice is through the customs and traditions accepted by all members.

*Source*: Schweigert, F. (2002). "Moral and Philosophical Foundations of Restorative Justice." In J. Perry (ed.), *Repairing Communities through Restorative Justice*, pp. 19-37. Lanham, MD: American Correctional Association, p. 25.

included job training/placement, drug treatment, and housing assistance, as these are identified as the major problems of those released from prison.

Another aspect that has been noted is that ex-offenders lose civil liberties that most of us take for granted. In most states, ex-offenders no longer have the right to vote (14 states permanently take away this right), serve on juries (31 states permanently take away this right), or possess firearms (28 states permanently take away this right). In about half of all states, ex-offenders cannot hold public office, and close to half of all states allow imprisonment to be used as a reason for permanent deprivation of parental rights.[10] You might think that these deprivations are either rightfully withheld from those who broke the law, or that the offender should have thought of this result before they committed the crime, but the opposing argument is that we want the offender to become a productive, law-abiding citizen. If he or she does so, is it fair to withhold all the rights of citizenship indefinitely?

The following quote is from the report of the Reentry Policy Council, a bi-partisan agency that brings together federal, state, and local representatives, as well as representatives from institutional corrections, community corrections and law enforcement, to address the problems of reentry for criminal offenders.

Although the re-entry phenomenon is currently understood as a criminal justice issue, solutions to the challenges that are posed by so many people returning to their neighborhoods from prison cannot be found within the justice system alone. Instead, these solutions will require a coordinated effort among a range of actors stretching from state officials to neighborhood associations.[11]

## 3. Restorative Justice Programs

Restorative justice programs basically change the paradigm of the justice system. Instead of finding guilt or innocence and inflicting punishment, restorative justice seeks to "restore" all individuals to a state of wholeness. While this may involve restitution to the victim or some form of compensation in response to injury or loss, the approach also takes into consideration the relative needs of the victim and offender. Community members are also involved to help resolve the issues that led to the criminal event. Restorative justice efforts, in effect, reduce the need for reentry programs because, in many cases, the offender never leaves the community. Without banishment to state prison or county jail, there is no re-entry difficulty.

Many different types of programs fall under the restorative justice umbrella, but they all have in common the idea of doing more than simply punishing the offender. The roots of restorative justice go back as far as Roman or Grecian law, based on repayment to the victim rather than punishment of the offender.[12] In the 1960s and 1970s, during the rehabilitative and reintegration era, restorative justice programs were popular and fit in with the community empowerment and grass-roots model of President Johnson's "War on Poverty." Box 1 presents some of the ideas of restorative justice.

Examples of tribal justice are often used to illustrate the origins and philosophy of restorative justice. For instance, the family group sentencing conference that is used by the Maori people of New Zealand, or the Peacemaking Panel of the Skokomish tribe in North America, are examples where tribal justice is more interested in resolving and repairing the harm done by the crime than inflicting punishment on the offender. All community members are involved in the resolution and participate in the decision-making in these types of models.[13]

Four types of restorative justice models related to criminal justice sentencing and corrections are:

*Victim-offender mediation.* This is the most common and is more than 20 years old. Some programs are called Victim-Offender Reconciliation Programs or Dialog Programs. There are more than 320 programs in the United States and many more in Europe. They involve the victim and offender meeting and discussing the event and coming to an agreement about restitution and reparation. The idea is to promote healing on the part of the victim, and responsibility on the part of the offender. The program may be implemented as a diversion from prosecution or as a condition of probation. Research has found that victims are more satisfied when they have an opportunity to go through these programs (79 percent compared to 57 percent). Victims were also significantly less fearful of being victimized. Offenders were more likely to complete their restitution and recidivism was lower for those who went through mediation as compared to traditional sentencing.

*Community Reparative Boards.* This model has been more common in the juvenile system and has been in use since the 1920s. It re-emerged with greater popularity in the 1990s and may be called youth panels, neighborhood boards, or community diversion boards. The goals of the program are to promote citizen ownership of the sentencing process, and provide an opportunity for victims and community members to confront the offender in a constructive manner. The idea is also to reduce dependence on formal justice processing. Basically, citizens are involved in a sentencing decision and the experience is more of a dialogue between the offender and the board, who look at long-term solutions rather than retribution.

*Family Group Conferencing.* This type of program comes directly from the dispute resolution tradition of the Maori as described above. In fact, it was adopted into national legislation in New Zealand in 1989. A similar model is taken from the Wagga Wagga people of South Australia and uses police officials to administer the conferencing. In these models, police (or another agency) set up a family conference of the offender, victim, and the families of both, as well as others involved. The goal is to have everyone participate, to have the offender come to a greater understanding of how the crime affected others, and to allow others to help make sure that the collective decision is carried out. Participants generally report higher levels of satisfaction than those who go through traditional justice models.

*Circle Sentencing.* This model is an updated version of tribal justice processes of North American indigenous peoples and is very similar to the models above. The key elements are that everyone involved with the victim and offender participates. In this model, they sit in a circle and everyone gets a turn to speak. After everyone has a chance to speak, the circle decides what should be done. The goal is to promote healing, to provide the offender an opportunity to make amends, to address the underlying causes of criminal behavior, to build a sense of community, and to promote and share community values.[14]

There are some criticisms and potential problems with the restorative justice concept. Some argue that it is not an appropriate response for serious violent crimes. Some argue that victims may not want to participate, or that they may feel pressured to forgive the offender or feel "ganged up" on by the offender's family and friends.[15] Generally, however, research indicates that victims are more satisfied when the focus is on their needs and when the offender takes responsibility for and makes right the offense.

## Exercise: In the State of …

Do a computer search to discover if there are any restorative justice programs in your state. If they exist, where are they? Which type of program exists?

Although restorative justice programs received a great deal of attention and even federal funding in the mid through late 1990s, after 9/11, federal dollars were shifted to other priorities. Restorative justice programs haven't gone away, but they tend to be localized and are more common with juvenile offenders than adult offenders.

## 4. Terrorism and our Response

Some people argue that this country was created by terrorism because the Revolutionary War began with attacks by dissidents against the established government of the king. "One man's terrorist is another's freedom fighter" is an overused phrase, but has some truth to it. Terrorist tactics have been used at various times in this nation's history by groups such as the Ku Klux Klan, which used lynching and burning to instill terror in newly freed slaves. Such tactics were revitalized during the Civil Rights movement of the 1960s. Race riots and arson have been episodic reactions by minorities in this country to the perceived oppression of the dominant majority. Even direct attempts to destabilize the government have occurred. Bolshevik terrorists attempted 38 bombings against capitalist figures such as J.P. Morgan and John D. Rockefeller in 1919, and the Weather Underground, the Symbionese Liberation Army, and the Black Panthers used armed robberies to finance their terrorism in the 1960s and 1970s, which included bombing public buildings.[16]

As terrorism has been present from the beginning of this country's history, so, too, have been government efforts to combat it. The first Alien and Sedition Acts were passed a mere 22 years after the birth of the United States in 1798. The Alien Act gave the government the right to deport those thought to be a danger to the country, and the Sedition Act gave the government the right to punish those who spoke against the government's actions. These Acts were criticized by many prominent individuals as being contrary to the First Amendment and eventually disappeared; however, the Bolshevik bombings and advocacy of communism led to the Espionage Act of 1917 and the 1918 **Sedition Act**. During the early 1900s, the United States government, fearful that Russian immigrants would import their revolution as well, had thousands arrested. Under the Sedition Act, anyone who expressed support for Communism could be arrested. Attorney General Palmer arrested 16,000 Soviet resident aliens in 1918 and 1919, and detained them without charges and without trial.

The government targeted emerging labor unions, especially the Industrial Workers of the World movement, as threats to the nation, and widespread violence occurred on both sides. The fear and official reaction to the Bolsheviks reached a pitch at the anniversary of the Russian revolution on November 7, 1919. The fear that they would begin a major assault on that day never materialized.[17]

The next chapter in the government's campaign against communism was carried out by Palmer's assistant, J. Edgar Hoover, who was appointed in 1924 and rose to prominence as director of the FBI. His continued investigation of Communists eventually led to the McCarthy hearings (House Un-American Activities Committee) in the 1950s. Throughout the 1960s and 1970s, the FBI continued to infiltrate and investigate groups and individuals that were considered threats to the nation. At one point, Hoover had a card index of 450,000 people who were identified or suspected of having left-wing political views.[18]

It should be noted that there were seriously violent groups that did advocate and use violence, such as the Symbionese Liberation Army, who utilized kidnapping and robberies and the Black Panthers, who used armed robbery and hijacking to advance their cause. However, the focus of investigations carried out by the government also included those who, in hindsight, did not pose a danger to the government, such as Martin Luther King Jr., Hollywood actors who espoused liberal views, and student and community groups that advocated nonviolent means of protest.

It was the abuses of the powers granted by anti-terrorist legislation, as well as the misuse of government intelligence, by those in the Nixon administration, that led to Congress dramatically curtailing the powers of federal law enforcement in the 1970s. The Senate created the Select Committee on Intelligence in 1976, and strengthened the Freedom of Information Act. In 1978 the Foreign Intelligence Surveillance Act (FISA) was created and mandated procedures for requesting authorization for surveillance. A secret court was created (the Foreign Intelligence Surveillance Court), which consisted of seven federal district court judges appointed by the Supreme Court's Chief Justice. Federal law enforcement officers were required to obtain permission from the court to conduct surveillance. They had to show that their target was an agent of a foreign power and information was in furtherance of counterintelligence. FISA originally approved only electronic eavesdropping and wiretapping, but was amended in 1994 to include covert physical entries, and later in 1998 to permit pen/trap orders and business records.[19]

Typical search warrants are obtained only on a showing of probable cause that the target of the search will be found in the location specified, and that it is evidence or an instrumentality of a crime. On the other hand, FISA approval may be obtained merely upon a showing that the target is a foreign power or agent and the search is relevant to a counterintelligence investigation. If the target is a U.S. citizen, there must be probable cause that their activities may involve espionage.[20]

After the Cold War ended, the United States shifted its attention to right-wing radical groups in this country who advocated violent means to oppose the government and, to a lesser extent, international groups, such as the PLO. Hamas and Hezbollah later became targets after they claimed responsibility for violent attacks and spoke out against the United States. Through the 1980s and 1990s, the activities and rhetoric of such groups became more and more anti-American and many analysts argued that the United States, in addition to Israel, was or would become a central target of terrorist actions.

The government did not sit idle, of course. President Reagan utilized National Security Decision Directives rather than seeking public laws from Congress to craft and employ a government response to the growing international threats. These directives established a hierarchy of authority regarding response to threats via aviation and kidnapping. Public Laws were also passed, including:

- Act to Combat International Terrorism (1984), which sought international cooperation
- Public Law 99-83 (1985), which allowed funding to be cut off to countries that supported terrorism
- Omnibus Diplomatic Security and Antiterrorism Act (1986), which expanded the jurisdiction of the FBI to overseas when investigating acts of terrorism against U.S. citizens abroad or at home [21]

Two of the most important pre-9/11 anti-terrorist laws were passed during the Clinton administration. The Omnibus Counterterrorism Act of 1995 greatly expanded the role of the federal government over local and state law enforcement in investigating and prosecuting acts of terrorism, such as bombings, within the boundaries of the United States, and also expanded the U.S. jurisdiction overseas when committed against U.S. embassies. It also criminalized fundraising for groups defined as terrorist. It

# BOX 2

*USA PATRIOT Act*

## Title I—ENHANCING DOMESTIC SECURITY AGAINST TERRORISM
- Amends Posse Comitatus Act
- Enhances President's power to confiscate property and assets

## Title II—ENHANCED SURVEILLANCE PROCEDURES
- Eliminated restrictions on and expanded federal surveillance practices
- Eliminated barrier between domestic and international investigations
- Expanded use of pen register and trap-and-trace devices
- Relaxed rules on obtaining warrants

## Title III—INTERNATIONAL MONEY LAUNDERING ABATEMENT AND ANTITERRORIST FINANCING ACT OF 2001
- Required banks to create anti-laundering procedures and audit functions
- Expanded reporting mechanisms for suspicious transactions

## Title IV—PROTECTING THE BORDER
- Increased the number of border security agents
- Improved monitoring capabilities

## Title V—REMOVING OBSTACLES TO INVESTIGATING TERRORISM
- Created domestic rewards for information leading to terrorist capture
- Relaxed rules of no communication between domestic crime and international investigations of terrorism
- Relaxed requirements for obtaining National Security Letters from "specific and articulable evidence" to "relevant"
- Removed any rights of terrorists to have privacy over DNA or records

### Title VI—PROVIDING FOR VICTIMS OF TERRORISM, PUBLIC SAFETY OFFICERS, AND THEIR FAMILIES

- Expedited processes for obtaining aid for victims and their families

### Title VII—INCREASED INFORMATION SHARING FOR CRITICAL INFRASTRUCTURE PROTECTION

- Expanded the eligible participants in federal grants for information sharing

### Title VIII—STRENGTHENING THE CRIMINAL LAWS AGAINST TERRORISM

- Included acts of terrorism and assisting terrorists in the federal criminal code
- Criminalized the act of providing funds to terrorist organizations
- Removed statute of limitations for some crimes
- Further delineated cybercrimes

### Title IX—IMPROVED INTELLIGENCE

- Restated removal of the "wall" between investigations of international terrorists and domestic criminals
- Set priorities for national intelligence mission and policies

### Title X—MISCELLANEOUS

- Defined critical infrastructure components
- Addressed fraudulent charitable solicitations
- Prohibited anyone involved in money laundering from entering the country

expanded federal law enforcement authority to use "pen registers" and "trap and trace" devices, which track telephone calls. It also created the power of federal law enforcement to seek a wide range of personal and business documents with "national security letters," rather than warrants, when investigating terrorism.

This Act was replaced by the Anti-Terrorism and Effective Death Penalty Act of 1996, which incorporated most of the provisions discussed above, and added others, such as expanding the authority of INS to deport accused terrorists and other resident aliens, and increasing the penalties for such crimes. The other part of the Act applied to all offenders, and changed habeas corpus protections, eliminating multiple appeals and removing legal barriers to executions.[22]

Prior to 9/11, few of us were aware of this nation's counter-terrorism laws and few citizens gave serious thought to the threat of terrorism. There were prior events that should have alerted us to the possibility of a major attack: the 1993 bombing of the World Trade Center, the attacks on the USS Cole and the attacks on U.S. embassies in Africa, and the stated aim of Osama Bin Laden to "cut off the head of the snake," meaning the United States and, more specifically, United States' economic dominance in the world. Generally, however, the FBI was largely concerned with domestic terrorism. This focus was not misplaced given the tragedy of the Oklahoma City bombing by Timothy McVeigh and Terry Nichols and the presence of other radical groups that still exist and have expressed and indicated a willingness to use violence to advance their goals.

In the aftermath of the terrorist attacks on September 11, 2001, Congress enacted the USA PATRIOT Act to combat terrorism and created the Homeland Security Council, and then later the Department of Homeland Security. These two actions have had tremendous consequences for the organization and powers of investigative and justice agencies in the United States. We will discuss the USA PATRIOT Act first and then the Department of Homeland Security.

## 4.1 USA PATRIOT Act

On October 11, 2001, the 107th Congress enacted Public Law 107-56, which is titled "Uniting and Strengthening America by Providing Appropriate Tools Required to Intercept and Obstruct Terrorism Act." This Act is known as the **USA PATRIOT Act** of 2001. The purpose of the Act is "to deter and punish terrorist acts in the United States and around the world, to enhance law enforcement investigatory tools, and for other purposes." What many people don't realize is that there were already counter-terrorism laws in existence. As mentioned above, the 1996 Anti-Terrorism Act was signed by President Clinton and included most of the provisions of the USA PATRIOT Act. What was added to the USA PATRIOT Act were provisions that were expressly rejected by Congress in the earlier law. The numerous sections of the Act are included under 10 titles as set out in Box 2.

Title VIII of the Patriot Act, "Strengthening the Criminal Laws against Terrorism" revised Chapter 113B, titled "Terrorism" in the United States Code. The earlier Chapter included criminal penalties for a series of acts relating to terrorism, including: Use of Weapons of Mass Destruction, Acts of Terrorism Transcending National Boundaries, Financial Transactions, Providing Material to Terrorists, and Providing Material Support or Resources to Designated Foreign Terrorist Organizations.

Title 18 U.S.C. § 2331, as it existed prior to the PATRIOT Act, defined international terrorism as activities that "involve violent acts or acts dangerous to human life that are a violation of the criminal laws of the United States or of any State, or that would be a criminal violation if committed within the jurisdiction of the United States or of any State" and that appear to be intended to do one or more of the following:

(i) to intimidate or coerce a civilian population;
(ii) to influence the policy of a government by intimidation or coercion; or
(iii) to affect the conduct of a government by assassination or kidnapping; and
(C) occur primarily outside the territorial jurisdiction of the United States, or transcend national boundaries in terms of the means by which they are accomplished, the persons they appear intended to intimidate or coerce, or the locale in which their perpetrators operate or seek asylum;

The PATRIOT Act amended § 2331 of Title 18 to include "by mass destruction, assassination or kidnapping" as one of the acts that constitutes terrorism. In addition, "domestic terrorism" was included and defined as those acts "dangerous to human life that are a violation of the criminal laws of United States or of any State and that appear to be intended to do one of the following:

(i) to intimidate or coerce a civilian population;
(ii) to influence the policy of a government by intimidation or coercion; or

(iii) to affect the policy of a government by mass destruction, assassination, or kidnapping; and

(C) occur primarily within the territorial jurisdiction of the United States.

Section 2332b is titled "Acts of Terrorism Transcending National Boundaries." This section expanded the concept of terrorism to include the actions of individuals who attack Americans outside of the boundaries of the United States. This expansion allowed for the prosecution of John Phillip Walker Lindh, who was charged under this Act with conspiracy to murder nationals of the United States, including American military personnel and other government employees serving in Afghanistan. He was not convicted of violating the statute, but was found guilty of other offenses.[23]

Title 18 U.S.C. § 2339A, "Providing Material Support to Terrorists" provides that whoever, within the United States, provides material support or resources or conceals or disguises the nature, location, source, or ownership of material support or resources, knowing or intending that they are to be used in preparation for carrying out a violation of the sections indicated, or in preparation for, or in carrying out, the concealment or escape from the commission of such violations, shall be fined under this title, imprisoned not more than 10 years, or both. This section was amended by the USA PATRIOT Act by striking out "within the United States" and by adding sections of the law covered by the Act. The effect of deleting "within the United States" makes the provisions enforceable when the acts described occur outside the United States.

Title 18 U.S.C. § 2339B, "Providing Material Support or Resources to Designated Foreign Terrorist Organizations" was amended in part by the PATRIOT Act to include the idea that foreign terrorist organizations were defined by the federal government, specifically the President, and an individual who contributed money to such an organization for its charitable activities would still be guilty of violating the law and subject to a long term of imprisonment.

The other elements of the PATRIOT Act that have been controversial are those that expand federal powers of investigation. Title II, "Enhanced Surveillance Procedures," substantially changed the provisions of the FISA described earlier. Specifically, the Act lowered the standard required to obtain permission to use surveillance against suspects; roving wiretaps were authorized that allowed agents to tap any phone the suspect might use; further, pen registers were allowed that followed any phone number called by the suspect. The PATRIOT Act also authorizes law enforcement agencies charged with investigating terrorism to share investigative information with domestic law enforcement investigators and vice versa.

In summary, some of the provisions that are most controversial include:

- Expanding the range of crimes trackable by electronic surveillance
- Allowing the use of roving wiretaps to track any phone a suspect might use
- Allowing the "sneak and peek" search (not notifying suspects of searches)
- Allowing federal warrants to search records with less than probable cause
- Lowering barriers of information sharing between domestic and international investigations
- Creating new tools for investigating money laundering (by requiring banks to file reports on suspicious behaviors).

On March 7, 2006, Congress approved the renewal of the USA PATRIOT Act. Three provisions of the Act will be reviewed in four years, the other provisions of the Act have been made permanent. The bill created a "National Security Division" in the Department of Justice. It continued the "roving wiretap" provision of the USA PATRIOT Act, as well as the power of federal officials to access library, business, and medical records without probable cause.[24]

Generally, the public has been supportive of the USA PATRIOT Act. In 2003, only 28 percent of those polled believed that it gave the government too much power over individual liberties, and 51 percent believed that people had to give up some individual freedom to fight terrorism.[25]

## 4.2 The Department of Homeland Security

Nine days after 9/11, President Bush created the Homeland Security Council and a cabinet-level position was created called the Homeland Security Advisor, with Tom Ridge appointed to fill the position. Then, in March 2003, the Department of Homeland Security was created with the mission to prevent terrorist attacks within the United States and to minimize damages from any attacks. The Department of Homeland Security consolidated 22 federal agencies and more than 180,000 federal employees under one umbrella agency. It had a budget of $30 billion in 2005 and $31.4 billion in 2006.[26]

The major impetus for the agency was 9/11 and the finding that one of the reasons the terrorists were able to accomplish their goal was poor communication among the FBI, the CIA, and the FAA. For instance, while the CIA knew that two of the hijackers had attended Al Qaeda meetings in the Middle East, the FBI knew (or at least a field office knew) that several of the hijackers were acting suspiciously by taking flying lessons. Together, those bits of information might have been enough to prevent the disaster.[27]

While the CIA is not one of the agencies that has been merged into the Department of Homeland Security, the idea of a national intelligence center is at the heart of the effort, and the CIA director is no longer the titular head of the U.S. intelligence function, as that role has shifted to the Department of Homeland Security. The Immigration and Naturalization Service was dismantled and the functions distributed to two agencies, U.S. Immigration and Customs Enforcement (ICE), and the U.S. Customs and Border Protection Agency, which also subsumed and redistributed the functions of the Border Patrol and U.S. Customs. The Customs and Border Protection Agency has about 40,000 employees; together, the two agencies employ 55,000 people.

We have all felt the effects of the nation's efforts to prevent terrorism. Travelers endure searches and a constant revision of rules concerning what can be carried onto airplanes. The national threat alert system is a routine part of news broadcasts, although whether people pay any attention to them is another matter. The vigilant efforts have met with success because there has not been a single successful terrorist incident within the borders of the country. Since 2001, nearly 200 suspected terrorists or associates have been charged with crimes and, according to authorities, 100 terrorist plots disrupted.[28]

## 4.3 Other Responses to Terrorism

In addition to the PATRIOT Act and the creation of the Department of Homeland Security, the United States has been involved in other actions in response to the threat of terrorism. The war in Iraq is beyond the scope of this book, but some of the controversial decisions of the Bush administration are extremely relevant to the system of criminal justice because they illustrate the centrality of law in our lives. Issues such as detaining "enemy combatants," limiting habeas corpus, the use of torture during interrogation, and conducting wiretaps without court orders are legal issues, and our earlier discussion of due process is directly relevant.

When the United States is engaged in war, and soldiers are captured on the battlefield, the Geneva Convention (1864/1949) specifies how they should be treated. The Convention, which the United States joined, dictates that no ordinary soldier should be tried and punished for fighting, as long as he had not committed war crimes, as defined by treaty and convention. Further, certain minimum standards exist for the care of prisoners of war, and they are supposed to be protected from interrogation, other than the information of name, rank, and serial number.

President Bush signed an Executive Order shortly after the invasion of Afghanistan that defined those captured as "enemy combatants" rather than soldiers. As such, they were said to be outside the protections of the Geneva Convention. Eventually, 680 "enemy combatants" were transported to Guantanamo Bay, Cuba, and held in a military installation there, without charges, without access to attorneys, and without any constitutional or legally recognized protections. The use of the "enemy combatant" status had not been used since World War II, when it was applied to six German spies who entered the United States illegally to conduct sabotage. The Bush Administration's position has been that the individuals held in Guantánamo were not captured in a normal war and they are not soldiers in the traditional sense, therefore the protections of the Geneva Convention do not apply, including the protection against interrogation (and the use of coercive and torture-like tactics) to obtain information.

Opponents argue that the Executive Order places limitless power in the President to define anyone as an unlawful combatant outside the oversight of any other body, including the Supreme Court. In an earlier case, the Supreme Court held that holding detainees without access to federal courts was illegal according to current law; however, the justices indicated that Congress could enact a new law that would allow such action. In response, Congress passed the Military Commissions Act, which stripped habeas corpus protections from detainees and subjected them to a military tribunal rather than due process via the courts. The writ of **habeas corpus** is an ancient due process right that protects individuals from the power of the government to hold them unlawfully or unfairly. Amidst a firestorm of controversy, the Supreme Court declined to hear the case that challenged this provision of the Act. However, in late June, 2007, the Supreme Court reversed itself and decided to hear the case, which is scheduled to be heard as early as December of 2007.[29]

In the meantime, less than half of the detainees are still being held. Many of them have been released to their home countries. Some are now suing the United States for illegal detention and torture in international courts.[30] The administration's position was that enemy combatants were not subject to the protections of the Geneva Convention and there have been news reports of the use of extreme interrogation tactics at Guantanamo, as well as at the infamous Abu Ghraib prison in Iraq. Opponents argue that by ignoring the mandates of the Geneva Convention, American prisoners have less protection from enemy forces. For instance, presidential contender John McCain, himself a prisoner of war and victim of torture during the Vietnam War, was a staunch opponent of the Bush Administration's attempt to short-circuit Congress's condemnation of torture tactics. These issues illustrate differences between what some consider legally and ethically appropriate in war against our enemies, and what is legally and ethically appropriate against American citizens. Yet it was inevitable that some American citizens would also become identified as participating in terrorist actions.

The definition of enemy combatants was later extended to American citizens fighting against coalition forces in Afghanistan and Iraq. José Padilla is an American citizen who was arrested on American soil as an enemy combatant. In 2002, shortly after he was arrested at O'Hare Airport under a material witness warrant, he was transferred to a military base under a presidential order that he be declared an enemy combatant. Governmental authorities alleged that he was instrumental in a plot to explode a "dirty bomb" in this country. What they did know was that he had probably been in a terrorist training camp in Pakistan or Afghanistan. Advocates argued that he could not be considered an enemy combatant because he was an American citizen, and these advocates fought to restrict the ability of the government to use the enemy combatant status against citizens who were not members of foreign armies. The Supreme Court sent the case back for technical reasons and, after it had been through the federal appellate process again, declined to issue a writ of certiorari. However, before it was scheduled for a final appeal, the government asked for and received permission to remove the case from the military tribunal system to a federal district court in Miami. After being tried in a civilian federal court, on August 16, 2007, after being held for about five years, Padilla was convicted of all charges, including conspiracy to murder, kidnap, and maim U.S. citizens, and conspiracy to provide material support for terrorists. The government had dropped all the other charges.

Proponents of governmental actions argue that the U.S. government has every right to provide a different type of due process to those accused of being terrorists and that military tribunals are an acceptable alternative to the court system. They argue that civilian courts are unable to hear cases involving terrorists because juries might feel intimidated, that governmental security prohibits the exposure of much of the evidence relied upon, and that it is too difficult to try such cases with the evidence and procedural rules of such courts. On the other hand, opponents argue that American citizens should never be held without access to the courts and that many citizens could be labeled as enemy combatants, given the vagueness of the term.

In 2006, a controversy arose after it was revealed that federal officers had been using wiretaps without warrants. A Presidential Order signed in 2002 allowed the National Security Agency to monitor international telephone calls and international e-mail messages of thousands of people inside the United States without first obtaining a warrant. The concern expressed by opponents of the practice is that the National Security Agency has traditionally been involved in investigations external to the borders of the United States and that the secret court (Foreign Intelligence Surveillance Court) has hardly ever turned down a government request for a warrant when asked for one. The 1978 law that created the court has been interpreted to bar all domestic wiretapping, even for national security, unless it is sanctioned by a warrant, and the secret court was created to grant such warrants. On the other hand, the administration's position is that Congress authorized the President to take any and all steps required to combat terrorism in the wake of 9/11.[31] This issue remains unresolved.

The process of **rendition** is when federal agents find, detain, and carry away suspected terrorists in other countries without the country's approval or permission and against their sovereign laws. The United States argues that it has the jurisdiction to do so as a protection for its own security. Other countries argue that such actions are simply criminal. There are outstanding warrants in Italy against a CIA Bureau Chief and several agents for the rendition of an Italian citizen; Italy defined such action as kidnapping. Renditions are also associated with **torture-by-proxy**, the practice of the United States to hand over suspects to governments that use torture methods condemned by international treaties that the United States has signed. While some argue that extraordinary threats call for extraordinary methods; others argue that the United States is very quickly losing international support and by flouting the criminal laws of other countries, it encourages lawlessness and may be sowing the seeds of new terrorists by these actions.

## 4.4 State and Local Law Enforcement

Local law enforcement has obviously been greatly affected by the challenge of terrorism. As we all know, the first responders to a terrorist attack such as 9/11 are local and state public servants. Firefighters and police officers were the first to respond to the attacks on the World Trade Towers and the Oklahoma City federal building, and among those who died.

Since 9/11, more resources have been directed to **first responder training.** This type of training gives law enforcement officers the skills to approach, engage, and coordinate responses to major threats, such as terrorist actions. Local police, especially those in major metropolitan areas, must assume that they will be first responders when targets of terrorist attacks are located in their city. Bridges, buildings, schools, transportation, sports complexes, other venues where there are large crowds, and nuclear reactors and power plants are the likely targets of terrorists. Actually, there are a wide range of targets that might be vulnerable to terrorist attacks. In addition to those already mentioned, the water supplies of major cities can be contaminated with toxic agents, the banking industry can be immobilized by computers, the nation's ports can be blocked with explosions, or the nation's oil and gas supplies can be sabotaged—bringing to a standstill industry, commerce, and basic services. Federal agents are unable to protect all these targets. Police are the first line of defense, both in terms of preventive observation and surveillance, as well as response and intervention.

Narco-terrorism refers to the pattern of terrorist groups to use narcotics to fund their activities. Since 9/11, several major drug raids have uncovered ties between drug dealers and terrorist groups, such as Hezbollah. Opium from Afghanistan, although condemned by the Taliban, is now believed to be one of the largest sources of funding for Al Qaeda. It is clear that local drug investigations may end up becoming investigations of international terrorists. One of the biggest challenges, in fact, is to improve the communication between local law enforcement intelligence and federal Homeland Security personnel. Local law enforcement officials complain that the communication pattern tends to go one way only when they are expected to collect intelligence for federal agencies, but are not informed of threats in their jurisdiction. The lack of communication between the CIA and the FBI has been widely cited as one of the reasons that the 9/11 plot was not discovered and prevented, but the wider problem is the complete lack of any coordinated information sharing among the 20,000 law enforcement agencies and the Department of Homeland Security.

State and local law enforcement are now receiving more resources to address these new responsibilities. For instance, civilian analysts may be employed by state and metropolitan police agencies. These analysts track and analyze information that might lead to uncovering terrorist plots. Joint task forces between local and federal agents have also been funded. State anti-terrorism agencies have also been created to coordinate local law enforcement agencies in the state.

It is clear that, despite the importance of state and local law enforcement in preventing future terrorism, at present they may not have the training or resources to be as effective as they might be. Their arsenal of weapons may not even match that of a well-armed militia group, the surveillance equipment may be inadequate to monitor suspected terrorists, and their communication networks may be deficient. Further, local officers may not be trained to investigate even domestic cybercrime, much less terrorists who use cybertactics. Further, local agencies may not have the expertise to investigate, or training, to recognize biological threats.

Hurricane Katrina was a natural disaster, but many point to this as an example of how poorly prepared the United States is when responding to massive events such as 9/11 or a hurricane that devastates a major city. FEMA is the federal agency that is charged with responding to disasters of this magnitude and, many argue, the weaknesses of the agency were apparent. Local law enforcement did not escape criticism either and the event pointed out that more training and operational procedures are necessary to prevent the panic and disorganization that characterized the aftermath of Katrina.

Local law enforcement has also been faced with difficult decisions in balancing their investigative activities against individual liberties. Federal law enforcement has sometimes taken aggressive actions in response to the threat of terrorism, especially in regard to Muslim residents and individuals of Middle Eastern descent. Immediately after 9/11, more than 5,000 resident aliens were detained without charges. Many were subsequently deported for minor immigration violations. Those who were released alleged that they were subject to illegal detention and abuse during their imprisonment. The FBI also asked local law enforcement agencies to conduct surveillance and/or question Muslims and foreign residents without any reason other than their nationality or religion. The Portland, Oregon, Police Department gained notoriety when they refused the FBI's request that they conduct interviews with all foreign students in the area. Portland police supervisors thought that they had no authority to do so because the FBI did not articulate any reasonable suspicion, the questions were in areas that were constitutionally protected, such as their religion, and did not relate to criminal matters.[32]

Racial profiling was held to be unconstitutional when it is used as the only element in a decision to stop a minority as a suspect in drug crimes. After 9/11, however, racial profiling of Middle Eastern-looking men was used by airline employees, federal agents, and local law enforcement officers, and continues to lead to greater scrutiny of this group of travelers. Federal guidelines clearly condemn the use of racial profiling *except* for investigations involving terrorism or national security.[33]

Another area of controversy between federal and local law enforcement is the enforcement of immigration laws. Some cities and their police departments have refused to notify federal authorities when they may have reason to believe victims or witnesses of crimes are violators of immigration laws. Police departments that refuse to be the enforcers of federal laws argue that their role is domestic and involves only local security and crime fighting. These so-called sanctuary cities basically respond to crime victims or criminals, for that matter, without regard to any suspicion that the individual is an illegal alien. One assumes that even those departments, however, will cooperate with DHS authorities when the individual who comes to their attention may be even peripherally involved with others who may be terrorists. The fact is that immigration control is one of the most critical areas of protecting this nation from terrorists.

In these examples, as well as many others, it is clear that local law enforcement is a vital element in protecting the United States against terrorism. The legal issues involved when balancing due process and civil liberties against security are difficult and, ultimately, affect us all.

## 5. Conclusion

In this chapter we have examined the concept of community. Criminology has long identified the community as a crucial element in crime causation. In our response to crime, we have swung back and forth between banishment and involving the community in correctional responses. Early forms of parole and probation were based on a belief that the offender should be in the community if at all possible. Older forms of justice involved the community in developing the response to offenders that would take into account the needs of the offender, the victim, and the community. Today these programs are known as restorative justice.

There are such things as criminogenic communities—those where social capital is weak and the community is unable to utilize private and parochial controls on its members. These communities have high rates of incarceration, but also have high rates of poverty and a disproportional use of governmental services, such as TANF. Because offenders will return to these same communities while on parole, probation, or diversion programs, it is essential to consider the community and not just the offender in any response to crime.

Ironically, just as restorative justice efforts picked up momentum, we had a far greater threat to our national peace of mind than crime. The threat of terrorism has led to a massive restructuring of the federal investigative and justice agencies. State and local law enforcement have also responded, and funding priorities, training, and the mission of local law enforcement have changed. Terrorists are thought of as outside the community and, certainly, the Middle Eastern men who hijacked and crashed the airplanes on 9/11 can be considered outsiders in very fundamental ways.

On the other hand, it is important to remember that there is also the threat of domestic terrorists, and these individuals were born and raised in the communities of the South, the Northwest, and other regions of the country. They grew up and lived in our communities and, for very specific reasons, decided that violence was an appropriate and acceptable response to their needs, in much the same way that an armed robber or a hired killer decides that violence is an acceptable solution. Even the Middle Eastern men who were "sleepers" and came from other countries spent years in this country, even raising families here. To what extent did the community affect them?

José Padilla, the citizen who was accused of being an enemy combatant, came from a poor Puerto Rican immigrant family. He was involved with gangs and had been in trouble with the criminal justice system since his youth. In fact, it is believed that he converted to Islam in prison. So we come full circle. We see that the challenge of responding to the threat of terrorism is not unrelated to the challenge of responding to crime. It is not difficult to imagine that the threat of future terrorism may lie within our own cities and communities. Poor and disenfranchised citizens who do not believe that the great wealth and opportunities that exist in this country are available to them are prime subjects for indoctrination by those spouting anti-American rhetoric. An individual like José Padilla might, in a previous decade, have spent his life in and out of prison for "ordinary" crimes. Instead, he felt the need to travel to the Middle East to join a group committed to this country's destruction. How many more Padillas exist in the tenements, streets, lockups, and prisons of this country? What methods will we approve to prevent them from hurting us? Is it possible that strengthening communities, meeting the needs of victims and offenders, scrupulously adhering to the law and ideals of due process, and making it clear that everyone is a valued part of the community, regardless of what they have done, might help to prevent terrorists as well as criminals? In the twenty-first century, the criminal justice system will most probably be dealing with the prevention of terrorism as well as crime.

## Discussion

Millions of Americans remember in detail where they were on the morning of September 11th, 2001. I was a lieutenant on my way to a jail management school with Sergeant Tom Loy. We were both assigned to our Tactical Response Team. We had just arrived at the San Bernardino County Sheriff's main jail. As we walked into the classroom, the television caught my eye. I watched in horror as two planes hit the Twin Towers. I knew at that moment we were at war. My cell phone lit up so Tom and I went back to the Monrovia Police Department, activated our team and went to work.

Days after the 9/11 attacks, I vividly remember a conversation with my parents about Pearl Harbor. I was astonished how the 911 attacks made them remember in incredible detail, that fateful moment, as they heard the news about the Japanese attacks on Pearl Harbor in Hawaii. My son, Glenn and I had visited Pearl Harbor so I could visualize the Japanese attack as my parents talked about their memories of the event.

The day after the attack on Pearl Harbor, my father, Wallace E. Lacher, enlisted in the Army and fought the Germans in Europe. The attacks on 9/11 had occurred almost 60 years before Pearl Harbor, and now, twelve years have passed since I stood glued to that television as the planes hit the towers.

In November 2001, the CIA and Army Special Forces linked up with the Northern Alliance and brought war to the Taliban. Thousands of American and Coalition troops are still fighting that war. When my son Glenn T. Lacher, Army Airborne, deployed to Afghanistan I bought him a leg holster for his M-9 pistol. I also gave him a tactical holster that I had purchased and carried when I was assigned to our Tactical Response Team. I wanted a part of me to go with my son to help him fight the war on terror.

The events of 9/11 were a paradigm shift for law enforcement, the courts and corrections. The prospect of nuclear, biological, and chemical attacks on U.S. soil became a reality. The probability of suicide bomber attacks on soft targets such as malls and entertainment venues became reality. The 911 attacks also changed how Americans lived their lives.

My department bought and issued gas masks and hazardous-material suits to our employees. We issued injectable medications to our officers in the event they were gassed. The FBI actually sat down with us to discuss terrorist targets in our community. A couple weeks after the attack, our region started meeting on a regular basis with federal law enforcement officials to share vital terrorist intelligence information. The war on terror was in full swing.

## Questions for Discussion

1. What other significant attacks on American interests have occurred before or after September 11, 2001?

2. What is the significance of narco-terrorism and what impact does it have on American law enforcement and corrections?

3. What impact has the USA PATRIOT ACT had on the war on terror? How has the act been abused by the government?

4. How safe are our borders with Mexico and Canada from attacks by terrorist groups? What political factors have prevented the U.S. from effectively securing our border with Mexico?

## Activities for the Professor

1. Assign the discussion questions in on-line chats or in the classroom.
2. Assign the students to write a short paper on the USA PATRIOT Act and discuss their finding with the class.
3. Assign the students to prepare a Power Point presentation on narco-terrorism and present their findings with the class.
4. Assign the students to write a reflection paper on how 9/11 has impacted them and their workplace.

## Notes

1. See, for instance, Shaw, C. & H. McKay (1942). *Juvenile Delinquency and Urban Areas*. Chicago: University of Chicago Press.
2. See, for instance, Sampson. R. (1988). "Local Friendship Ties and Community Attachment in Mass Society: A Multilevel Systemic Model." *American Sociological Review* 53: 766–779. Sampson, R. & W. Groves (1989). "Community Structure and Crime: Testing Social-Disorganization Theory." *American Journal of Sociology* 94: 774–802.
3. Carey, M. (2005). "Social Learning, Social Capital, and Correctional Theories: Seeking an Integrated Model." In American Correctional Association, *What Works and Why: Effective Approaches to Reentry*, pp. 1–33. Lanham, MD: American Correctional Association, p. 9.
4. Bursik, R. & H. Grasmick (1993). *Neighborhoods and Crime: The Dimensions of Effective Community Control*. New York: Lexington Books.
5. Zatz, M. & E. Portillos (2000). "Voices from the Barrio: Chicano Gangs, Families, and Communities." *Criminology* 38, 2: 369–401.
6. Reentry Policy Council (2005). "An Explanation of Justice Mapping: Three Examples." Retrieved 12/30/05 from: www.reentrypolicy.org/report/justice-mapping.php.
7. Clear, T., D. Rose & J. Ryder (2001). "Incarceration and the Community: The Problem of Removing and Returning Offenders." *Crime and Delinquency* 47, 3: 335–351; Clear, T., D. Rose, E. Waring & K. Scully (2003). "Coercive Mobility and Crime: A Preliminary Examination of Concentrated Incarceration and Social Disorganization." *Justice Quarterly* 20, 1: 33–64.
8. Clear, T., D. Rose & J. Ryder (2001). "Incarceration and the Community: The Problem of Removing and Returning Offenders." *Crime and Delinquency* 47, 3: 335–351.
9. Lynch, J. & W. Sabol (2004). "Assessing the Effects of Mass Incarceration on Informal Social Control in Communities." *Criminology and Public Policy* 3, 2: 267–294.
10. Hemmens, C. (2001). "The Collateral Consequences of Conviction," *Perspectives* 25, 1: 12–13.
11. Reentry Policy Council (2005). "An Explanation of Justice Mapping: Three Examples." Retrieved 12/30/05 from: www.reentrypolicy.org/report/justice-mapping.php.
12. Schweigert, F. (2002). "Moral and Philosophical Foundations of Restorative Justice," In J. Perry (ed.), *Repairing Communities through Restorative Justice*, pp. 19–37. Lanham, MD: American Correctional Association, p. 21.
13. Schweigert, F. (2002) "Moral and Philosophical Foundations of Restorative Justice," In J. Perry (ed.), *Repairing Communities through Restorative Justice*, pp. 19–37. Lanham, MD: American Correctional Association, p. 28.

14. Braithwaite, J. (2002). "Linking Crime Prevention to Restorative Justice." In J. Perry (ed.), *Repairing Communities through Restorative Justice*, pp. 55–66. Lanham, MD: American Correctional Association.

15. Braithwaite, J. (2002). "Linking Crime Prevention to Restorative Justice." In J. Perry (ed.), *Repairing Communities through Restorative Justice*, pp. 55–66. Lanham, MD: American Correctional Association, p. 85.

16. Fagin, J.(2006). *When Terrorism Strikes Home: Defending the United States*. Boston: Allyn and Bacon.

17. Fagin, J. (2006). *When Terrorism Strikes Home: Defending the United States*. Boston: Allyn and Bacon, p. 39.

18. Fagin, J. (2006). *When Terrorism Strikes Home: Defending the United States*. Boston: Allyn and Bacon, p. 51.

19. Cole, D. & J. Dempsey (2002). *Terrorism and the Constitution*. New York: Free Press.

20. Ward, R., K. Kiernan, & D. Mabrey (2006). *Homeland Security: An Introduction*. Newark, NJ: Lex-isNexis/Matthew Bender, p. 254.

21. Fagin, J. (2006). *When Terrorism Strikes Home: Defending the United States*. Boston: Allyn and Bacon, p. 57.

22. Fagin, J. (2006). *When Terrorism Strikes Home: Defending the United States*. Boston: Allyn and Bacon, p. 62.

23. *United States v. Lindh*, 227 F. Supp. 2d 565 (E.D. Va. 2002).

24. Cable News Network. Retrieved 7/4/06 from: www.cnn.com/2006/POLITICS/03/07/patriot.act/.

25. Cited in Fagin, J. (2006). *When Terrorism Strikes Home: Defending the United States*. Boston, MA: Allyn and Bacon, p. 77.

26. Ward, R., K. Kiernan, & D. Mabrey (2006). *Homeland Security: An Introduction*. Newark, NJ: Lex-isNexis/Matthew Bender, p. 68.

27. Ward, R., K. Kiernan, & D. Mabrey (2006). *Homeland Security: An Introduction*. Newark, NJ: Lex-isNexis/Matthew Bender.

28. Cited in Fagin, J. (2006). *When Terrorism Strikes Home: Defending the United States*. Boston, MA: Allyn and Bacon, p. 127.

29. Hawke, A. (2007). *Primer: Guantanamo Detainees' Rights*. National Public Radio. Retrieved 8/25/07 from: http://www.npr.org/templates/story/story.php?storyID=11600605.

30. Barnes, R. (2007). "Justices to Weigh Detainee Rights." *Washington Post*, Sat. June 30, 2007, A01.

31. Ward, R., K. Kiernan, & D. Mabrey (2006). *Homeland Security: An Introduction*. Newark, NJ: Lex-isNexis/Matthew Bender, p. 254.

32. Cited in Fagin, J. (2006). *When Terrorism Strikes Home: Defending the United States*. Boston, MA: Allyn and Bacon, p. 71.

33. Cited in Fagin, J. (2006). *When Terrorism Strikes Home: Defending the United States*. Boston, MA: Allyn and Bacon, p. 305.

# Credits

## Text Selections

Richard R.E. Kania, "Future Issues in Criminal Justice Management," Managing Criminal Justice Organizations: An Introduction to Theory and Practice, pp. 237-249. Copyright © 2008 by Elsevier Press. Reprinted with permission.

Gary W. Cordner and Kathryn E. Scarborough, "Contemporary Issues in Police Administration," Police Administration, pp. 443-470. Copyright © 2010 by Elsevier Press. Reprinted with permission.

"The Impact of the Economic Downturn on American Police Agencies," http://www.cops.usdoj.gov/files/RIC/Publications/e101113406_Economic%20Impact.pdf, pp. iii-iv, 1-41. U.S. Department of Justice, 2011. Copyright in the Public Domain.

Lawrence F. Travis, III, "Issues in Community Supervision," Introduction to Criminal Justice, pp. 419-450. Copyright © 2008 by Elsevier Press. Reprinted with permission.

Mark P. Lagon, "Trafficking and Human Dignity," Policy Review, no. 152, pp. 51-61. Copyright © 2008 by Hoover Institute. Reprinted with permission. Provided by ProQuest LLC. All rights reserved.

Justin Mankin, "Gaming the System: How Afgan Opium Underpins Local Power," Journal of International Affairs, vol. 63, issue 1, pp. 195-209. Copyright © 2009 by Journal of International Affairs. Reprinted with permission. Provided by ProQuest LLC. All rights reserved.

Kent C. Jurney and Steve Cader, "School Security: Best Practices," http://www.securityinfowatch.com/article/11004500/how-to-mitigate-shootings-and-other-violent-events-on-school-grounds. Copyright © 2013 by Cygnus Business Media. Reprinted with permission.

Joycelyn M. Pollock, "Looking Toward the Future: Criminal Justice in the 21st Century," Crime and Justice in America: An Introduction to Criminal Justice, pp. 369-393. Copyright © 2008 by Elsevier Press. Reprinted with permission.

## Images

Afghan Women and Children: Source: Glenn Lacher.
Afghan Riding in Horse Cart: Source: Glenn Lacher.
Typical Afghan Village: Source: Glenn Lacher.
Fortified Afghan house: Source: Glenn Lacher.
Enemy Detainee with Weapons: Source: Glenn Lacher.
Afghan Mud Huts: Source: Glenn Lacher.
Afghan 9 Year Old Boy: Source: Glenn Lacher.
Afghan Poppies: Source: http://commons.wikimedia.org/wiki/File:Afghan_poppies.jpg. Copyright in the Public Domain.
Nomadic Kuchi People: Source: http://commons.wikimedia.org/wiki/File:Nomadic_Kuchi_people.jpg. Copyright in the Public Domain.

CPSIA information can be obtained
at www.ICGtesting.com
Printed in the USA
FSHW020755060520
69943FS

9 781626 617469